FACT-CHECKING THE SCIENCE OF READING

FACT-CHECKING THE SCIENCE OF READING

OPENING UP THE CONVERSATION

Robert J. Tierney
P David Pearson

VANCOUVER - BERKELEY
2024

© Robert J. Tierney and P David Pearson, 2024

ISBN 978-1-0688195-0-6 (paperback)

An online version of this work is published at https://literacyresearchcommons.org.

All versions of this work may contain content reproduced under license from third parties. Permission to reproduce this third-party content must be obtained from those third-parties directly. They can be contacted at rob.tierney@ubc.ca & ppearson@berkeley.edu.

References to Internet websites (URLs) were accurate at the time of writing. The authors are not responsible for websites that may have expired or changed since the book was prepared.

Figure 2: *Scarborough's Reading Rope* (p.57) is reprinted with permission of Guilford Press. Catherine Compton-Lilly and her co-authors provided permission to reproduce Table 6 (p.110) originally published in: Compton-Lilly, C., Spence, L.K., Thomas, P.L. & Decker, S.L. (2023). Stories grounded in decades of research: What we truly know about the teaching of reading. *The Reading Teacher,* 77(3), 392-400.

Research and Editorial Associate: Caroline Hamilton
Cover Art, Editorial and Graphic Design: Logaine Navascués
Cover Photography: Robert J. Tierney
Digital Support: Anthony Whalen, MARSworks

Acknowledgements

There is an element of uncertainty with the writing and publication of this monograph. From the outset we found ourselves wrestling with the merits of a project directed at fact-checking the Science of Reading. Our goal was to delve into the credibility of the evidence enlisted for the claims being made and the mandates being imposed. Our hope was that we could do so in a manner that was neither biased nor negative but represented a form of fair witnessing with an eye to supporting more discerning decisions by educators and increased civility in a field often characterized as contentious.

We overcame our reluctance with support from one another and several colleagues whose own engagements with these matters have been inspirational. We would like to send special thanks to several individuals who served as models for us and provided vital support. They include: Maren Aukerman, Richard Beach, Sam Bommarito, Brian Cambourne, Sam DeJulio, Gina Cervetti, Nell Duke, Barbara Flores, Rachael Gabriel, Judith Green, Jim Hoffman, George Hruby, Peter Johnston, James King, Carol Lee, Allan Luke, Dixie Massey, Lesley Morrow, David Reinking, Victoria Risko, Emily Rodgers, Donna Scanlon, Peter Smagorinsky, Norman Stahl, Diane Stephens, and David Yaden. We hope that they see merit to what we have done.

We are also indebted to the University of British Columbia and the University of California Berkeley and for two incredible associates—Caroline Hamilton who provided editorial and research expertise and Logaine Navascués who did the lay out of the material working with Anthony Whalen at Marsworks that hosts the book (https://literacyresearchcommons.org).

Finally, this project demanded a great deal of back and forth between the two of us amidst other challenges that arose in our lives. Our friendship and respect for one another were vital as were the patience and support of our partners—Barbara and Terry.

Table of Contents

List of Figures and Tables

CLAIM 7

CLAIM 8

Preface

The two of us have been in the field of literacy education research across a number of major developments. David started as a 5th grade classroom teacher in Porterville, California; Rob, as an elementary teacher in Australia. Throughout our careers as educators, we have remained connected to classrooms in our efforts to support learners, teachers, parents and school personnel in achieving their literacy goals. Our engagements have resulted in publications in leading journals and various outlets, and have been widely cited by educators. We have also served in numerous leadership capacities, including editing key journals and reference works. As a result, we have witnessed the ebb and flow of curricular movements through many cycles. Especially salient has been the periodic swing of the pendulum between curriculum-centered and child-centered philosophies of teaching and learning reading. The difference between these two perspectives is nuanced, but important:

- **Curriculum-centered** approaches ensure that **all** students get an opportunity to learn that which authoritative agencies and individual judges deem to be "the right stuff."
- **Child-centered** approaches ensure that **each** student gets access to the right—and unique—mix of opportunities and supports that build upon their lived experiences and meet their needs to achieve their potential and key outcomes.

Equally salient has been the frustration educators feel when they reflect on the fact that, despite our best and most sincere efforts, many students still fail to acquire the literacy abilities (particularly the reading competence) they need to be successful in school and everyday life. It is undoubtedly these frustrations that lead to the third salient feature of this literacy landscape: The never-ending quest to find panaceas or fail-safe approaches to teaching reading—in other words, the best methods that will ensure that every student becomes a reader. While these tensions and swings in perspectives are concerned with the whole span of reading development, their primary focus is on the earliest stages of learning to read. There they center on the question of whether the earliest emphases should be on cracking the code (i.e., through a systematic phonics approach) or on reading for sense-making (i.e., where the code is taught as one of many components in a comprehensive or balanced approach that enables novice readers to understand and interpret the texts they encounter).

Each of us has written about these matters in the past (Pearson, 1989, 2000, 2004; Tierney, 1992, 2001, 2009, 2018), most notably in a book we co-authored (Tierney & Pearson, 2021) about the waves of research and practice that have ebbed and flowed in the literacy education field. But never have we witnessed anything like this current push for a return to foundational skills that flies under the banner of the "Science of Reading" (SoR). We became involved in the current debate in a reactive rather than a proactive way, as we witnessed the deluge of commentary in books, journal articles, and print, broadcast, and social media—all culminating in a common plea to return to the systematic teaching of phonics as the first and foremost teaching obligation of schools. The more we read, listened, and viewed, the more we recognized the same arguments, terrain, and recommendations from earlier iterations of the debate—often framed using military metaphors, such as the Reading Wars (DeJulio et al., 2024; Kim, 2008; Pearson, 2004). But we also noticed something new in the current SoR version: A self-assured attitude among those carrying the SoR flag, who assert a clarity and a confidence about the return to phonics that leaves little if any doubt about what the research demonstrates about early reading. Their consistent message is that phonics, first and fast, is settled science—and it is high time to get on with the policies and legislative action needed to ensure that every child in the U.S. (as well as Canada, the U.K., Australia, New Zealand, and any other English-speaking country) is provided direct access to the code as the first step in the process of becoming a reader.

Our initial reaction was to say to ourselves, "Have they been reading the same research we have?" Why? Because our reading of the research—across the many reports, syntheses, and consensus documents produced since the landmark year of 1967 (the publication year of Jeanne Chall's book, *Learning to Read: The Great Debate*, as well as that of Bond and Dykstra's

First-Grade Studies)—prompted us to reach a very different conclusion, something like this:

> The inclusion of code-based instruction, as a part of a comprehensive early reading curriculum, yields consistently positive and moderately-sized effects on isolated measures of word reading—but inconsistent and small effects on comprehension.

This reading of the findings led us to reach a much more nuanced policy stance: A code-emphasis component is warranted as a part of a comprehensive curriculum—namely, one that orchestrates synergies among a range of necessary developmental facets, including:

1. Foundational skills (including letter-sound knowledge and phonemic awareness);
2. Language (especially the language of schooling);
3. Knowledge (especially knowledge of the natural, social, and cultural worlds in which we live);
4. Writing (so that students benefit from moving back and forth between oral and written language registers);
5. Motivation (so that students are highly engaged in their reading); and
6. Relevance (so all students can capitalize on their cultural and personal assets in learning to read).

Whereas SoR advocates were granting 3 cheers to phonics, we were proposing 1.5, maybe 2. This discrepancy between our reading of the research and the readings we encountered in both the professional literature and public and social media led us to take a closer look at the circulating discourse, with the intention of making a public statement about these differences—addressing why they exist, and what conclusions we reached after weighing the arguments and evidence behind SoR claims.

Undoubtedly, for both of us, the precipitating event was Emily Hanford's (2022) release of the six-part podcast, *Sold a Story*, broadcast by American Public Media beginning in late 2022. Hanford's series motivated us to accelerate our response for many reasons—two of which were most pressing to us:

1. A consistent misinterpretation of the relevant research findings; and
2. A mean-spirited tone in her rhetoric, which bordered on personal attacks directed against the folks Hanford considered to be key players in what she called the Balanced Literacy approach to teaching early reading.

In particular, Hanford identified Kenneth Goodman, Marie Clay, Lucy Calkins, and the team of Gay Su Pinnell and Irene Fountas as culpable in advancing approaches to teaching early reading that included elements beyond decoding. Goodman was singled out for his contributions to a child-based theory of reading called "Whole Language," which encouraged novice readers to focus on reading for meaning—a process that might include drawing on context or other elements to predict a word, instead of first decoding the print through phonics. Lucy Calkins and the team of Fountas and Pinnell were assailed as creators of commercially-popular published reading programs built on Whole Language, or Balanced Literacy, principles. Marie Clay was criticized for promoting, among other practices, reliance on the three-cueing system. Hanford clearly and unambiguously lay the blame for what she described as a crisis in America's reading performance at their collective feet. Both her substantive errors and personal attacks accelerated our motivation to take on this review of the whole SoR movement.

As fate would have it, Rob had been asked to present a paper on the socio-cultural chasm in the Science of Reading at the American Educational Research Association's (AERA) Annual Meeting in Chicago in April 2023. Rob invited David to co-author the paper with him, and that provided the catalyst for this effort. In our discussions about how to frame our response, we were taken with the recent trend in print journalism in which news reporters and columnists fact-check the claims made by politicians about policy proposals and personal achievements. The general approach is to:

1. State the claim, preferably in the politician's own words;
2. Unpack the argument and evidence (allegedly the facts) provided in support of the claim;
3. Evaluate the validity of the "facts" (as it turns out, they are often other claims rather than facts) in evidence, as well as how those facts are used in the argument to support the claim;

4. Reach a conclusion about the validity of the claim, especially the degree to which it can be supported by the evidence.

We wondered whether we could apply the same approach in addressing the many claims made by those researchers and policy advocates aligned with the SoR. Thus, we began the process. Early on, we settled on a tentative title, *Fact-Checking the Science of Reading*, and we expected that the simple 4-part approach to analyzing each claim we encountered would serve us well in writing the essay.

Well, it did and it didn't. On the one hand, we were able to locate a provisional set of claims—statements like:

- All students benefit from an early emphasis on the code.
- Learning to read is an unnatural act.
- Reading is best defined as recognizing and understanding words that are a part of one's oral language repertoire.
- The three-cueing system has been debunked.
- Good readers don't guess, and poor readers shouldn't.
- Social, cultural, and contextual factors may influence learning more broadly, but their influence does not shape the basic act of reading.
- Reading performance is on the decline, as evidenced by national assessments, and these declines can be attributed to neglect of phonics.
- Teacher education programs have been delinquent in not preparing teachers to teach phonics.

But when we tried to apply the four-part structure, we realized that it did not lend itself to the kind of careful, nuanced, and deliberate consideration of the conceptual, methodological, and political issues that lay just beneath the surface of each claim. Hence, while this book does fact-check a set of important claims that are circulating in the public sphere, it is more about the issues that these claims bring to the table than it is about the validity of the claims themselves. For example, the section on whether learning to read is a natural act brings up several contrasts, such as:

- Learning to speak versus learning to read in one's home language.
- School-based acts of literacy versus everyday acts of literacy at home and in the community.
- Learning to read versus learning many other things, such as how to add or ride a bike; the capitals of Europe; the causes of the Civil War; etc.

Similarly, the relatively straightforward claim about the alleged three-cueing system masks a complex array of theoretical (e.g., the linguistic and epistemological resources that shape the basic socio-cognitive processes involved in reading) and practical issues (e.g., what advice should we offer novice or low-performing readers when they "get stuck" on words or meaning?). When we learned that some of the most prestigious reading researchers (e.g., Rayner et al., 2001) defined reading in a highly constrained manner (as identifying and understanding words that are a part of one's oral language repertoire), we realized that in that single statement, they removed reading from any obligation to account for most if not all of the social, cultural, and contextual factors that the learning sciences have implicated as central to all facets of learning, including learning to read.

Things got even more complicated after Rob traveled to Chicago to deliver the AERA paper. Following that conference, we collaborated with the International Literacy Association to plan, and eventually deliver, a webinar, "Fact-checking the Science of Reading." It took place about 5 weeks after the AERA presentation, in late May of 2023. We then did a second webinar (a kind of fact-checking 2.0) on the same set of ideas for Rutgers University in September.

What this meant for us as authors—and what it means for you as readers—is that each of the sections of this book turned out to be more an extended conversation about the issues surrounding a specific claim than a direct and simple "fact-checking" of one statement. We get to the fact-checking, but in most cases only after, or sometimes while, unpacking those issues. What began as a "collage" of mini-essays extended to a longer version, involving a form of iterative fact-checking as we dug deeper into each claim.

Introduction

The reading field has been a site of passionate debate about curriculum, teaching, and learning (Chall, 1967; Johns, 2023; Mathews, 1966; Pearson, 2004) since the mid-19th century. Some of the most salient questions in dispute have included:

- Is reading a quest for meaning, or a search for the code (to map letters onto sounds)?
- Is it phonics, or whole words?
- Is it part-to-whole, or whole-to-part?
- Does reading come to us as naturally, as with oral language?

First raised by scholars such as Horace Mann in the 19th century (see Mathews, 1966), these questions and more have persisted for nearly 200 years. They have ebbed and flowed with shifts in the leading philosophical views (e.g., child-centered versus curriculum-centered) and research foci (e.g., basic processes versus instructional practices) that have guided the teaching and learning of reading across different eras.

Historical Precedents

These issues reached a crescendo in the United States in the 1960s, when two seminal studies dominated discussions of beginning reading. In one of its early efforts to fund experimental research, the U.S. Federal government (via the Cooperative Research Branch of the then Office of Education) funded what came to be called the First-Grade Studies (Bond & Dykstra, 1967)—a search for the best method of teaching beginning reading. This undoubtedly remains the largest—before or since—direct comparison of various methods of teaching reading in grade one (including various phonics- or code-based approaches). The findings from this project led to the conclusion that no one method exhibited consistent advantages over others (Bond & Dykstra, 1967), suggesting that we would be better off examining the all-important role of teachers in their delivery of a range of approaches.

In that same year, Jeanne Chall's (1967) classic book, *Learning to Read: The Great Debate*, was published. Like the First Grade Studies, Chall emphasized the critical role of the teacher. In a famous conclusion, Chall pleaded for both an effective method (code-emphasis) and an effective teacher: "But a good method in the hands of a good teacher—that is the ideal" (p. 309). Unlike the First Grade Studies, Chall's book acknowledged the wide range of approaches that emphasized cracking the code as the first order of business in early reading curricula. Chall didn't just address the issue of the best method for teaching beginning reading; she dealt with a number of other issues as well, including: a) Content, and addressing enduring themes in the human experience; b) More challenging texts at every grade level; (c) New tests, both single-component skill tests and assessments that require the orchestration of many skills; and (d) Increasing the quality, relevance, and transparency of reading research (see Pearson, 2000, p. 163). Nevertheless, the major recommendation was still to ensure that an early code-emphasis was infused into all early reading programs—a priority that would endure across the decades.

Despite the popularity of Chall's book, both at the time of its publication and in the half century to follow, it did not settle the debate about the most effective method of teaching beginning reading. Instead, it would take many government-sponsored reports, legislative actions, scholarly volumes, and grassroots movements—and 60 years—to get us from Chall's version of the debate to today's. During that period, the field witnessed the advent of psycholinguistics; the cognitive revolution; socio-cultural and critical perspectives examining and supporting learner- and meaning-centered early literacy development; and several pendulum swings toward or away from the emphasis on mastery of the code. Although meaning-centered work dominated this period (i.e., that focused on basic processes and instructional practices), support for a code emphasis did not diminish—especially among psychologists and educators with a strong commitment to understanding and improving teaching and learning for both young and vulnerable readers.

This was apparent in the numerous attempts to reach a definitive conclusion on the matter of code emphasis—a persistent thread throughout research syntheses, consensus processes, and mandates. As seen in Table 1, the U.S. based initiatives included several large-scale studies and publications. On the empirical front, the National Institute of Child Health and Human Development (NICHD; see Foorman et al., 1998) also sponsored an influential quasi-experiment during the revival of code approaches in the mid-1990s; later, the U.S. Department of Education sponsored two large-scale quasi-experimental studies during the No Child Left Behind, Reading First era (Gamse et al., 2008; Jackson, et al., 2007), comparing code-emphasis with more broadly-based, business-as-usual approaches.

Table. 1
U.S.-Based Initiatives

1985	*Becoming a Nation of Readers. The report of the Commission on Reading. National Academy of Education, National Institute of Education, & Center for the Study of Reading* **(Anderson, Hiebert, Scott, & Wilkinson)**
1990	*Beginning to Read: Thinking and Learning About Print* **(Adams)**
1998	*Preventing Reading Difficulties in Young Children: A Report of the National Research Council* **(Snow, Burns, & Griffin)**
2000	*Report of the National Reading Panel: Teaching Children to Read* **(NRP & NICHD)**
2010	*Developing Early Literacy: Report of the National Early Literacy Panel* **(NELP& NICHD)**

The US was not unique in these initiatives; similar debates emerged elsewhere. For example, in the U.K. and Australia, the ebb and flow of discussions pertaining to phonics and language matters was evidenced in various government reports in the 60s and 70s—as well as those from recent years (Table 2).

Table 2

Initiatives in the U.K. and Australia

1966	*Standards and Progress in Reading* **(The Morris Report on Reading in England and Wales; see Morris)**
1967	*Children and their Primary Schools* **(The Plowden Report on Reading in the U.K.; see CACE)**
1975	*A Language for Life* **(The Bullock Report on Language and Reading; see Bullock)**
2005	*Teaching Reading: Report and Recommendations* **(see Rowe and the National Inquiry into the Teaching of Literacy, Australia)**
2006	*Independent Review of the Teaching of Early Reading* **(The Rose Report on the Teaching of Early Reading in the U.K.; see Rose)**

Consistent across these efforts to identify the best approach for teaching early reading is the argument that the explicit and systematic teaching of phonics (defined as the cipher that helps students map letters onto speech sounds) serves as a key component of comprehensive, well-integrated and orchestrated reading program. If and when phonics instruction is approached in this explicit and systematic way, students will experience greater success in early reading. Most of the reports also emphasize the important role of learning letter names as well as phonemic awareness training, usually in conjunction with the teaching of letter-sound correspondences. While the U.K.'s Rose Report (Rose, 2006) went further in recommending synthetic phonics (e.g., teaching the parts of the word, such as "buh-ah-tuh," before blending into the whole word, "bat"), the others stopped at "explicit and systematic" in their phonics recommendations. All of these recommendations came with the qualification that the results were more substantial on measures of word reading than comprehension, but that did not deter champions of phonics from mobilizing these claims for policy endorsements.

The Current Situation

Since about 2016, these debates have taken a turn toward a more strident insistence on making the code the centerpiece of early reading instruction. Flying under the banner of the Science of Reading (SoR), code-based advocates—some from the reading research community and some from the policy advocacy community—have accused the education establishment of resisting the "settled science" by supporting curricula based on tenets of Balanced Literacy and/or Whole Language. Within the ongoing public debates across social media and the popular press, we have witnessed a confluence of forces, all pointing to a greater early emphasis on cracking the code that links written to oral language (see Table 3).

Table 3

Key Sources and Indicators of Science of Reading (SoR) Advocacy across Media

- Concerns over meeting the needs of struggling readers, especially those diagnosed with dyslexia (e.g., International Dyslexia Association, 2020) have suggested that teaching systematic phonics is the most urgently needed reform (Buckingham, 2020).
- A resurgence of interest in the line of government-sponsored reports on preferred approaches to early reading instruction.
- Articles in major print and broadcast media (e.g., The New York Times, The New Yorker, The Washington Post, The Times, Education Week, The Globe and Mail, and National Public Radio, among others).
- Social media blogs, videos, and podcasts advocating a return to phonics-first, most influentially those of broadcast journalist Emily Hanford (e.g., 2018, 2022)
- Books by eminent psychologists unpacking the scientific research on the nature of the reading process, such as:
    - Wolf (& Stoodley, Illus., 2008): *Proust and the Squid: The Story and Science of the Reading Brain*
    - Dehaene (2009): *Reading in the Brain: The New Science of How We Read.*
    - Willingham (2017): *The Reading Mind: A Cognitive Approach to Understanding How the Mind Reads.*
    - Seidenberg (2017): *Language at the Speed of Sight: How We Read, Why So Many Can't, and What Can Be Done About It.*
    - Johns (2023): *The Science of Reading: Information, Media, and Mind in Modern America.*

The combination of SoR forces has been remarkably effective in shaping public opinion and conversations about the superiority of phonics (over Whole Language or Balanced Literacy approaches to instruction) as well as regional and national legislation and policy. As a result, a growing number of legislatures in jurisdictions across the U.S., Canada, New Zealand, and Australia have been mandating educational policies that require schools and teachers to make code-based instruction the first priority in beginning reading.

The expectation of both scholars (e.g., Buckingham, 2016; 2019a, 2019b; Seidenberg, 2017; Rayner et al., 2001) and policy advocates (Hanford; 2018; Moats, 1999; 2000; 2020), sometimes implicit and sometimes explicit, is that upon entry to schooling, children can use their existing language and knowledge expertise to comprehend text—once the words have been identified and understood. Deeming phonemic awareness and the ability to recode print into speech as paramount, SoR advocates express concerns about the insufficient preparation of teachers to support beginning and struggling readers (Ellis et al., 2023). Lobbying for changes to teacher preparation programs and instructional practices, they insist that teachers learn how to teach phonics more effectively.

They do so based on claims that the science of reading is "settled," and that teaching alphabetic skills is the essential starting point for beginning reading instruction and the naming of words. Moreover, SoR advocates lean on common rationales and key works by eminent scholars to explain why word learning is the most important goal for novice readers. Leading the list are:

- Gough & Tumner's (1986) Simple View of Reading;
- Chall's (1983) Stages of Reading Development;
- Perfetti & Hart's (2002) Lexical Quality Hypothesis;
- Share's (1995) account of phonics as a self-teaching mechanism; and
- Ehri's (2014; 2020) views about orthographic mapping.

Stemming from this work, systematic phonics has been positioned by authorities, policymakers, and pundits across various countries as the mainstay of the early reading curriculum. Similar to earlier eras, advocates for a code emphasis have been quick to add that while phonics is a necessary condition for early reading success, it is, by itself, not sufficient, and must therefore be complemented by curricular foci on language, especially academic language, as well as knowledge of the natural, social, and political world in which we live (Castles, Rastle, & Nation, 2018; Rose, 2006; Seidenberg, 2023b; Wexler, 2023). Interestingly, however, our own perusal of the policies and media representations suggests to us that even when the calls for policy reform include greater emphasis on language development, knowledge acquisition, and comprehension, the popular discussion has focused almost exclusively on a return to phonics as the most foundational of skills for early success. Phonics, in the public, social, and academic media, has become first among equals.

In several states in the U.S., the legislation has been so detailed as to specify that certain educational practices may not be taught in schools (see Olson, 2023, for an account of passed or proposed legislation). These include practices such as the three-cueing system, which encourages students to use both meaning and orthographic cues to unlock unknown words. Some states have gone as far as to ban the three-cueing system from being taught as a pedagogical strategy in teacher education programs. Key to these debates over method is the starting point of reading—and what counts as reading. Based upon the intricacies of the alphabetic system of writing (e.g., Castles, Rastle, & Nation, 2018; Seidenberg, 2017; Wolf & Stoodley, 2008), both phonemic awareness and letter-sound knowledge are deemed essential for learning to read. Meaning is viewed more as a product of decoding rather than as a means of supporting it. As Castles, Rastle, & Nation (2018) stated:

> If a child learns to decode that symbol-to-sound relationship, then that child will have the ability to translate printed words into spoken language, thereby accessing information about meaning. (p. 9)

These scholars build their approach using a mix of sources, including research on effective curricular approaches, the history and the evolution of the alphabet system, and neurological evidence about the areas of the brain that are activated in response to print stimuli. At the same time, they make claims from national and international test results—speculating that the ebb of test results and the shortfall in improvements for struggling readers might be ascribed to the failure of other, often meaning-based, approaches. Specifically, they point to Whole Language and Balanced Literacy—sometimes claimed to be Whole Language in disguise (Moats, 2000)—as the likely culprits in these alleged declines (e.g., Hanford, 2018; Moats, 2020).

While not wanting to diminish the merits of the overriding goal of meeting the needs of students—especially those struggling to learn to read—the nature of these efforts, their underlying assumptions, and their adoption are sobering if critically examined against and held accountable to a fuller consideration of research. With the support of some parent groups and the media, advocates of systematic phonics have been an influential force in shaping legislation and policy in over 40 states in the U.S. (Olson, 2023). In the U.S., Australia, New Zealand, and the U.K., SoR campaigns have led to mandates for major curriculum changes for beginning reading, based upon claims that phonics is key to reading development. The sometimes explicit, sometimes implied accompanying claim is that alternative approaches to reading instruction—including Whole Language (Altwerger, Edelsky, & Flores, 1987; Goodman & Goodman, 1982), Reading Recovery (Clay, 1993; 1998; Pinnell, DeFord, & Lyons, 1988), Guided Reading (Fountas & Pinnell, 1996), and Balanced Literacy (Calkins, 2019; Calkins et al., 2022; Salinger & Weinberg, 2021)—have contributed to reading failures. Specifically, according to SoR advocates, these approaches promote misguided emphases (e.g., enlisting meaning based cueing systems) and espouse faulty assumptions (e.g., reading is natural) stemming from work by Frank Smith (1971/2012, 1973, 2015) and Ken Goodman's model of reading as a psycholinguistic guessing game (Goodman, 1967, 1968, 1969).

Taking Stock of the SoR: Fact-checking

Certainly, these developments in our knowledge—about the need for more emphasis on the code—merit taking stock and fact-checking to assess the validity of the claims. To that end, we will examine the assumptions, the evidence, and the reasoning used to support the claims that are prevalent in SoR discourse. Our fact-checking is not exhaustive, but it does address what we consider key issues driving the controversies involved in this new instantiation of the Reading Wars (Castles, Rastle, & Nation, 2018; Kim, 2008; Pearson, 2004).

Our goal is to raise questions and to engage all parties with a stake in this conversation—educators, parents, scholars, legislators, the public, and the media—in finding a path forward to meet the needs of all students, their parents, and their teachers in the diverse communities that comprise the societies in which we live. To these ends, we are attempting to understand the views of those who align themselves with the SoR. At the same time, we are holding them to account—asking what evidence and warrants exist for their claims, and whether their arguments merit the influence they currently have over national and international discussions, legislation, and mandates for teaching reading.

We hope that our comments contribute to opening conversations—consistent with the concluding views expressed in Adrian John's (2023) recently published history of the Science of Reading:

> We should look much further and more deeply, not only at the science of reading, but at the reading of science—or rather, at the act of reading in science. One way to resolve the alleged crises of the scientific enterprise may lie in an understanding of those practices. (p. 427)

Claims Suggesting that the Science of Reading is Settled

So, what are the claims that emanate from scholars and policy advocates who align themselves with the Science of Reading (SoR)? A recurring position is that important aspects of reading development are settled science. The most common, and surely the most significant in terms of its current influence on policy in many states (Olson, 2023) and other English-speaking countries (Rose, 2006; Rowe et al., 2005), are the claims about pedagogy (Table 4).

Table 4
Systematic phonics instruction is the key to effective beginning reading instruction.

Related claims include:

- The Simple View of Reading (Reading Comprehension is the product of Decoding and Listening Comprehension, or RC = D x LC) provides an adequate theoretical account of skilled reading and its development over time.
- Reading is best defined as the ability to identify and understand words that are part of one's oral language repertoire.
- Phonics facilitates the identification of unknown words that, with multiple exposures, become immediately recognizable at sight, thus permitting readers to devote more and greater cognitive resources to making and monitoring meaning.
- The Three-Cueing System (Orthography, Semantics, and Syntax) has been soundly discredited.
- Learning to read is an unnatural act.

Other assertions are not so much claims about the nature, development, or instruction of reading as they are complements to these more basic claims. They tend to be more about the settings, policies, research methods, or theoretical perspectives that inform the more basic claims (Table 5).

Table 5

Settings, Policies, Methods, & Theories Informing Basic SoR Claims

- Balanced Literacy and / or Whole Language approaches bear the responsibility for the low or falling National Assessment of Educational Progress (NAEP) scores the U.S. witnessed in the past decade or so.
- Recent neuroscience research bolsters our confidence in the central role of phonological processing and phonics instruction in supporting early reading development.
- Broad contextual perspectives, such as sociocultural models of reading and literacy, are not needed to explain reading development. They may bear on literacy and learning, broadly construed, but not on reading.
- Literacy teacher education programs are not preparing teachers in the Science of Reading.

We address the question of just how settled each claim is, but first we deal with the broader question of what it means to possess, or even talk about, "settled science."

The Overall Claim: The Science of Beginning Reading Instruction is Settled

In their volume examining the generalizability of research, Ercikan and Roth (2009) raised what may be the most important question about classroom instruction: Which matters more—the mean (what works "on average") or the variation (what it would take to find approaches for even the outliers in a classroom)?

> The teacher, to design appropriate instruction for individual students, is interested precisely in the variation from the trend, that is, she is interested in the variation that in statistical approaches constitutes error variance.... we need to provide her with forms of knowledge that are simultaneously sufficiently general to provide her with trends and with forms of knowledge that are sufficiently specific to allow her to design instructions to the specific needs expressed in the variation from the trend. (p. 5)

Such a tempered position seems counter to the political reality—the spread of legislation mandating practice—but not inconsistent with recent scholarship focused upon interrogating the "Science of Reading."

When a wide range of scholars were recently given an opportunity to critically examine the Science of Reading in a special collection of *Reading Research Quarterly*, most of the participating authors asserted, suggested, or implied that we are "not there yet"—in terms of being able to offer firm, scientifically unambiguous guidance to teachers about teaching and learning for diverse classrooms and learners. A number of the authors (e.g., Alexander, 2020; Cervetti, et al., 2020; Graham, 2020; Hoffman, Hikida, & Sailors, 2020; Seidenberg, Borkenhagen, & Kearns, 2020; Shanahan, 2020; Woulfin & Gabriel 2020) expressed restraint in linking practice too tightly to the basic science of reading (see also Yaden, Reinking, & Smagorinsky, 2021).

For example, Mark Seidenberg—a vocal advocate for enhancing our professional commitment to science as the backbone of understanding reading and its development (e.g., Seidenberg, 2017)—and his colleagues (Seidenberg, Borkenhagen, & Kearns, 2020) seemed more set upon suggesting future directions, needs, and hypotheses than providing prescriptions. Indeed, they advocated a broad set of efforts, including multiple cross-disciplinary endeavors; studies of teaching practices; avoidance of a limited focus (e.g., on phonics); more studies on what might be done in different contexts to enhance early learning, and a more inclusive focus on all learners; and an examination of the systems needed to implement change. Ironically, in spite of the restraint called for—even by scientists aligned with the SoR—policy and legislation marches on, often citing research that scholars regard as not quite ready for policy implementation (Seidenberg, 2023c).

While we endorse, even champion, the notion that research contributes to improving our understanding of literacy development and how to support it through curriculum, we do so cautiously and carefully. Certain practices with select students in particular situations have merit. But it is a step too far to assume that all students would profit in the same ways from high-fidelity implementation of particular practices; evidence from the crucible of the classroom is required before any blanket mandates are implemented. Research and best practices represent possibilities for consideration rather than mandates that might override varied needs, interests, backgrounds, and development pathways of students. Particularly problematic are extrapolations to practice derived from research comparing the practices of good and poor readers; they often leave the unwarranted conclusion that we should teach all poor readers to do exactly what good readers can do. We believe that all research can—or should—do is provide hypotheses for careful classroom design, further research, and experimentation. Our position should not be viewed as discounting research findings. Both of us have spent our careers conducting and reporting on research conducted following a wide range of methodological traditions and in a diverse array of school settings. We believe that research is one of our most important tools for evaluating theories and for documenting the efficacy of instructional practices. But so too are cultural practices that are involved in our approaches to and uses of research as guides for theory development and practices. As Johns (2023) stated:

> Much that the modern science of reading investigates and everything that it claims to know about the practice, turns out to be cultural "all the way down." This is all the more apparent as the science and history of this field converge on a shared understanding—an understanding that reading is indefinitely multiform and unsettled. It is shaped by cultural experience, by history itself. (p. 426).

Our position is that practice should be guided by research. However, we would quickly add, we should always rein in the tendency to overgeneralize from research to practice—particularly from basic research to practice. Rather, a kind of dialectical conversation should arise out of discussions of the generalizability of educational research. The general must always respect its limits by recognizing variability in the particulars. Thus, we need an ongoing conversation that is dialogical rather than monological. We regard setting (the total context of teaching) as the starting point for addressing, celebrating, and taking advantage of the diversity students bring to classrooms. Teaching practices, it follows, should be responsive to the students and settings in which teachers teach and students learn. This principle aligns with what statisticians call interaction effects—the observation that the effect of an intervention may not generalize across learners, tasks, or sites.

These issues are not restricted to education. In medicine, for example, the generalizability of results from carefully controlled research is frequently tempered in applications to patients' different circumstances. Doctors prepare for the possibility that "every case will vary from the norm." In medicine, the appreciation of the science is yoked to an understanding of its modesty, and a recognition that medical science is always unsettled—thereby avoiding overgeneralization and inviting critique and counterevidence. Practices in medicine could provide an aspirational model for education. A convergence of developments in healthcare have led to what the World Health Organization has described as a rebalancing of rights and authority for determining health care protocols with patients and communities in particular health care settings (WHO Regional Office for the Western Pacific, 2007). This reflects a concern regarding what Helfand, Aguilar-Gaxiola, and Selker (2009) have characterized as overgeneralized medicine:

> When we prescribe these treatments widely even though we know little about them, we practice "overgeneralized medicine;" for most patients, we do not even know the likelihood of benefit in the short run, or anything about the benefits and risks in the long term. "Overgeneralized medicine" persists because physicians are usually willing to prescribe widely even when little is known about the actual long-term benefits and harms. In many cases, it takes years for it to become evident that the supposed benefits were less impressive than we hoped, and the harms worse than expected. (p. 444)

Shifts in approaches to healthcare also reflect a recognition of medical support as formative and transactional, tied to ethics of care, reciprocity, and respect. In promoting the needs of the individual patient in their community context, they position medical practice within an ethic of cultural safety. As Curtis et al. (2019) suggest:

> ...cultural safety encompasses a critical consciousness where healthcare professionals and healthcare organisations engage in ongoing self-reflection and self-awareness and hold themselves accountable for providing culturally safe care, as defined by the patient and their communities, and as measured through progress towards achieving health equity. (p. 16)

Culturally responsive (Gay, 2000), culturally relevant (Ladson-Billings, 1995), and culturally sustaining (Paris, 2012) may well be the educational counterparts of Curtis et al.'s notion of culturally safe medical practice. Likewise, there are similar practices in law, suggesting refrain in generalizing findings across different sites or circumstances. A key notion in law, for instance, is precedence as distinct from universal principles. Findings from other cases might inform, but should not be applied without regard to context-specific differences (Pattinson, 2015).

Methodological and Epistemological Diversity in Educational Research

We recognize the role for carefully controlled experimental studies in education, but we also see the need for more dynamic, iterative, and inclusive approaches to educational research and development—those that capitalize on many ways of knowing and many ways of collecting and analyzing evidence. Pearson (2004, 2020), in discussing the unintended consequences of various skirmishes in the Reading Wars, has argued strongly for a methodological compatibilism (Howe & Eisenhart, 1990), based on the idea that the problems and dilemmas we face in education are too important and too complex to leave in the hands of any one methodological tool.

Our claim is that "it takes a full and complementary satchel of methods, lenses, and epistemologies to make a science of reading" (Pearson, 2021, p. 99). We accept the premise (see National Research Council, 2002) that complexity demands complementarity in our search for explanation and improvement. Surely, then, we will want—even demand—randomized field trials for policy guidance, especially on pedagogical matters.

We demand such trials for vaccines and new medical or pharmaceutical practices; we should demand no less for education (Shanahan, 2020). But those randomized trials in medicine are the last 10% of the story of science. We must not privilege that small portion of the scientific journey over the other 90%, in medicine or education. We also need:

- Careful descriptions of phenomena in their natural settings (which biologists, chemists, and physicists have done for centuries);
- Examinations of natural correlations among variables in a particular setting (so we can judge the cumulative effect of persistent covariation); and
- Natural experiments (where serendipity does by circumstance what experiments do by intention).

To accomplish these goals, we also need other tools in the satchel, including:

- Data gathered in the name of theory-building and evaluation (not unlike some of the basic research driving the SoR). This is to ensure a rich pipeline of insights about how cognition interacts with culture and context to promote the magic of reading;
- Design experiments—those planful, incremental approaches to examining features of interventions in real learning situations (to ensure that we understand how things work "out there," (see Hoffman, Hikida, & Sailors, 2020); and
- Qualitative forays into the worlds of teaching and learning and implementation, using tools such as ethnography and critical discourse analysis. Specifically, such tools would help to unearth:
  - Plausibilities up front;
  - Consequences (both intended and unintended) on the back end;
  - Up close and personal accounts of practices, to provide better explanations of why things do and don't work—and, when they work, what "active ingredients" propelled them; and
  - Situated understandings and generalizations about how and why things work the way they do.

But all these tools will be useless if we cannot, or do not, accept the fundamental premise—that the role of research, in a democracy that espouses commitments to equity, opportunity, and justice, is to improve the quality of the lives for all of its citizens.

Situated Scholarship

Additionally, and in pursuit of equity, opportunity, and justice, all educational research needs to be well-situated in the contexts within which it is conducted. It should be built upon the premise that situation matters. Most importantly, it must recognize the social and cultural circumstances and engage in research befitting partnerships or respectful consultations, rather than detached objectivity and standardized deployment. Consistent with the model Schnellert, Butler, and Higginson (2008) have proposed, we opt for research-into-practice efforts that are driven less by top-down mandates or implications from the research and driven more by engaging multiple stakeholders in coordinated, and/or collaborative inquiry as a means to support teacher decision making and practices. These collaborative practices should apply to the full range of school- or community-based research, including testing practices; observational procedures; measurements; analyses; and the interpretation of the results, as well as their use en route to taking stock and implementing change.

We need to extend our research—by moving beyond basic research conducted in laboratory settings, or drawing from studies of adults to address teaching and learning for different students in different situations. To such ends, we envision a more interactive and situated approach: Transformative research and development endeavors in classrooms, clinical settings, or communities, enlisting ethical tenets that extend beyond objectivity and anonymity to respect, relevance, and reciprocity (Lather, 2004; Luke, 2011; Smith, 2000; Smith, 1999, 2005). Shanahan (2020), Allington (2007), and Stephens (2023) all offer this advice: Curriculum and pedagogy deserve their own science, lest we end up limiting the warrants for our claims about classroom practices to basic research that has only the remotest of links to practice. There is a need to nurture a science of reading development that seeks evidence-based findings across at least three layers of diversity—diverse *learners* experiencing diverse *pedagogies* in diverse *settings*.

The translation of research findings to classroom practice is not straightforward, even in tightly controlled studies of teaching, as evidenced by attempts to achieve fidelity across classrooms. Practices are apt to vary across classrooms and schools as teachers strive to respond to the needs of their students. At minimum, variability ought to be documented in some manner, either through fidelity checklists or careful descriptions of what actually happened inside classrooms (see Taylor et al., 2000; Taylor et al., 2002). We should also consider models that embrace variability—rather than regard it as error variance that compromises the analyses and generalization of treatment effects. The first step in achieving such a goal would involve an orientation to ongoing inquiry that is iterative rather than settled—grounded in the particulars of classrooms, and open to the variability of learners, their teachers, and their learning experiences.

A variability-oriented view of educational science is compatible with the recent and powerful developments in the learning sciences—what have come to be referred to as design studies (Gutiérrez et al., 2017; Gutiérrez & Penuel, 2014; Hoffman 2023; Sailors & Hoffman, 2019; Simon, 1969/1996, 1973; Van den Akker et al., 2006). Gutiérrez and Penuel (2014) describe design research in critical spaces of transformation that reinvent experimentation, transforming the traditional fixed approaches with readily measurable outcomes into more open-ended socially embedded experiments that involve ongoing mutual engagement (p. 20). As Hoffman (2023) recently suggested, one of the keys of design research involves "seeing everyday practices in new (and critical) ways and then using design research to explore the 'what could be'" (p. 478). For Hoffman, like Gutiérrez & Penuel, such studies form an essential contrast with large-scale studies because they are small in scale and locally situated; context is not a nuisance to be "eliminated or controlled but studied for its influence. The power of design research comes in the interaction of researchers across different contexts engaging with similar challenges and similar design paths" (Hoffman, 2023, p. 478).

For teacher educators and historians in our field, such an orientation should be considered more reassuring than radical. This represents forms of research that recognize the diversity of learners and the saliency of their socio-cultural experiences. These views align with research on teaching and the overriding influence of the teacher variable in the teaching of reading. They complement the tenets of action research and reflective practice espoused by Schon (1983), Kincheloe (1991), and others. In a recent book chapter (Tierney & Pearson, 2023), we have recommended a move away from the notion of best *practice* to best *practicing* to emphasize the principle that practices

> ...are evolving understandings not stable prescriptions. They are aspirations, not facts. Yesterday's best practice must give way to today's, and today's, to tomorrow's. They require constant adaptation and updating. (p. 462)

We also echo García and Kleifgen's (2020) commitments, in their discussions of multilingual teaching and learning, that educators "must respond to the specific interaction, in the specific place, and with the specific interlocutors and objects in which the spontaneous performance happens" (p. 13).

Essentially, what all these efforts have in common is a commitment to a paradoxical principle: If your goal is to know what works in general, start by figuring out what works in a specific setting, with a particular set of students, teachers, and local cultural resources. Regardless of whether you are testing hypotheses, observing to unearth patterns of behavior, seeking answers, or just refining questions, research involves discovery. A useful metaphor for cutting to the core of this perspective comes from legal discourse. Cases are adjudicated not just on legal principles, but also on legal precedents. The precedents are particular cases that serve as exemplars to guide future legal judgments; in fact, it is commonplace to use the name of the case (Plessy v. Ferguson; Miranda; Roe v. Wade; Dobbs) to refer to the principle, as well as to ground it in particulars. We think the idea of precedents of particularity might be a useful way to think about what is needed to improve the impact of educational research on practice. Such a venture would certainly highlight the importance of situating our scholarly principles in particular settings.

Modesty as a Core Research Value

These thoughts on situatedness lead directly to our last note regarding just how settled science is. Any general views of a Science of Reading—or any other research endeavor that aspire to wear the mantle of science—need to adopt an appropriately modest and skeptical view of just how certain and settled scholarship ever is. We agree with Reinking, Hruby, and Risko (2023) view that the notion of a "settled science is an oxymoron":

> Scientists are never entirely comfortable that their current data and explanations are fully explanatory. They are continually testing the veracity and utility of current theories, findings, and interpretations. They look for anomalies in their data, and they set an extremely high bar for any conclusions that might approach certainty. What attracts them to science is that nothing is entirely settled. They live in the realm of perpetual ambiguity and what-ifs. Scientists seek final truths only in the abstract, knowing that the best they can do is reduce ignorance.
>
> ...Scientists aren't satisfied with determining what works or not. They want to understand how, why, and in what circumstances different approaches may or may not be a good fit. Multidimensional continua, not binaries, are the stuff of science, especially when science is applied to real-world decisions in the realm of instructional practice.
>
> ...Science, used this way, is not a means of inquiry toward better understanding or to obtain better results, but something that requires uncritical deference and genuflection. It suggests that the aim of science is to reach a state where no further understanding is possible, where no more questions need to be asked, where no more evidence needs to be considered, where no other perspectives or interpretations can be reasonably offered, and where anyone who thinks otherwise is a misguided, if not a heretical denier of immutable truth. Such perspectives are not science, especially in matters of teaching and learning, which are always embedded in an incredibly complex social system that entails cultural norms, values, and beliefs, including issues of equity and justice. (p. 123-124)

It is neither necessary nor wise to regard some science as settled. Instead of touting that science is settled, we look at how its history documents an inherently provisional endeavor—always prepared to be modified, or even overturned, by the next challenge from empirical evidence or the next shift in theoretical paradigms.

Evaluating the settled character of key SoR claims

We turn now to the specific claims emanating from the SoR discourse of "settled science." As a reminder, we review each claim in three steps: a) Unpacking the evidence presented for its validity; b) Offering our reading of that evidence; and c) Concluding with a revised version of the claim that we can support. In terms of the sequence of claims, we considered many options—but settled on using our perceptions of their prominence in the current SoR discourse, either in scholarly or policy contexts, as our standard. To operationalize the prominence standard, we examined their ubiquity in books, professional journals, the popular press, and social media.

CLAIM 1

Explicit systematic phonics instruction is the key curricular component in teaching beginning reading.

The Evidence Marshalled in Support of the Claim

A prototypical example of the evidence for phonics appears in an article for *Reading Research Quarterly*, in an issue dedicated to analyses of the Science of Reading (SoR). In a section of the article entitled, "Compelling evidence in the science of reading" (p. S270), Petscher and colleagues (2020) provided a clear and definitive endorsement of the role of decoding instruction in the learning and teaching of reading:

> Since the publication of the National Reading Panel's (2000) report, and supported by subsequent research (e.g., Foorman, Beyler, et al., 2016; Gersten, Jayanthi, & Dimino, 2017), it is clear that a large evidence base provides strong support for the explicit and systematic instruction of the component and foundational skills of decoding and decoding itself. That is, teaching students phonological awareness and letter knowledge, particularly when combined, results in improved word-decoding skills. Teaching students to decode words using systematic and explicit phonics instruction results in improved word-decoding skills. (p. S271)

They went on to identify how these findings about decoding bear out in studies of specific populations:

> Such instruction is effective both for monolingual English-speaking students and students whose home language is other than English (i.e., dual-language learners; Baker et al., 2014; Gersten et al., 2007), as well as students who are having difficulties with learning to read or who have an identified reading disability (Ehri, Nunes, Stahl, & Willows, 2001; Gersten et al., 2008). (p. S271)

This endorsement is typical of many we found in our perusal of both scholarly and policy advocacy literature. Looking across many endorsements of early phonics, many different syntheses of studies are cited, but the single most cited evidentiary source for this stance on reading is the meta-analysis in the Alphabetics section of the National Reading Panel (NRP) Report, commissioned by the National Institute for Child Health and Human Development (NICHD) (2000). Bowers (2020), emphasizing its influence, noted that the NRP report has been cited over 24,000 times. The chair of the Alphabetics subgroup, Linnea Ehri, along with colleagues Nunes, Stahl, and Willows, summarized that section's findings in the *Review of Educational Research* (Ehri et al., 2001)—a piece that also subsequently became a popular evidentiary source for the efficacy of phonics instruction (with over 1500 citations as of August 2023). Other common but less frequently cited sources include the What Works Clearinghouse practice guide by Gersten et al. (2008), and a 2016 What Works Clearinghouse report on foundational skills to support reading in grades K-3, co-authored by Foorman and colleagues (Foorman et al., 2016). Increasingly, secondary syntheses (syntheses or analyses of syntheses)—such as the 2018 piece in *Psychological Science in the Public Interest* by Castles et al., the critical analysis by Bowers (2020), or the recent postmortem of the furor spawned by the Bowers piece (Brooks, 2023)—are also gaining favor as authoritative documentary sources.

There are some differences in the approaches and perspectives published in other countries. However, many of those reports have similar antecedents, including claims of unmet student needs; indications of falling national test results; and suggestions that certain educational approaches contribute to these declines. Likewise, there have been similar leanings in terms of recommendations, drawn from a comparable definition of reading from advisors with shared views.

Our Reading of the Evidence and the Claim

As suggested in our introduction to this monograph, debates over the efficacy of phonics-first approaches were lively and controversial matters in the 1960s. They retreated in the two decades following, as comprehension, text structure, and knowledge took center stage in conversations and policies about reading (Pearson & Cervetti, 2017). The 1990s ushered in new debates and a flurry of activity regarding the role of phonics in early reading. In the late

1980s, the U.S. federally-funded Center for the Study of Reading was asked to develop a report on beginning reading, which resulted in Adams' (1990) volume, *Beginning to Read.* This was followed by a major NICHD-funded quasi-experimental evaluation of three levels of phonics—directed code, embedded code, and implicit code (Foorman et al., 1998). The results, which showed small to moderate advantages for direct code on within-word tasks, were widely used in the media, including several *Education Week* articles (Manzo, 1997, 1998a, 1998b), and in state policy settings (see Manzo, 1998c; Taylor et al., 2000), seeming to claim a clear mandate. This prompted a short but sharp controversy (Taylor et al., 2000) about the role of research in warranting changes to policy and practice. The next major developments were a National Academy of Sciences and National Research Council report, *Preventing Reading Difficulties in Young Children* (Snow, Griffith, & Burns, 1998), followed, in short order, by the NRP and NICHD (2000) report, *Teaching Children to Read.* All of these efforts concluded that, according to the research, systematic phonics instruction provides a reliable advantage over non-systematic, opportunistic phonics (e.g., synthetic approaches, such as matching phonemes to graphemes, then blending to pronounce the word), especially on word reading outcomes. They also recommended policy changes that would feature systematic phonics as one key component (but certainly not the only component) in a comprehensive reading/language arts curriculum.

The National Reading Panel. In 1997, the NICHD was asked by Congress to assemble a National Reading Panel of "experts" to assess the status of research-based knowledge, including the effectiveness of various approaches to teaching children to read. Related to the claim about the best approach to beginning reading instruction, the key questions were:

- Does instruction in phonemic awareness improve reading?
- If so, how is this instruction best provided?
- Does phonics instruction improve reading achievement?
- If so, how is this instruction best provided? (p. 1-3)

Other questions focused upon the role of fluency instruction, comprehension instruction, vocabulary instruction, independent reading, technology, and teacher education. To address these first two questions on phonemic awareness and phonics, the Alphabetics subgroup of the NRP, chaired by Linnea Ehri, engaged in a selective research review, meta-analysis. They restricted their examination of the research to peer-reviewed articles governed by traditional and positivistic experimental standards—namely, quasi-experimental and randomized experimental studies. In doing so, they excluded naturalistic studies (e.g., descriptive studies, ethnographies, and case studies of young learners). Among the exclusions were studies of print awareness; emergent reading and writing behaviors, engaging texts for a range of purposes—all topics and perspectives that would be difficult to study within experimental frameworks. Reviews, including our own, are never totally objective, nor are they inclusive or apolitical. To some extent, they reflect the studies included for consideration and the conceptual predispositions of the reviewers. The NRP report was no exception. The Panel's selective review of traditional experimental studies adopted the lens of meta-analysis in the hopes of gleaning, where possible, convergent findings. In terms of beginning reading, the focus of the Alphabetics subgroup review—driven by their guiding questions—was the influence of teaching phonemic awareness (sensitivity to the structure of sounds in spoken language) and phonics (learning letter-sound correspondences and patterns) on both word reading and comprehension. These approaches to word learning became their primary concern.

To draw conclusions from the set of experimental studies sampled, the NRP employed, where possible, meta-analyses, using effect sizes (i.e., the average difference, measured in standard deviations, between competing treatments) as the common metric. Their goal was to determine the most consistently effective approach to teaching early reading. While they reported in a tempered fashion that their analyses had yielded positive results for the effects of phonemic analysis on the identification of unknown words and the pronunciation of pseudowords, they reported no advantages of PA instruction in terms of transfer to reading comprehension. As they reservedly concluded:

> PA training does not constitute a complete reading program. Although the present meta-analysis confirms that PA is a key component that can contribute significantly to the effectiveness of beginning reading and spelling instruction, there is obviously much more that needs to be taught to children to enable them to acquire reading and writing competence. PA instruction is intended only as a critical foundational piece. It helps children grasp how the alphabetic system works in their language and helps children read and spell words in various ways. However, literacy acquisition is a complex process for which there is no single key to success. Teaching phonemic awareness does not ensure that children will learn to read and write. Many other competencies must be taught for this to happen. ... Whether the benefits are lasting will likely depend on the comprehensiveness and effectiveness of the entire literacy program that is taught. (NRP & NICHD, 2000, pp. 2-6–2-7)

The conclusions about phonics instruction, are similarly couched as cautious advice, with many qualifications:

> ...it is important to emphasize that systematic phonics instruction should be integrated with other reading instruction to create a balanced reading program. Phonics instruction is never a total reading program. In 1st grade, teachers can provide controlled vocabulary texts that allow students to practice decoding, and they can also read quality literature to students to build a sense of story and to develop vocabulary and comprehension. Phonics should not become the dominant component in a reading program, neither in the amount of time devoted to it nor in the significance attached. It is important to evaluate children's reading competence in many ways, not only their phonics skills but also their interest in books and their ability to understand information that is read to them. By emphasizing all of the processes that contribute to growth in reading, teachers will have the best chance of making every child a reader. (NRP & NICHD, 2000, p. 2-97)

In 2001, Ehri and her colleagues published a peer-reviewed version of ostensibly the same data that formed the basis of the NRP phonics meta-analysis. However, they reached a more optimistic, and much less qualified, conclusion:

> Systematic phonics instruction helped children learn to read better than all forms of control group instruction, including whole language. In sum, systematic phonics instruction proved effective and should be implemented as part of literacy programs to teach beginning reading as well as to prevent and remediate reading difficulties. (Ehri et al., 2001, p. 393).

Missing, in comparison with the NRP report, is the language about the other pedagogical supports and processes, in concert with phonics, that contribute to the development of competent, committed readers. After examining the conclusions from the 2000 National Reading Panel and the 2001 Ehri et al. article, Bowers (2020)—perhaps the most vocal critic of the NRP report—noted that a more apt conclusion from the evidence provided would be something much more modest. As he suggested: "Systematic phonics did provide a moderate short-term benefit to regular word and pseudoword naming, with overall benefits significant but reduced by a third following 4–12 months" (p. 687).

Reanalyses of the NRP Data. The data from the NRP meta-analysis on phonics have been reanalyzed on several occasions. Among the earliest were 2003 and 2006 attempts by Camilli and his colleagues to refocus the analysis on systematic (i.e., the treatment) versus unsystematic phonics, the latter of which Camilli took to be the status quo in U.S. classrooms (Camilli, Wolfe, & Smith, 2006; Camilli, Vargas, & Yurecko, 2003). Camilli et al. coded all of the treatment conditions across all of the analyzable studies as systematic phonics, unsystematic phonics, or no phonics. Additionally, Camilli et al. added codes for moderator variables not used in the NRP—namely, the regular use of language activities (shared writing or reading), tutoring, or basal programs. In the 2003 analysis, they did replicate the advantage for systematic phonics, but at a 50% reduction in effect size compared to the NRP. Additionally, they found reliable moderating effects for both language activities and tutoring, with both effect sizes larger than those for systematic phonics.

In their 2006 reanalysis, using multilevel modeling, they found even smaller effect sizes for systematic phonics. In 2008, Stuebing et al. reanalyzed the same Camilli datasets. In their critique, they noted that the different outcomes of the Camilli work, in comparison with the findings of the NRP, was not due to the use of slightly different data sets. Camilli et al. (2008) responded that same year with another defense of their findings and methodology.

In 2006, Torgerson, Brooks, and Hall, noting that the NRP had included studies that used both randomized and nonrandomized designs, carried out a reanalysis that corrected what they considered to be errors in applying inclusion criteria. The net effect was that while the word-reading effects remained, no comprehension or spelling effects proved significant. When Bowers (2020) examined the NRP report alongside the reanalyses conducted by Camilli et al. (2003, 2006) and Torgerson and colleagues (Torgerson, Brooks, & Hall, 2006), he concluded:

> ...a careful review of the NPR (2000) findings show that the benefits of systematic phonics for reading text, spelling, and comprehension are weak and short-lived, with reduced or no benefits for struggling readers beyond grade 1. The subsequent Camilli et al. (2003, 2006) and Torgerson et al. (2006) reanalyses further weakens these conclusions. (p. 691)

Other Major Syntheses. In addition to these reanalyses, several scholars (Adesope et al., 2011; Galuschka, et al., 2014; Hammill & Swanson, 2006; Han, 2010; McArthur et al., 2021; Sherman, 2007; Suggate, 2010, 2016) undertook new meta-analyses, with both old and new studies included, while Torgerson et al. (2019) and Bowers (2020) engaged in critical tertiary analyses of the many meta-analyses. Torgerson and his colleagues (2019) found that definitive conclusions about which approach to use would require more evidence from impeccably-designed randomized controlled trials—although, they noted, it was sensible to include some form of systematic phonics in curricula for younger readers. Bowers, however, took issue with the somewhat qualified conclusions of Torgerson et al. (2019). As he argued, because the control conditions in the NRP and the Torgerson et al. (2019) analyses included both unsystematic phonics (which Bowers claims to be characteristic of Whole Language) and no phonics conditions, neither the NRP nor Torgerson et al. can conclude that systematic phonics is superior to unsystematic (what we might call opportunistic) phonics. After examining an array of meta-analyses, reanalyses, and tertiary analyses, Bowers (2020) concluded (in *his* own tertiary analysis):

> In sum, the above research provides little or no evidence that systematic phonics is better than standard alternative methods used in schools. The findings do not challenge the importance of learning grapheme-phoneme correspondences, but they do undermine the claim that systematic phonics is more effective than alternative methods that include unsystematic phonics (such as whole language) or that teach grapheme-phoneme correspondences along with meaning based constraints on spellings (morphological instruction or structured word inquiry). (p. 705)

Bowers' critique did not go unchallenged by colleagues with a history of advocating for a strong phonics position (e.g., Buckingham, 2020; Fletcher, Savage, & Vaughn, 2021). Critics took issue with Bowers' goals, assumptions, and methods of critique. Both Buckingham (2020) and Fletcher and his colleagues (2021) revisited the same studies that prompted Bowers (2020) to conclude that the empirical support for systematic phonics over other approaches was extremely weak—only to conclude the polar opposite. Namely, they found that support for systematic phonics as a necessary—but not a sufficient—curricular feature was uniformly strong (although Fletcher, Savage, and Vaughn did note that "explicit" might be a more fitting term than systematic to describe the successful code-based interventions). Both parties also agreed that better randomized controlled trials were needed to evaluate the relative efficacy of competing approaches, including some (e.g., combining morphology and phonology in promoting letter-sound knowledge) that were not well-examined in pedagogical research. One statement in the Fletcher, Savage, and Vaughn (2021) response, taken from the abstract, stands out to us as emblematic of the unproductive nature of the debate we seem to experience again and again, with Groundhog Day-like regularity:

> We conclude that there is consistent evidence in support of explicitly teaching phonics as part of a comprehensive approach to reading instruction that should be differentiated to individual learner needs. The appropriate question to ask of a twenty-first century science of teaching is not the superiority of

> phonic versus alternative reading methods, including whole language and balanced literacy, but how best to combine different components of evidence-based reading instruction into an integrated and customized approach that addresses the learning needs of each child. (p. 1249)

Comments like this, from a group of scholars readily identifiable as "scientists of reading," makes us wonder why the debate endures—when there seems to be little left to debate (see our concluding section on our advice for a post-reading-war set of principles for moving the field ahead).

We would note that Bowers, throughout this repartee with colleagues, held steadfastly to several points: (a) Letter-sound correspondences (what he calls GPCs for grapheme-phoneme correspondences) must be learned; (b) Phonics is one way, but certainly not the only way, to promote such learning; and (c) As a field, we would do well to capitalize on the recent evidence supporting an emphasis on morphology. By developing pedagogical approaches that promote a dual emphasis on phonology and morphology, he argued, we could advance a more refined, transparent, and effective way of helping students learn how to link graphemic information to meaning.

Three more recent syntheses add to this consistent evidentiary trend (the phonics effect is stronger on word reading than on passage comprehension outcomes) and interpretive thread (phonics is a key part of a comprehensive and responsible reading program). Hall et al. (2023) conducted a meta-analysis of 53 experimental or quasi-experimental intervention studies conducted between 1980 and 2020 that aimed to improve reading outcomes for over 6,000 K-5 students with or at risk of dyslexia. They concluded that the effects on reading comprehension outcomes tended to be smaller than effects on word reading or spelling outcomes. In contextualizing their results, they noted:

> This finding corroborates results reported by Gersten et al. (2020 and Neitzel et al. (2022), who found that outcome domain statistically significantly moderated intervention effects. Gersten et al. determined that effects on word/pseudoword measures were greater than effects on passage reading or reading comprehension measures; Neitzel et al. found that effects on alphabetics (i.e., PA, print awareness, letter naming, phonics knowledge,

> decoding, and encoding) and passage reading fluency measures were larger than those on general reading performance measures. ...Although improvements in foundational skills would be expected to translate to improved reading comprehension (Hoover & Gough, 1990), reading comprehension was nevertheless a less proximal outcome for this corpus of studies. (p. 303)

Wyse and Bradbury (2022) reviewed evidence from national and international assessments, their own qualitative meta-synthesis of largely the same corpus of studies reviewed by Suggate (2016) and Bowers (2020), and a survey administered to a large sample of teachers in the UK (to gain a sense of practices actually being implemented in schools). Looking across this span of data, they concluded:

> The undue separation of the teaching of the alphabetic code from the context of whole texts as part of teaching of the alphabetic code from the context of whole texts in the teaching of reading in primary/elementary schools is unlikely to be effective as contextualized teaching of reading, and as such poses a significant risk to typically developing children's education and life chances because it is not optimal robust evidence-based teaching. If education policies also fail to sufficiently reflect the robust research evidence this risk is compounded. (p. 42)

They hypothesized that "phonics teaching is most likely to be effective for children aged five to six" (p. 42), and added that, in general: "A focus on whole texts and reading for meaning, to contextualize the teaching of other skills and knowledge, should drive pedagogy" (p. 42). Whereas Bowers' (2020) critique prompted the conclusion that systematic phonics was no more effective on key outcomes (word reading and comprehension) than unsystematic phonics (operationalized as opportunistic "teachable moments," often attributed to Whole Language or Balanced Literacy approaches), Wyse and Bradbury's conclusion is more affirmative: Focus on making meaning and use phonics to promote that broader goal. It is interesting to note that some 15 years earlier, Wyse, writing with Goswami (2008), noted that systemic but contextualized phonics instruction, when it was a part of a larger comprehensive curriculum, was equally as effective as any other phonics approach—and, in a few studies, proved to be the most effective approach on both word and passage level tasks.

The most recent critique we found before we went to press was a response by Brooks (2023), to both Bowers (2020) and Wyse and Bradbury (2022). Brooks (2023) claims that both parties misinterpreted the results from the studies included in their tertiary syntheses. In particular, he argues that Bowers over-relied on Camilli's work, which Brooks takes to be flawed in terms of categorizing teaching methods. Similar to Buckingham (2020) and Ehri et al. (2001), Brooks concludes:

> … the evidence in favour of systematic phonics seems robust, and the key implication for teachers of initial literacy is therefore that systematic phonics instruction should remain an essential element within their repertoire. (p. 2)

Brooks qualifies that strong endorsement in the conclusion to his essay. In the end, he aligns more with the conclusions offered by Fletcher, Savage, & Vaughn (2021) and the NRP report (NRP & NICHD, 2000)—arguing that phonics is an essential, but not the only, component of a comprehensive program:

> …in the current state of knowledge, the evidence in favour of systematic phonics instruction seems robust. This does not imply that it should be used to the exclusion of other aspects of instruction, but does imply that it should form an essential part of a rich and varied language and literacy curriculum. (p. 6)

Research, Evaluation, and Policy Studies. As a reminder, the two major quasi-experimental research studies in the U.S. (Gamse, et al., 2008; Jackson et al., 2007) came out of the No Child Left Behind Act of 2001. The legislation established the Reading First (RF) and Early Reading First (ERF) program initiatives, which stipulated that reading curricula and materials for elementary and preschool-age children, respectively, were expected to align with certain criteria. ERF preschool programs were meant to focus on developing skills in oral language, phonological awareness and awareness of print conventions, and alphabet knowledge. The RF programs were then expected to emphasize the five components of reading instruction: 1) Phonemic awareness; 2) Phonics; 3) Vocabulary; 4) Fluency; and 5) Comprehension.

The *Reading First* (RF) study by Gamse and colleagues (2008) concluded that RF schools (those which emphasized the 5 components) showed a modest but consistent advantage over non-RF schools, using a measure of word decoding in Grade 1, but not on comprehension measures at any grade level. The *Early Reading First* study (Jackson et al., 2007) showed strong effects on teacher knowledge and practices, but weak effects on student outcomes. In other words, compared to non-ERF preschools, the teachers in ERF preschools changed what they did to align with the guidelines—but these changes in practice had little impact on student performance. The only significant advantage for ERF schools was on print awareness (none on phonological awareness or oral language). By contrast to the national studies, several of the Reading First quasi-experimental evaluations carried out at the state level revealed that schools that followed the RF guidelines for program (i.e., the 5 components or pillars) outperformed non-RF schools with comparable demographic characteristics (see Coburn et al., 2011; Pearson, 2010), again suggesting that when phonics is a part of a more comprehensive program, it is associated with positive outcomes.

The U.S. has certainly not been alone in the quest for a panacea to reading development debates—nor have they been the only region in which systematic, sometimes synthetic, phonics have been positioned as the solution. Other countries have paralleled the U.S., in terms of the process undertaken for reviews, the premises that guide them, and the nature of expertise enlisted. In the United Kingdom, for example, the Secretary of State commissioned Sir Jim Rose to review the teaching of early reading; Rose's recommendations placed a major emphasis on teaching phonics systematically and synthetically (Rose, 2006). In Australia, the Australian Council of Educational Research commissioned a report on the teaching of reading, under the leadership of Kenneth Rowe (Rowe & National Inquiry, 2005). In Canada, in response to a concern spurred by the Canadian Supreme Court with regard to the rights of special education students in learning to read, the Ontario government commissioned a report that appears to similarly advocate for phonics-focused instruction (OHRC, 2022). A close examination of these reports, informed by the research syntheses and various meta-analyses we have just reviewed, reveals them to be generally in favor of phonics—again, not on its own, but as a key component in a more comprehensive curriculum. These are certainly more modest than the claims made in the media, blogs and other outlets by policy advocates (e.g., Buckingham, Wheldall, & Beaman-Wheldall, 2013; Hanford, 2018; Moats, 2000).

More Signs of Restraint. In addition to the consistent qualifications coming from research syntheses, signs of restraint come from scholars and policymakers both aligned with and skeptical of the SoR. Among the skeptics were Johnston and Scanlon (2022), who, in a policy statement for the Literacy Research Association, reviewed the research informing practices for students diagnosed with dyslexia. They questioned whether the science was "settled," the efficacy of synthetic phonics, and the importance of context versus cueing systems. With respect to phonics, they concluded that the evidence

> ...does not justify the use of a heavy and near-exclusive focus on phonics instruction, either in regular classrooms, or for children experiencing difficulty learning to read (including those classified as dyslexic). (p. 25)

They also argued that there was little evidence to suggest that phonics should be pursued synthetically or removed from other curricular practices (e.g., those targeting comprehension, vocabulary, contextual clues, etc.).

Reinking, Hruby, and Risko (2023) offered another critique of the SoR position. In an effort not unlike ours, they disputed the validity of several claims distilled from SoR advocates, including arguments made in articles in the popular press, professional archival literature, and social media posts. As they note, these claims include:

- Phonics is *the* essential component of learning to read.
- Phonics should be mastered before other components of a comprehensive curriculum are addressed.
- Differentiated instruction for mastering the code is not necessary.
- Synthetic phonics is preferred to other more analytic or opportunistic approaches.

- The vast majority of reading difficulties stem from incomplete mastery of, and can be remediated by, phonics.
- There is a crisis in reading performance in this country, and it can be explained by the education establishment's reluctance to accept phonics as the curricular key to early success.
- Phonics requires continued emphasis until it is mastered by students.
- The science behind these claims is settled.

The key point in their article is that while the research base for these claims is weak, they are nonetheless offered to legislators and policymakers at the state and local level as scientifically irrefutable and, therefore, appropriate for supporting wide-scale reforms that favor code-based standards for early reading instruction.

Mark Seidenberg (2017, 2023b/c), in contrast, is among the advocates of an early emphasis on phonics. In a recent blog entry, Seidenberg (2023c) expressed concern that in our zeal to ensure a good start for young readers, we might have overemphasized the necessity of phonemic awareness:

> The goal of teaching children to read is reading, not phonemic awareness. We know that learning to read does not require being able to identify 44 phonemes or demonstrate proficiency on phoneme deletion and substitution tasks because until very recently *no one* who learned to read had to do these things. Instruction in subskills such as phonemic awareness is justified *to the extent it advances the goal of reading*, not for its own sake. (para. 2)

In that same blog entry, he stated:

> The treatment of PA in the "science of reading"–the idea that a certain level of PA is prerequisite for reading, and that PA training should continue until the student becomes highly proficient at PA tasks regardless of how well they are reading–is emblematic of problems that have arisen within the SoR approach. It is an overprescription that reflects a shallow understanding of reading development yet has become a major tenet of the "science of reading". The PA situation and other developments suggest to me that the SoR is at risk of turning into a new pedagogical dogma, consisting

> of a small set of tenets loosely tied to some classic but dated research, supplemented by additional assumptions that are ad hoc and ill-advised. (para. 5)

Both in his blog and in his 2020 co-written piece for *Reading Research Quarterly* (Seidenberg, Borkenhagen, & Kearns, 2020), Seidenberg stressed the need to elevate our efforts to translate research into practice by enhancing the efficacy of translational research.

As noted, Sir Jim Rose (2006)—who managed to convince the UK Secretary of State to mandate synthetic phonics—was also known as an advocate of synthetic phonics. In his commissioned report from 2006, he concluded:

> Having considered a wide range of evidence, the review has concluded that the case for systematic phonic work is overwhelming and much strengthened by a synthetic approach.... (p. 20)

Earlier in that same report, however, Rose waffled a bit, as in this more tempered statement:

> It is widely agreed that reading involves far more than decoding words on the page. ...Phonic work is therefore a necessary but not sufficient part of the wider knowledge, skills and understanding which children need to become skilled readers and writers, capable of comprehending and composing text. (p. 4)

Rose even suggested that "leading edge practice bears no resemblance to a 'one size fits all' model of teaching and learning, nor does it promote boringly dull, rote learning of phonics" (p. 16).

One can include Gough in this list of phonics advocates who demonstrated restraint in their emphasis on the code in the early years of schooling (e.g., Gough & Hillinger, 1980; Gough, Hoover, & Peterson, 1996; Gough, Juel, & Roper-Schneider, 1983; Gough & Tunmer, 1986). Gough, as well as his colleagues Hoover and Tumner (Hoover & Gough, 1990; Hoover & Tunmer, 2018, 2020, 2022), assert that the cipher used to recode print into speech must be learned and probably must be taught to most novice readers. However, they stop short of any specific suggestions about the characteristics of that instruction.

Our Revised Version of the Claim

Looked at historically, the characterization of phonics—as a) exerting a greater effect on reading words and/or pseudowords than understanding text and b) one key piece in a larger and broader curriculum—is consistent with the cautions offered in a long line of efforts to determine the best method for teaching reading. The list begins in the 1960s, with Chall (1967) and the First-Grade Studies (Bond & Dykstra, 1967), and goes on to include major syntheses, such as *Becoming a Nation of Readers* (Anderson et al., 1985), *Beginning to Read* (Adams, 1990), *Preventing Reading Difficulties in Young Children* (Snow, Burns, & Griffin, 1998), and the *National Reading Panel Report* (NRP& NICHD, 2000). These were followed by the quasi-experimental studies funded during the Reading First era (Gamse et al., 2008; Jackson et al., 2007), alongside a similar lively debate in the UK (Rose, 2006). Everyone seems to be saying that a responsible curriculum—rationalized as part of the settled science of reading or as part of an ecologically-balanced program—will ensure that all students get full access to all the evidence-based pieces of the reading puzzle. So why are we—educators, researchers, policy advocates—still shouting at one another? We are not sure. We will take up this question again, after reviewing 9 more claims related to the debate.

Here's one working hypothesis to carry into the rest of the claims. Neither side really trusts the other to follow through on their statements of commitment. SoR folks seem to believe that a lot of educators (teachers, and especially teacher educators) keep their fingers crossed when they promise to provide students with access to the full range of code-based instruction. Folks with a balanced literacy perspective, on the other hand, seem to believe that SoR-oriented advocates want to marginalize language, comprehension, and critical thinking practices until all of the code-based knowledge is mastered. In short, we don't really trust one another to keep our promises. We will revisit this potential impasse at the conclusion of this monograph.

CLAIM 2

The Simple View of Reading provides an adequate theoretical account of skilled reading and its development over time.

The Evidence Marshalled in Support of the Claim

As developed by Gough and Tunmer (1986), the Simple View of Reading (SVR) maintains that reading comprehension (RC) is the product of decoding (D) and language comprehension (LC): (RC = D x LC). Those who champion the SVR are quick to point out both its empirical strengths (i.e., evidence available to document its validity—see Catts, 2018) and conceptual merits (i.e., its elegant simplicity—see Pearson, Madda, & Raphael, 2023). For instance, a common claim is that the SVR is supported by over 150 research studies (Seidenberg, 2023b; The Reading League, 2023). A typical citation documenting its empirical stature is captured in this statement from Castles, Rastle, and Nation (2018):

> Measures of decoding and of linguistic comprehension each predict reading comprehension and its development, and together the two components account for almost all the variance in this ability (e.g., Lervåg, Hulme & Melby-Lervåg, 2017). Early in development, reading comprehension is highly constrained by limitations in decoding. As children get older, the correlation between linguistic and reading comprehension strengthens, reflecting the fact that once a level of decoding mastery is achieved, reading comprehension is constrained by how well an individual understands spoken language (LARRC, 2015). (p. 27)

Much of the scholarship in support of the SVR also points to its conceptual integrity and economy—as a useful way to describe the many aspects of reading development (Catts, 2018; Lonigan, Burgess, & Schatschneider, 2018; Sleeman et al., 2022). In its original conceptualization (see Gough & Tunmer, 1986; Hoover & Gough, 1990) the SVR simply asserts that:

- The complex array of factors affecting reading comprehension (RC) can be conveniently placed into one of two big buckets:
    1. Decoding (D)
    2. Oral Language (or Language) comprehension (LC)
- The quality of RC can be determined by the product of these two clusters:
  (RC = D x LC)
- Most if not all of the variance in RC can and will be explained by this formula.

Additional claims in the original view maintain:

- D and LC are of equal importance in determining RC
- Both D and LC are necessary for RC, but neither is sufficient on its own. (Pearson Madda, & Raphael, 2023, p. 11)

Undergirding these arguments is statistical explanatory power, and a leap—from correlational data, emanating from a subset of measures, to causal claims. The causal link seems presumptuous, but tempting; for once D and LC are entered into a statistical model designed to explain reading comprehension outcomes, there is little if any variance left for other factors to explain (Castles, Rastle, & Nation, 2018; Lonigan, Burgess, & Schatschneider, 2018).

It is also important to note that the SVR is and has always been silent on the question of the specific instructional protocols best suited to building those skills (Hanford, 2020; Hoover & Gough, 1990; Hoover & Tunmer, 2018). Nevertheless, Gough and his colleagues (see Hoover & Tunmer, 2020) were clear that students in grades K-1, while reasonably assumed to be experts on the Language Comprehension side of the equation, were likely in need of explicit instruction to develop the Decoding side. The SVR is often, indeed almost universally, cited by advocates of early phonics instruction who employ SoR rhetoric. Hanford (2020), for example, after agreeing with its founders that the SVR does not specify how to teach reading, goes on to say that the SVR "... makes clear that the first task of the beginning reader is to learn how to decode the words he or she knows how to say" (para. 34).

Our Reading of the Evidence and the Claim

Many of the sympathetic reading researchers who extol the SVR—and readily refer to the 150+ studies validating it—have also been conducting research to evaluate and revise the model; in short, to improve it! Most of these endeavors attempt to add complexity within the SVR's current parameters, such as incorporating new features within the Decoding and Language Comprehension buckets. Some have also attempted to replace the model with a more complex alternative.

Increasing Complexity for the Simple View. Much of SVR research over the past 20 to 30 years has focused on improving and fine-tuning the SVR model. Ironically, this line of scholarship seems directed toward enhancing the complexity of the simple view—suggesting that it may not be so simple after all (see LRRC & Chiu, 2018; Cervetti, et al., 2020; Francis, Kulesz, & Benoit, 2018; García & Cain, 2014; Kim, 2017). In general, SVR studies illustrate that a combination of decoding and language comprehension proficiencies has a more powerful effect on reading comprehension than either component alone—indicating that there are facets of each that bolster one another toward increasing competence over time. As such, some studies have identified important prerequisites to effective word recognition and decoding-related skills, such as phonological awareness, rapid word identification, and letter knowledge. Other scholars have noted that vocabulary, grammar, and the ability to read extended text are important predictors of language comprehension, which has come to include working memory, inferencing, and background knowledge (Cromley & Azevedo, 2007; Francis et al., 2018). In short, reading comprehension is thought to be a multidimensional, complex cognitive act.

Cervetti and her colleagues (2020) summarized the SVR studies conducted in the 2010 IES-funded Reading for Understanding initiative. Across multiple sites, these studies documented the importance of early oral language skills—those often overlooked by SoR advocates—that support both decoding and oral language comprehension in young readers. In keeping with other scholars, Cervetti et al. (2020) found that the skills contributing to RC within the D and LC clusters varied across the grades (see also Catts,

2018; Lonigan et al., 2018). For instance, while word-level skills and fluency (within the D cluster) have a significant impact in the early grades, starting in third grade, skills within the LC cluster become a more important determinant of RC. Researchers have attributed this shift in impact to increases in the vocabulary, grammar, and discourse demands of the texts students encounter after the primary years (Pearson et al., 2020).

Overall, the SVR work over the last two decades shows that the two clusters still provide, at a broad level of consideration, a useful—and simple—heuristic for thinking about how word-level and language-level skills and processes contribute to reading comprehension. At the same time, they also illustrate how that seductively simple formula (RC = D x LC) masks an increasing amount of complexity. There's a lot to be considered and developed through rich learning experiences, once you take off the lid!

From Simple to Active. With these studies in mind, what progress have we made in refining the SVR for a more complete account of reading comprehension? Duke and Cartwright (2021) created a new model that essentially answered that question. Their extensive review of the research over the past two decades demonstrated that the SVR becomes more complex when we deconstruct what is inside—and between—the language comprehension and decoding clusters. Considering the overlap between the two, they offered compelling evidence that many other factors not represented in the initial equation contribute to reading performance. They proposed a more comprehensive model than that represented in the SVR: The Active View of Reading, or AVR (Figure 1). Their recent empirical investigation of the validity of the AVR (Burns, Duke, & Cartwright, 2023) found that the new model was able to explain additional variables that the SVR could not—providing what they argued would be a more thorough evidence-based foundation for reading interventions (albeit a modest improvement; see Shanahan, 2023).

Figure 1

Duke & Cartwright's (2021) Active View of Reading

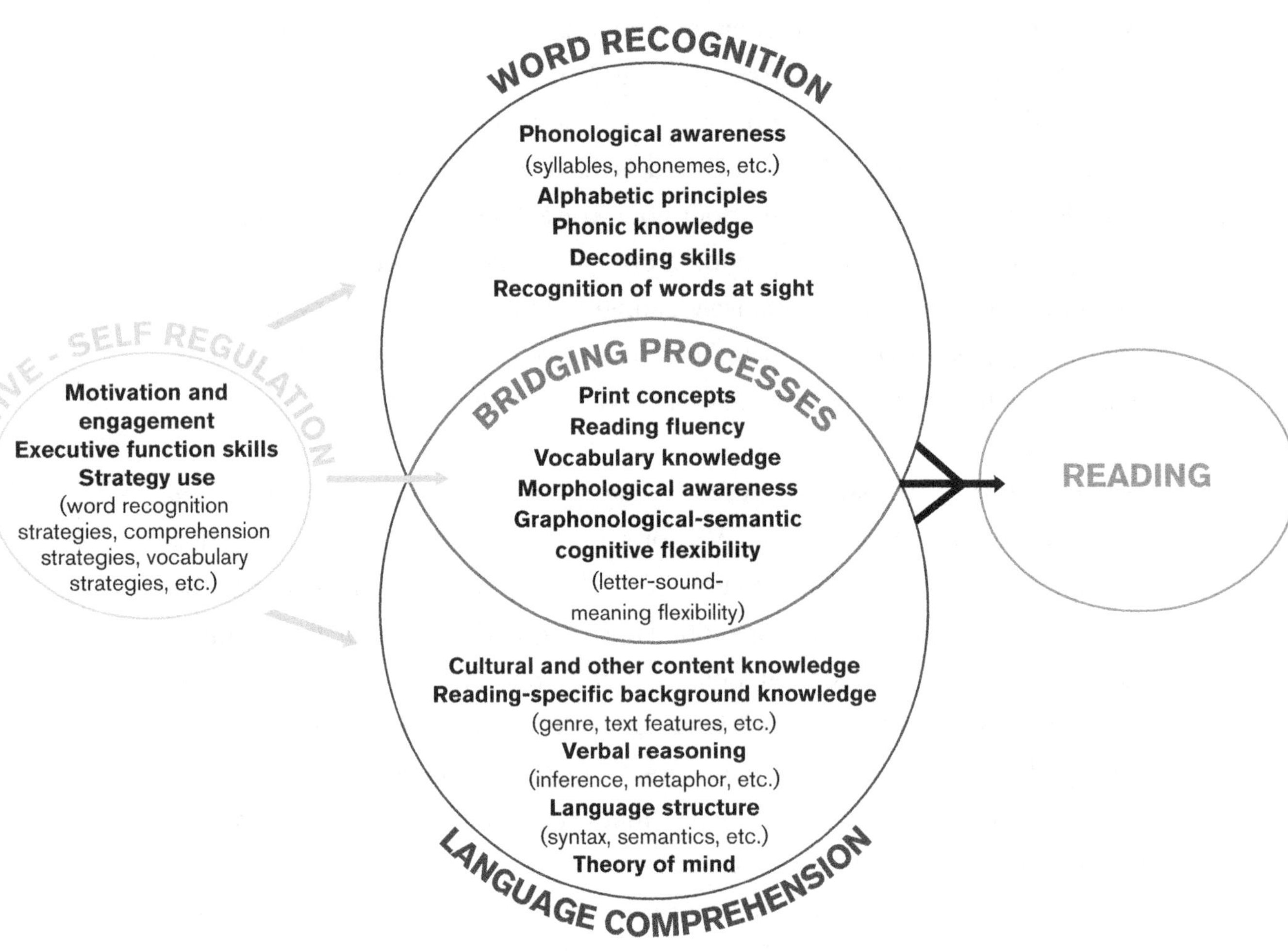

This is a reader model. Reading is also impacted by text, task, and sociocultural context.

Duke, N. K., & Cartwright, K. B. (2021). The science of reading progresses: Communicating advances beyond the simple view of reading. Reading Research Quarterly, 56(1), S25-S44.

Our Revised Version of the Claim

In spite of these endeavors over the years to add nuance and explanatory power to the SVR, advocates in the Science of Reading debate continue to marshal the Simple View as justification for claims that reach beyond the evidence provided by the research. Claims in social media and the popular press—specifically, that the SVR carries direct implications for specific instructional approaches—are those that Gough and his co-theorists, Tumner and Hoover, explicitly avoided. In fact, the only claims about teaching and learning by its originators were that: 1) The cipher that provides a map from print to speech must be learned; and 2) For most novices, the cipher will have to be taught—because they are unlikely to discover it on their own.

So where do we stand on the Simple View of Reading? We believe that the adjective *simple* in the model's name more aptly modifies the word *view* than the word *reading*. In other words, the SVR is a simple way of conceptualizing the complex phenomenon we call reading. It may be that the very complexity of reading demands a simple heuristic; with so many moving parts, we need these two big buckets to mentally store all of the components.

Despite the attention that the Simple View of Reading has received, other models and metaphors have been offered in an effort to draw together and provide an intelligible rendering of the nature of reading acquisition. Among the most notable has been the depiction of reading acquisition as a Reading Rope, offered to parents and educators by Hollis Scarborough (Scarborough 2001, 2023). Although not intended as a formal testable empirical model, it has become popular as a metaphor to support parents and educators in their understanding of reading acquisition. Figure 2 provides a representation of the metaphor, incorporating the two intertwining sets of strands involved in the development of skilled reading (i.e., the fluent execution and coordination of word recognition and language comprehension). The elements constituting the strands are not intended to exist independently, but interactively, as they support one another in a fashion that is synergistic.

Figure 2

Scarborough's Reading Rope (Scarborough, 2001)

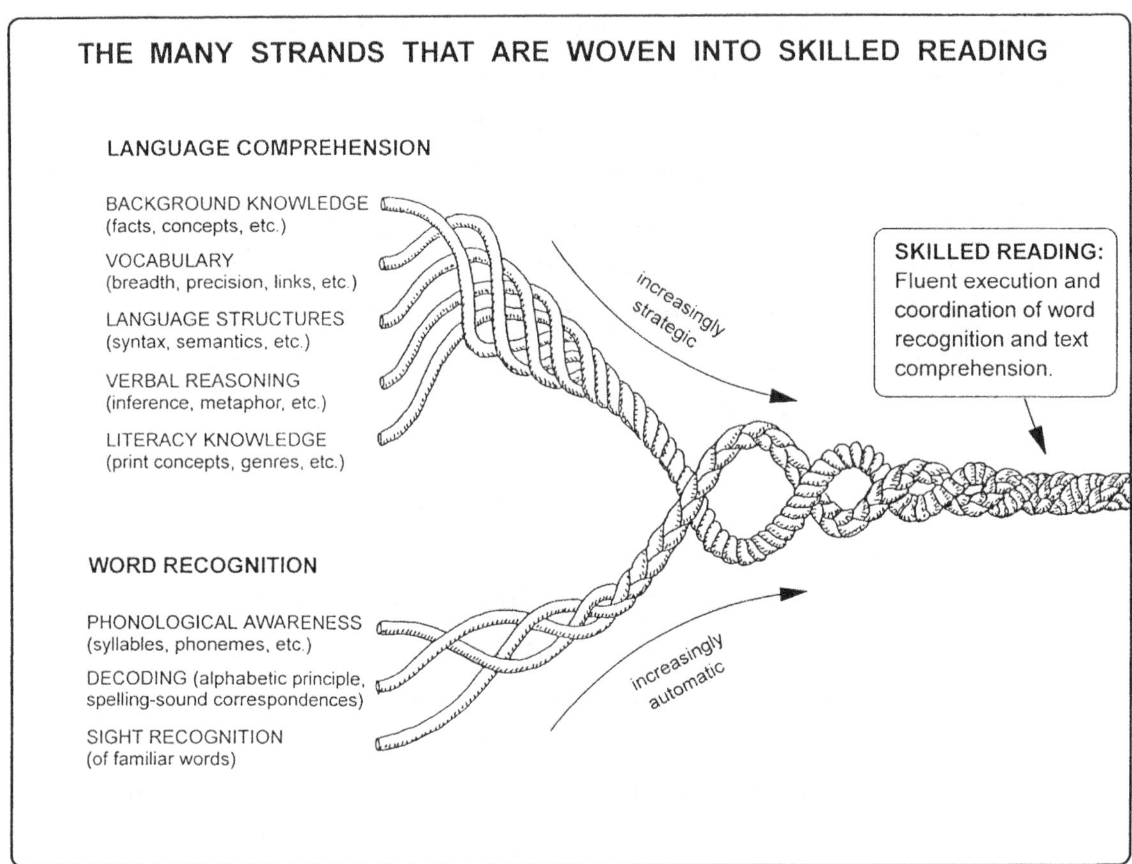

Scarborough, H. S. (2001). "Connecting early language and literacy to later reading (dis)abilities: Evidence, theory, and practice." In S. Neuman & D. Dickinson (Eds.), *Handbook for research in early literacy* (pp. 97-110). New York: Guilford Press.

Unfortunately, in the fast-paced and chaotic world of social media, the adjective *simple* gets applied to the reading process as a whole—and then to the teaching of reading. This chain of unwarranted inferences guides educators and parents to reach the conclusion that if we *simply* teach phonics first—and fast—each and every student will be able to read and understand any and all words and text that is within their listening repertoire. And that will be as good as it gets.

While we can live (and indeed, have lived) with the SVR, we believe there are no credible theoretical, empirical, or practical reasons for making do with an adequate model. That is, we see no compelling ideas, research findings, or implications from those findings regarding classroom teaching that require us to put square pegs in round holes, especially when we have a more fulsome model (a sociocultural view of reading) available. We will unpack this framework in our treatment of Claim 9.

CLAIM 3

Reading is the ability to identify and understand words that are part of one's oral language repertoire.

The Evidence Marshalled in Support of the Claim

An authoritative, highly-respected account of this claim appeared in a November, 2001 issue of *Psychological Science in the Public Interest*, in a piece authored by an equally-renowned team of psychologists: Keith Rayner, Barbara R. Foorman, Charles A. Perfetti, David Pesetsky and Mark S. Seidenberg. After comparing the relative merits of very broad versus very specific definitions, they arrived at what they believed to be a mid-level definition of reading:

> In focusing on reading's distinguishing features, we define learning to read as the acquisition of knowledge that results in the child being able to identify and understand printed words that he or she knows on the basis of spoken language. (Rayner et al., 2001, p. 34)

The rationale they offered for this claim sheds light on why the debate over teaching early reading seems so entrenched and difficult to resolve. In that same piece, prior to defining reading, they distinguished *reading* from *literacy*:

> To see the value of the narrower definition, it is useful to make a distinction between literacy and reading. Literacy includes a variety of educational outcomes—dispositions toward learning, interests in reading and writing, and knowledge of subject-matter domains—that go beyond reading. These dimensions of literacy entail the achievement of a broad range of skills embedded in cultural and technological contexts. An extended functional definition is useful in helping to make clear the wide range of literacy tasks a society might present to its members. (p. 34)

The Rayner et al. (2001) definition has experienced remarkable staying power over the past two decades. It has been implicitly relied upon by researchers (e.g. Seidenberg, 2017) who assert that the reading novice's first learning priority is to crack the code that maps written onto oral language. It has also showed up in social and news media—in press that supports an early emphasis on teaching systematic phonics (e.g., Kristoff, 2023; Hanford, 2018; Moats, 2020).

Our Reading of the Evidence and the Claim

A common ploy in academic debates is to ask opponents to define their terms. The debates over early reading pedagogy provide compelling evidence as to why this is actually good advice. For instance, contrast the Rayner et al. (2001) definition with this one by Patricia Alexander (2020), offered in the *Reading Research Quarterly* issue on the SoR:

> The reality is that reading does not begin or end with phonics or whole-word instruction (Seidenberg, 2013). It is far broader and more complex. Reading, broadly conceived, is any interaction between a person—be it a child, adolescent, or adult—and written language (Pearson & Cervetti, 2013). That interaction can involve written language at many levels, from words and sentences, to paragraphs, to entire volumes (Shanahan, 2019). Also, reading can be performed for many reasons, from purely personal to largely academic, and in many contexts, both in and out of school, as well as online or in print (Ito et al., 2013; Singer & Alexander, 2017). (p. S90)

Or, consider another broader definition of reading comprehension from the 2026 National Assessment of Educational Progress (NAEP) Reading Assessment Framework (NAGB, 2021):

> **Reading comprehension is making meaning with text,** a complex process shaped by many factors, including readers' abilities to
>
> - engage with text in print and multimodal forms;
> - employ personal resources that include foundational reading skills, language, knowledge, and motivations; and
> - extract, construct, integrate, critique, and apply meaning in activities across a range of social and cultural contexts. (p. 5)

These definitions of reading provided by Alexander and the 2026 NAEP were not the first to challenge narrow interpretations. As early as 2002, shortly after the definition by Rayner and his colleagues (2001) appeared in print, the RAND Reading Study Group (RRSG, 2002) published a definition oriented more toward sociocultural than cognitive frameworks. Reading comprehension, the RRSG asserted, is "the process of simultaneously extracting and constructing meaning through interaction and involvement with written language. We use the words *extracting* and *constructing* to emphasize both the importance and the insufficiency of the text as a determinant of reading comprehension" (p. 11). Proposing that the process of reading comprehension entails three primary elements—the reader, the text, and the activity (in which comprehension is a part)—they then emphasized that it always occurs in a sociocultural context, "that shapes and is shaped by the reader and that interacts with each of the three elements" (p. 11). Clearly, both the Alexander and 2026 NAEP definitions share more in common with the RRSG (2002) definition than that of Rayner et al. (2001).

Over the years, scholars have brought different assumptions and goals to the debate—leading to incommensurable definitions of reading and complicating, if not dooming, conversations across perspectives. According to Rayner et al. (2001), the distinctive essence of reading is the process of decoding print to speech. As such, their definition intentionally excludes passage-level (connected discourse) factors—along with the social, cultural, and contextual resources available to all readers. The Alexander and NAEP definitions, on the other hand, attempt to move beyond decoding—emphasizing instead the social, cultural, and functional applications of reading, such as inquiry, knowledge acquisition, or perhaps even action, in real world settings. This also has implications for instruction: For instance, notice how easy it is to leap from the Rayner et al. definition to a pedagogical emphasis on cracking the code. By contrast, see how easy it is to leap from the Alexander or NAEP definitions to a comprehensive approach that attends to the contexts, functions, and applications of reading to learning or problem-solving.

It should not be underemphasized that Rayner and his colleagues limited what counts as reading to the naming of words and the understanding of their decontextualized meanings. Not phrases, sentences, discourse, or genres, but words. In the definition proposed by Rayer et al. (2001), the understanding of units larger than words is not a part of "reading"—so it must be accomplished by knowledge and processes that are a part of literacy. Hence, larger units arise in functional situations (real world contexts) in which we learn to read worlds, including texts that describe those worlds. In short, the Rayner et al. (2001) focus on word naming comes at a conceptual cost—assigning all things social, cultural, contextual, epistemological, and motivational to literacy and learning. For our part, we would rather keep them front and center within the construct of reading!

Our Revised Version of the Claim

What counts as reading? This remains a key question at the center of the SoR debate. If reading is defined as identifying and understanding words that are a part of one's spoken language, then it makes sense to focus on what many novices lack when they enter school (i.e., the cipher that maps print to speech, acquired through systematic decoding instruction). However, if reading is defined more broadly, then it makes sense to offer a comprehensive curriculum that orchestrates those many processes and types of knowledge—in terms of the code; word meanings and relationships; language; and (perhaps most important) the social and cultural worlds in which we use reading, writing, and language to make sense of things. With such disparate perspectives, it is little wonder, then, that our debates are seldom resolved. Nowhere is this tension between competing definitions more active than in the models of the reading process, including models of how it develops (as noted in Claim 2, concerning the adequacy of the SVR).

To be crystal clear, we side with broader, more inclusive definitions of reading (as further addressed in Claim 9, on the sociocultural models of reading). We take this stance mainly because we believe that the narrow definition pushes most of the important variables in the quest for making meaning into another category—one we might label literacy and learning—where those phenomena and corresponding parts of the school curriculum (e.g., science, social studies, or integrated studies) do the heavy lifting. We see few advantages, and a host of disadvantages, in this definition—and its consequences. Conversely, we see—and will try to convince readers of—the many advantages of a sociocultural model, especially on standards of ecological validity, diversity, and equity.

CLAIM 4

Phonics facilitates the increasingly automatic identification of unfamiliar words.

The Evidence Marshalled in Support of the Claim

One of the great insights of scientific reading research conducted over the past 40 years is that as students become more proficient readers, they develop increasingly accurate and automatic word identification skills. These skills become so accurate and automatic that readers can identify the pronunciation and meaning of most of the words they encounter in print, without the arduous or even cursory recoding of each letter to its corresponding sound realization. As recently described by Ehri (2021), this is how the process works:

> When children are taught **decoding skills,** they can apply this knowledge to written words by learning to convert the sequence of letters (graphemes) into blended sounds (phonemes) to pronounce unfamiliar words. Once the words are decoded a few times, their spellings are bonded to their pronunciations and are retained in memory, so that children read them automatically or "by sight." This process of storing words in memory is called **orthographic mapping** and acts like **glue,** bonding the spellings of words to their pronunciations. When the meanings of the words are activated, they also become bonded to the spellings. Once these processes are established in memory, students are able to look at written words and immediately recognize their pronunciations and meanings, which allows them to focus on the meaning of the text rather than on decoding the words. All words that are sufficiently practiced—not just high frequency words or irregularly spelled words—become sight words through this process and are then read from memory automatically. (para. 3)

Dubbed the "self-teaching" hypothesis by David Share (1995), this function of phonics, or decoding, has been featured in a long line of research demonstrating how readers get from laborious, letter-by-letter, sounding out of words and their parts to the fluent, automatic, and accurate processing that characterizes expert reading at any age. It is this combination of Share's self-teaching hypothesis and Ehri's notion of orthographic mapping (Ehri, 2014) that explains what Ehri considers to be the typical course of reading development. Additional insights come with these new constructs—namely, that we cannot explain what expert reading looks like by assuming that: a) Readers continue to recode each graphemic unit (letter or letter grouping) into its corresponding speech sound (phonemic realization of the unit); or b) Readers simply learn all words as intact "wholes" (in the manner assumed by the classic look-say approaches popular in the first half of the 20th century). Additionally, this led to at least two meanings of the term "sight word" in reading theory and pedagogy. In one, sight word indicates all those high frequency words with devilish spellings that don't map easily onto their pronunciations (e.g., *the*; *of*; *give*; *have*; *hear* versus *heart*; *will read* versus *have read*). In another, sight words refer to all the immediately identifiable words in a student's portfolio—words that have passed through the portals of self-teaching and orthographic mapping and no longer present as arduous orthographic puzzles. Fluent expert reading at any level of sophistication is readily explainable by these constructs.

Ehri (2014, 2021), in commenting on the pedagogical implications of her orthographic mapping research, suggests several desirable, perhaps necessary, elements in early literacy programs:

1. **Grapheme-Phoneme Relations**. Letter-sound correspondences should be carefully laid out in scope and sequence (although she does not specify a specific sequence).
2. **Phonemic Segmentation.** The ability to segment the stream of speech into independent phonemes is critical to learning letter-sound correspondences. This is to guarantee that readers connect the grapheme to only that sound associated with the letter (e.g., the s in sum only with the *sssss*, and not with the *uuuu*), and to facilitate decoding, the next step in the process.

3. **Decoding**. This involves using the knowledge and skill obtained in the first two elements to sound out words that are novel and unfamiliar so that readers can read and spell them accurately.
4. **Spelling**. Though not strictly required for ensuring grapheme to phoneme connections, requiring students to also spell words helps to ensure bonding—not only of orthographically predictable words (e.g., *bat* or *fin*), but also for the predictable portions of orthographically unpredictable words (e.g., the *s* and *d* in *said*; the *d*, *e*, and *t* in *debt*).
5. **Correct Word Pronunciation.** Pronouncing words correctly in order to ensure that their spellings are bound to their pronunciations.
6. **Text Reading Practice**. In general, readers should independently read material that is relatively easy. When reading more challenging texts, readers should receive appropriate scaffolding from others (i.e., teachers or tutors). Ehri notes that this step is essential for many of the high frequency but very abstract and often orthographically unpredictable "glue" words of English, such as *was, said, held,* or *with*—words whose meanings require context to be activated.
7. **Use of Context**. Ehri's (2021) description of this element comes with clear restrictions. As she describes, the role of contextual information—i.e., semantic, syntactic, and (perhaps) pragmatic—is to "monitor their comprehension to make sure the words they read make sense in that context (para. 11)." However, Ehri (2021) cautions: "If they use context to guess the words and skip over spellings without processing letter-sound connections, unfamiliar words will not be secured as sight words in memory" (para. 11). In short, readers should read by first decoding or identifying words at sight—using context to verify and confirm those initial understandings.

Our Reading of the Evidence and the Claim

We have no quarrel with this formulation of the development of expert, efficient reading. We accept the idea (and the research supporting it) that expert readers develop (i.e., over time and with appropriate experiences, pedagogy, and exposure to texts) a large portfolio of immediately identifiable and understandable words (i.e., words whose pronunciations and meanings are readily available for meaning making). We do, however, quarrel with the pedagogical recommendations that accompany the underlying theory and research of reading development. Our quarrel is largely empirical rather than theoretical, focusing on the evidence that runs counter to the claims in the pedagogical implications.

First, we challenge the assertion that orthographic mapping (the creation of the portfolio of immediately identifiable sight words) is developed through—and only through—multiple attempts to decode a word (i.e., by employing some combination of phonemic segmentation and grapheme-phoneme knowledge). What if orthographic mapping were developed through multiple attempts to read the word, either through decoding, contextual prediction, or some combination of the two? We are not aware of any evidence that suggests that context cannot aid the development of orthographic mapping. To the contrary, we know from the work of Scanlon and her colleagues (see Scanlon & Anderson, 2020; Scanlon et al., 2024) that the Interactive Strategies Approach (ISA), which features a menu of cues to assist in identifying unknown words (what Scanlon calls "word solving"): a) Results in better performance than a phonics-only approach with a range of readers, including those identified with decoding difficulties; and b) Over time, nurtures readers to develop an increasing reliance on orthographic cues with an accompanying decrease in reliance on contextual cues. Assuming that students using the ISA also experience growth in their orthographic mapping portfolio, then decoding may not be the only pathway to this all-important store of words that can be read and understood at sight.

Our Revised Version of the Claim

We have mixed views on the acceptability of this claim. The act of reading for meaning may or may not entail word-by-word reading, especially if the reader is engaged in reading for meaning (e.g., engaging in visualizing, inferencing, etc.). In other words, an emphasis upon word-by-word reading may not support a reader's enlistment of an array of comprehension processes, important over time, for reading for meaning.

However, if accurate, word-by-word reading is your goal, we can support this version of the claim: "A range of word-solving strategies, including recoding letters into sounds, facilitates the increasingly automatic identification of unfamiliar words." This version of the claim is more consistent with the empirical research we have reviewed. Most important for us as a profession is to consider either version of the claim as provisional—awaiting a robust program of pedagogical research designed to examine the efficacy of various practices in supporting the development of these important sight word repertoires.

Again, assuming the importance of accurate word-by-word reading, equally important is developmental research demonstrating how these expansive sight word repertoires facilitate comprehension for students at different ages. The theory, which underlies both the self-teaching hypothesis and orthographic mapping development, is that when most word identification is automatic, it releases cognitive capacity and attention that can be directed toward text understanding. It's a compelling and plausible hypothesis, and deserves (and awaits) compelling documentation. But it does rest on the presumption that naming words is key to learning to read and whether such a definition is overly restrictive.

CLAIM 5

The Three-Cueing System (Orthography, Semantics, and Syntax) has been soundly discredited.

The Evidence Marshalled in Support of the Claim

Defining the three-cueing system is the first step in explaining the resistance to it by both scholars and advocates within the SoR community. Easier said than done.

Three-cueing is often depicted as a Venn diagram (Figure 3) of three sources of knowledge (cues). According to this model, as readers unlock word pronunciations and meanings on the way to comprehension, they consult: 1) Orthography (letter to sound patterns); 2) Syntax (sentence structure and morphological knowledge); and 3) Semantics (word meanings and relationships among words).

Figure 3

The Three-Cueing System

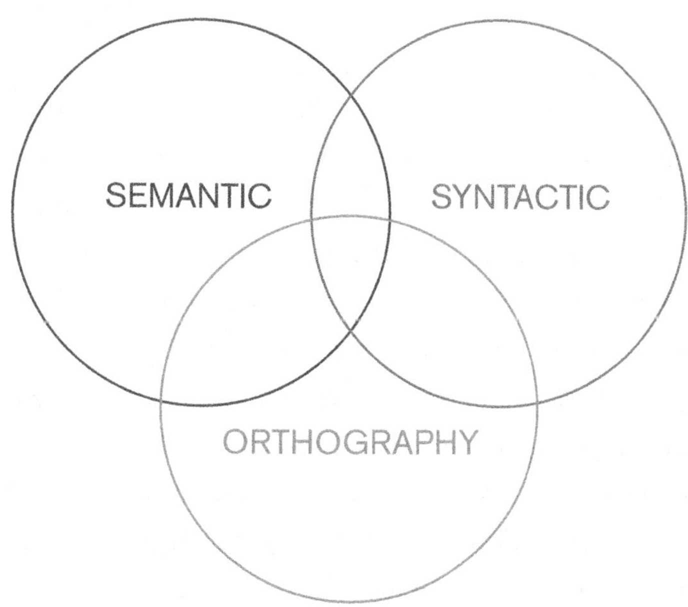

In tandem with the shift to practices aligned with the SVR, the discrediting of the cueing system became commonplace. In the U.K., advocacy for a model of learning to read that focused upon the enlistment of the cueing system (referred to as the Searchlights model) was displaced as teachers were directed to focus on decoding alone. Teachers were directed as follows:

> ... attention should be focused on decoding words rather than the use of unreliable strategies such as looking at the illustrations, rereading the sentence, saying the first sound or guessing what might 'fit'. Although these strategies might result in intelligent guesses, none of them is sufficiently reliable and they can hinder the acquisition and application of phonic knowledge and skills, prolonging the word recognition process and lessening children's overall understanding. Children who routinely adopt alternative cues for reading unknown words, instead of learning to decode them, later find themselves stranded when texts become more demanding and meanings less predictable. The best route for children to become fluent and independent readers lies in securing phonics as the prime approach to decoding unfamiliar words. (Primary National Strategy, 2006, p. 9)

Indeed, the use of cueing systems (e.g., Goodman, 1965; 1967; 1969) has become one of the most contentious issues in discussions of the SoR. SoR advocates contend that the three-cueing system is predicated on the mistaken belief that as readers develop expertise, they become increasingly nimble and skilled at orchestrating their use of all three cues. Drawing on Keith Stanovich's (1980; 1984) interactive compensatory model and Charles Perfetti's (1980) verbal efficiency model, these de facto critics of three-cueing models (e.g., Hanford, 2018; 2019) define learning to read instead as, first and foremost, a form of word mastery. As beginning readers gain experience, they compile a store of words (presumably those already in their oral language repertoire) that they immediately recognize en route to reading for meaning (as we describe in Claim 4 regarding orthographic mapping).

Critics cite studies comparing good and poor readers (e.g., Schwartz & Stanovich, 1981; Stanovich & West, 1979), which suggest that apart from their engagement with predictable texts (e.g., Martin and Carle's 1983 book, *Brown Bear, Brown Bear, What Do You See?*), struggling readers have a tendency to over-rely on context clues and pictures to develop hypotheses (the word "guess" is often used by the critics) regarding the pronunciation and meaning of words. Consequently, poor readers fail to develop the decoding skills necessary for facile word identification, and their accuracy and fluency appear to flounder. Good readers, on the other hand, are able to successfully enlist phonemic awareness and letter-sound correspondences to decode, and then understand, words. These differences between good and poor are taken as evidence that accurate and automatic word recognition is key to developing fluent reading and reading for meaning. This view lends credence to the argument that phonics is the more expeditious approach to beginning reading expertise—and that approaches enlisting multiple cueing systems are flawed, misguided, and perhaps even harmful to young readers (Hanford, 2018; 2019; Moats, 2000).

Criticisms of the three-cueing system are based on a combination of anecdotal evidence and opinion (Seidenberg, 2017; Moats, 2000), including extrapolations from static comparisons of the strategies of good and poor readers. They do not examine specific interventions involving the three-cueing system, such as the Interactive Strategies Approach (Vellutino & Scanlon, 2002; Scanlon et al., 2024), or the work of Marie Clay (1993; 1998) on Reading Recovery. For example, Marilyn Adams (1998) described the limitations of the three-cueing system after conducting occasional conversations with teachers and surmising their lack of clarity on how to guide students in the use of different cues. Mark Seidenberg rationalized an exclusive focus upon phonics skills in order to simplify what is taught and what students are expected to learn. He postulated that, as a matter of expediency (at least partially), restricting "... the range of alternatives to one that works may be more effective than offering multiple cues (Seidenberg, 2017, p. 303).

In fact, Seidenberg (2017; 2023b) argues that early advocates for cueing systems, such as Kenneth Goodman, have the roles for orthographic and contextual processing backwards; that is, word recognition comes first, followed by other contextual factors. Disagreeing with Goodman's (1967) premise that reading is "a psycholinguistic guessing game," Seidenberg dismisses approaches by other literacy educators that might provide, either directly or indirectly, evidence for the use of cueing systems (beyond letter-sound correspondences). Yet he also takes issue with the Simple View of Reading (SVR) and Scarborough's Reading Rope (RR). Recognizing the inadequacies of those models as well, Seidenberg (2023b) in a recent blog post calls for a new approach:

> Classic ideas such as the SVR and the RR are fine places for the "science of reading" to start and poor places to stop. If you don't know about this work it's new to you. If you do know about it, you'll respect the fact that the studies don't address basic questions about instruction or learning, and thus are consistent with many different approaches, including poor ones. I encourage people to embrace this work for what it offers—some important general insights about reading—and move on.
>
> Rather than components of reading such as print and language we need an account of what, when, and how. We need a developmental perspective that considers the relationships between different types of knowledge, how the information is learned, and how learning changes as knowledge grows. (paras. 30-31)

Our Reading of the Evidence and the Claim

The only way we can make sense of the arguments marshalled against the three-cueing system is to infer that the opponents object to its use in pedagogy rather than in reading theory. Many of the most vocal critics of the three-cueing system either espouse or support models of the expert reading process that posit an important role for all three of these information sources. They describe how readers recognize and understand words and connected discourse through the combined processing mechanisms for orthographic information, semantic information, and syntactic information (as well as other sources, like letter features).

David Rumelhart's (1977) popular Interactive Model of Reading, from which Keith Stanovich (1980; 1984) devised his interactive-compensatory model, is most transparent on the importance of all three processors of information (see Figure 4). According to Rumelhart, each processor works independently to send its working hypotheses about the word the reader is trying to identify to an executive "Pattern Synthesizer." The Pattern

Synthesizer, using all the information available, then provisionally commits to a given word. The moment more information becomes available, the reader takes that into account to confirm or alter their working hypothesis. We liken this model to a committee meeting of department heads: The committee chair (Pattern Synthesizer) asks for hypotheses about what word is represented by the graphemic information in the Visual Information Store (VIS). Each committee member (Knowledge Source) filters the information under scrutiny through their knowledge base to develop the most plausible hypothesis about the word's identity. The Pattern Synthesizer compiles all these hypotheses (dare we say educated guesses?) to arrive at a consensus and provisional identification of the word. As each Knowledge Source gains access to the hypotheses of the other sources, takes in more graphemic information in the VIS, and refines their hypothesis about the word's identity, they allow the Pattern Synthesizer to come up with a new, and presumably more informed, consensus hypothesis. This cycle continues until the Pattern Synthesizer is ready for input from a new graphemic string (e.g., a word), and the process repeats itself.

Figure 4

Rendition of Rumelhart's (1977) Interactive Model

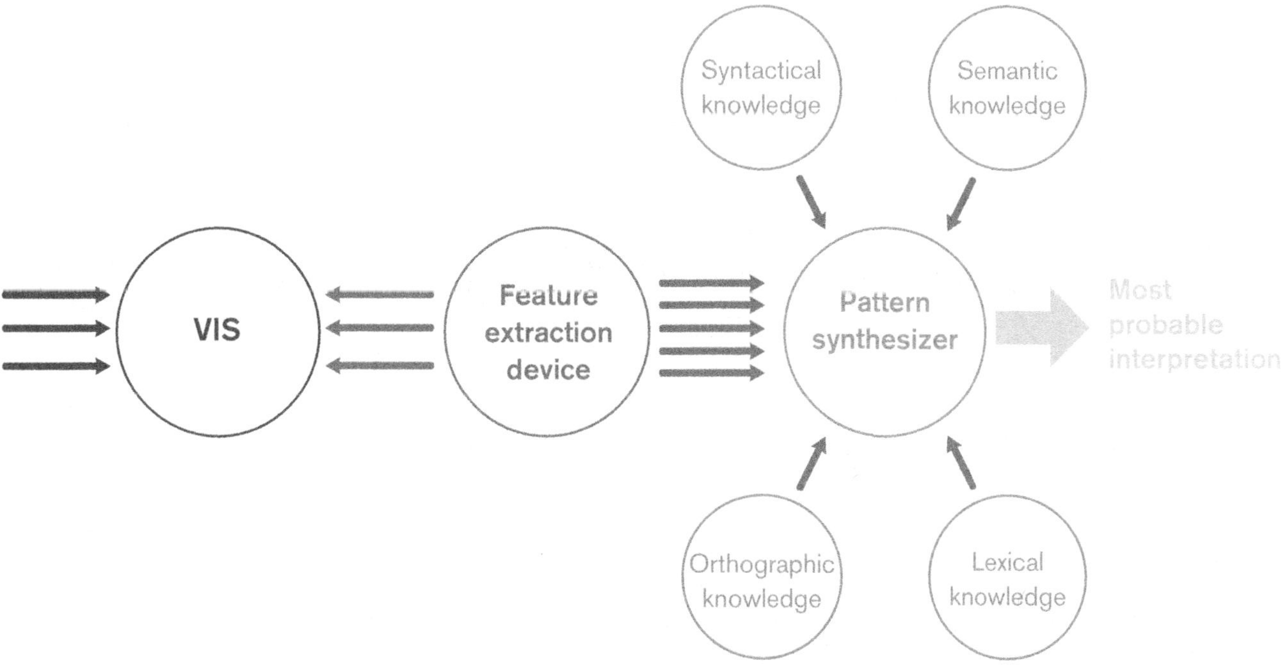

Gough's (1972) "one second of reading" model (see Figure 5), which undergirds his Simple View of Reading (Gough & Tunmer, 1986), similarly features processors for various kinds of information: A pattern recognizer and a character register for orthographic information; a decoder to get from orthographic to phonologic inputs; a librarian to access word meanings; and an executive, dubbed Merlin, to consult with syntactic and semantic rules, and put it all together.

Figure 5

Rendition of Gough's (1972) One Second of Reading Model

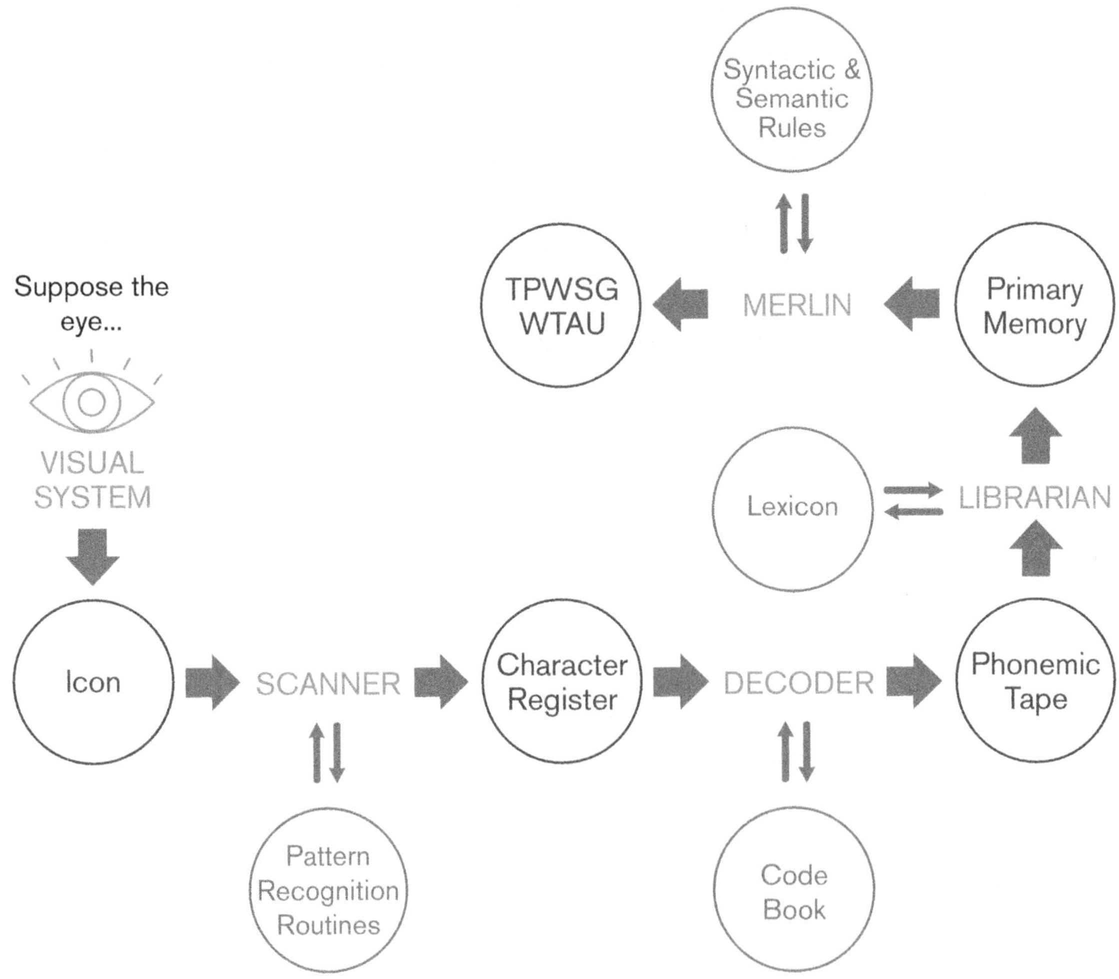

Even the strongest critic of the three-cueing system, Marilyn Adams (1990), leaned on the then-emerging parallel distributed processing model of reading (e.g., Rumelhart & McClelland, 1986; see Figure 6). Like the Rumelhart and Gough models, the parallel distributed processing model posits that processors for orthographic, phonological, and semantic information are deployed en route to identifying and understanding both words and connected discourse.

Figure 6

Rendition of Rumelhart & McClelland's (1986) Parallel Distributed Processing Model of Reading

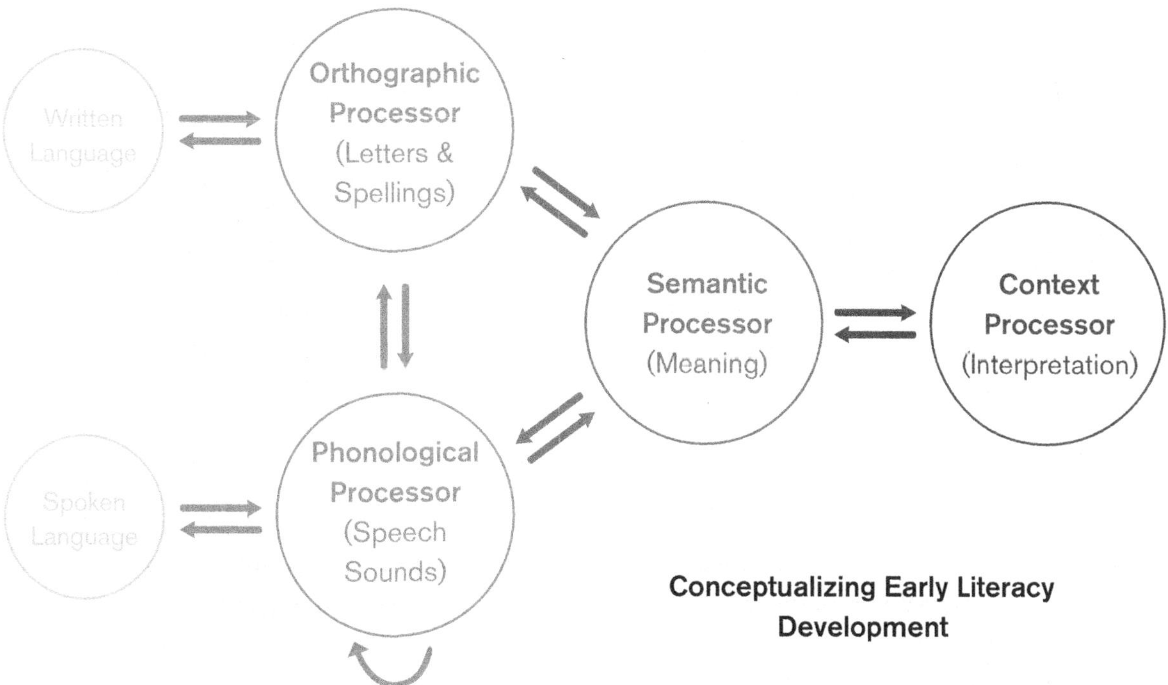

Given the widespread support of such models, objections to the three-cueing system must not be directed at theories of expert word and discourse comprehension. This leaves us to conclude that it is the use of three-cueing systems to guide instruction that many find objectionable. Indeed, several scholars with recorded opposition to the three-cueing system espouse eclectic orientations to theories of reading—supporting notions of the orchestrated interdependency of processes, and the simultaneous engagement of phonics with cueing systems related meaning making. Perfetti, for example, emphasizes the synergies between comprehension and meaning making in reading development from an early age. In an interview with David Boulton for the *Children of the Code* project website (Boulton & Perfetti, 2005), Perfetti suggests that there is a reciprocity between comprehension and the development of word identification, noting how "components can develop in tandem in ways that mutually reinforce each other" ("Reciprocal Relationship"). He goes on to call for an approach to reading that recognizes how "all parts of the system.... mutually support and strengthen each other."

Likewise, in her landmark book *Beginning to Read: Thinking and Learning About Print*, Adams (1990) discusses at length the importance of simultaneously engaging the cueing systems, thereby coupling phonics and with meaning making skills. As she states:

> In both fluent reading and its acquisition, the reader's knowledge must be aroused interactively and in parallel. Neither understanding nor learning can proceed hierarchically from the bottom up. Phonological awareness, letter recognition facility, familiarity with spelling patterns, spelling-sound relations, and individual words must be developed in concert with real reading and real writing and with deliberate reflection on the forms, functions, and meanings of texts...All of its component knowledge and skills must work together within a single and interdependent system. And, it is in that way that they must be acquired as well: It is not just eclecticism that makes a program of reading instruction effective; it is the way in which its pieces are fitted together to complement and support one another. (pp. 422-423)

Adams also supports, rather than criticizes, the contributions of Reading Recovery as developed by Marie Clay (1993). Despite some opposition to Reading Recovery and Clay's work (Chapman & Tumner, 2011; 2015; Nicholson, 2011; Reynolds & Whedall, 2007), several scholars have pointed to its effectiveness in balancing the various interdependent elements, including foundational skills, needed in learning to read (see Schwartz, 2005; 2015: Schwartz et al., 2009). As Robert Schwartz (2015) noted:

> Clay's (2001) theory incorporates a more-complex view of early literacy learning that incorporates direct phonics and phonemic awareness instruction and links that knowledge to monitor word recognition decisions while reading (Doyle, 2013; McGee, Kim, Nelson, & Fried, 2015; Schwartz, 2015; Schwartz & Galllant, 2011). This emphasis on monitoring during the reading of connected text helps many struggling beginners to construct the elaborate set of orthographic knowledge that Tunmer and Nicholson (2011) call the cipher. (p. 5)

In her approach to Reading Recovery, Clay (1993, 1998) suggested teachers provide readers with focused, strategic ways of enlisting phonics and the other cueing systems as they develop and monitor their reading across various texts (e.g., word analysis and sound blending activities; see Clay, 1993; 1998). Clay's notion of the self-improving system—which interestingly bears a family resemblance to Share's (1995) self-teaching hypothesis for recoding—submits that readers, like conductors of an orchestra (see Anderson et al., 1985), acquire the ability to manage multiple strategies for reading. Within this model, different cueing systems offer a means by which the reader can "cross check" their word recognition and meaning making as they read. Clay therefore did not suggest displacing grapho-phonemic approaches; she merely suggested ways in which readers might be guided to deploy cueing systems interdependently. Advocates of Whole Language, such as Yetta Goodman and her colleagues (Goodman, Burke & Sherman, 1980; Goodman & Marek, 1996), also suggest the importance of learning to orchestrate multiple cues, even promoting strategy lessons and retrospective miscue analyses to support readers as they engage with multiple diverse cueing systems (see Gibson & Levin, 1975, on teaching a "set for variability").

Evidence Supporting Multiple Cueing Pedagogy. Significant support for a more inclusive orientation has also emerged from several studies comparing multiple cueing approaches with a singular emphasis on phonics. Scanlon and Anderson (2020) summarize work that was initiated by Vellutino and Scanlon (2002) and refined over several decades (see Scanlon, et al., 2024). They specifically examine the Interactive Strategies Approach (ISA), a technique intended to help readers develop word solving strategies that enlist the use of orthographic, phonological, syntactic, semantic, and lexical cues. As Scanlon and Anderson (2020) state:

> The ISA involves extensive attention to the development of phonological/phonemic awareness and phonics skills and the application of those skills in combination with the development of strategic word-solving skills in context. In the ISA, substantial emphasis is placed on the interactive and mutually supportive roles of contextual and alphabetic information in the process of word solving. It involves explicit instruction and guidance in the use of word-solving strategies and in the underlying skills and understandings that enable the use of those strategies (Anderson, 2009; Scanlon, Anderson, & Sweeney, 2017). (S21-S22)
>
> ...
>
> According to the theoretical model that underlies the ISA, students at the early stages of learning to read need to understand the communicative purposes and conventions of print, develop facility and fluency with the alphabetic code, learn to use both code- and meaning-based word-solving strategies in interactive and confirmatory ways, and be provided with supportive opportunities to orchestrate these understandings in both structured tasks and authentic reading contexts (Vellutino & Scanlon, 2002). (p. S22)

Drawing from 25 years of research regarding the use of this approach with beginning and struggling readers as well as middle grade students, they found that the ISA, more so than other approaches, offers readers a form of self-teaching. This advantage supports readers' successful, ongoing enlistment of phonics for word learning in the context of their engagement with "natural" texts (i.e., texts that are not contrived to ensure a preset repetition of selected words or word families, or not specifically designed for research purposes).

Our Revised Version of the Claim

Critics of the three cueing systems hold the view that teaching beginning reading should focus on developing a reader's ability to recognize words accurately and automatically. They argue that decoding is key to developing the automatic word identification—thus freeing up the cognitive resources for constructing meaning. Accordingly, they question Goodman (1967) and other literacy educators whose approaches either directly or indirectly might perpetuate the use of cueing systems (other than phonics)—arguing that these are distractions from the crucial work of decoding.

In our view, however, SoR advocates have been too quick to dismiss the positive contributions of multiple cueing models and approaches—namely, that they support word identification and understanding, as well as the development of word learning, word solving, and orthographic mapping. Reading requires an orchestration of various factors across words and sentences. It seems overly limiting to discredit the use of cueing systems based on what some might consider a restrictive assumption—that reading is entirely the accurate naming of words, rather than an act of meaning making that involves hypothesizing. To dismiss the use of context as an over-reliance on "guessing" or "predicting" ignores important evidence. The essence of most theoretical models of reading involves semantic, syntactic, *and* orthographic processing, We also find some of the arguments against cueing systems (i.e., the view that the use of context or syntactic, semantic or pragmatic cues, even when coupled with phonics, may detract from word learning) to require the out of hand dismissal of important lines of research. Opponents of cueing systems fail to consider research that might counter their position. They suggest the need for, but sometimes fail to examine, studies considering these matters more directly with students as they learn to read. And, despite the danger of extrapolating from comparisons of good and poor readers, they use those studies to support their critique of an emphasis on context or the use of cueing systems (Seidenberg, 2017). As a result, Whole Language and other popular approaches (e.g., Balanced Literacy) have been maligned as having a phonics gap and a flawed allegiance to cueing systems.

Deep down, we also suspect that many scholars have experienced a kind of knee-jerk reaction to Goodman's (1967) name for this approach—"reading as a psycholinguistic guessing game." Arguably, Goodman's extended discussions of the reading process indicate that his use of "guessing" in the title was meant to convey a disposition to predicting, inferring, cross-checking, and hypothesizing. And while some of us might wish he had called it something else, like "informed hypothesis testing," or even "educated guessing," he didn't.

It is time, we think, to recognize that there is always a tentative and provisional character to both word identification and meaning construction. Meanings change across settings, and no matter how good we are at reading, we don't always get things right the first time around. That is precisely why Gibson & Levin (1975) proposed the necessity of a "set for variability" in the development of readers' word-solving repertoires. To rely on extrapolations from comparisons of good and poor readers while ignoring research on the efficacy of multiple cueing pedagogical approaches seems short-sighted. Prudently, in her discussions of cueing systems, Adams (1998) did not deny their possible role, but instead suggested the need for more research on their use with beginning readers. We believe that the work of Scanlon and her colleagues (2024) has answered Adams' call by demonstrating that a "full tool box" of word solving strategies, as reflected in their ISA interventions, enhances word solving, word reading, orthographic mapping, and understanding connected text.

CLAIM 6

Learning to read is an unnatural act.

The Evidence Marshalled in Support of the Claim

The notion that learning to read is unnatural is one of the core arguments for phonics-first approaches to reading. The phrase was memorialized in classic pieces by Goodman and Goodman (1976; 1979) entitled, *Learning to Read is Natural*, and by Gough and Hillinger's (1980) *Learning to Read: An Unnatural Act.* As Moats (2000), a key spokesperson for a decoding emphasis in beginning reading, has argued: "Learning to read is not natural or easy for most children" (p. 14). In a similar vein, physician and learning development scholar Sally Shaywitz (Boulton & Shaywitz, 2004), whose research focuses on dyslexia, noted in an interview:

> We're not hardwired for written language. Many societies on earth indeed rely solely on an oral language. So whereas spoken language is instinctive and natural—you don't have to teach a baby to speak, you just expose that baby to a spoken language and that baby will learn, eventually, to speak—reading has to be taught. It's artificial, it's acquired. (from the section, "Brain Not Wired for Reading")

Maryanne Wolf, in her 2018 book on reading in a digital era (Wolf & Stoodley, 2018), seems to espouse a more extreme position on this matter (especially in comparison to her earlier writing; see Wolf & Stoodley, 2008):

> ...human beings were never born to read. The acquisition of literacy is one of the most important epigenetic achievements of Homo sapiens. To our knowledge, no other species ever acquired it. The act of learning to read added an entirely new circuit to our hominid brain's repertoire. The long developmental process of learning to read deeply and well changed the very structure of that brain's circuitry, which rewired the brain which changed the nature of human thought. (p. 1-2)

Wolf goes on to say that while oral language is a "basic human function" (p. 17)—acquired with minimal if any instruction—reading is an unnatural, cultural act:

> We human beings have to learn to read. This means we must have an environment that helps us to develop and connect a complex assortment of basic and not-so-basic processes, so that every young brain can form its own brand-new reading circuitry. (p. 18)

Mark Seidenberg (2017) likewise highlights that reading is not simply the "handmaiden of spoken language" (p. 20)—and that word-level deciphering is the "necessary bridge between print and speech" (p. 119). As he argues:

> Whereas talking with children guarantees that they will learn to speak... reading to children does not guarantee that they will read. Children learn a spoken language through exposure and use, but reading requires systematic guidance and feedback, more than occurs in casual reading to children. In short, reading to children is not the same as teaching children to read.... Reading to children is important but not sufficient, children benefit from it quite a lot, but it neither obviates the role of instruction nor vaccinates against dyslexia.

While Seidenberg notes there are exceptions—children who "teach themselves" (p. 114)—he underscores that "grasping the alphabetic principle" (p. 119) is the first step in teaching reading:

> It should be clear why becoming alphabetic is a major hurdle that requires instruction, feedback, and practice. The child has to think phonemically, which involves both phonology and orthography, and learn arbitrary cross-modal associations between graphemes and phonemes...The amount of instruction required depends upon the child and how they are taught. (pp. 119-120)

The arguments in support of decoding by Seidenberg (2017) and Wolf (Wolf & Stoodley, 2008; 2018) draw upon a history dating back to the advent of alphabetic systems. In such views, writing systems represent degrees of decontextualization (or recontextualization) that require multiple processes of mediation—from symbols to sounds to meaning. Advocates of word learning will sometimes characterize learners as non-readers until they can decode words—an "unnatural" skill that demands systematic intervention to be acquired. As Castles, Rastle & Nation (2018) contend:

> ...it is clear that the fundamental insight that graphemes represent phonemes in alphabetic writing systems does not typically come naturally to children. It is something that most children must be taught explicitly, and doing so is important for making further progress in reading. Fortunately, however, the foundational knowledge required to trigger this insight is not extensive and, once acquired, puts children on a path to accruing further knowledge and firmly establishing their alphabetic decoding skills. (p. 11)

Threaded throughout these arguments is support for the explicit teaching of word level decoding—presented as the alternative to leaving learners to their own resources. Direct interventions focused upon the mastery of phonics are especially stressed in cases where learners might struggle with learning to read (such as children diagnosed as dyslexic), or might have missed the rich literacy experiences afforded to other young children.

Our Reading of the Evidence and the Claim

As noted, some who argue that learning to read is unnatural also acknowledge that this is not universal to all learners (e.g., Castles, Rastle & Nation, 2018; Seidenberg, 2017). They recognize that exceptions exist; indeed, they do not exclude the possibility that some beginning readers and writers draw upon something akin to a natural prowess for discerning, applying, and refining reading and writing skills.

Missing Perspectives. Missing from these discussions of the unnatural nature of reading is research describing the connection between learning to read and the ways in which learners become involved in experiences with print and other symbolic representations prior to schooling (e.g., by engaging with representations, objects, gestures, and other forms of communication; see Perry, 2023; Siegel, 2006). By facilitating the development of print awareness and an appreciation of different contexts, print conventions, genres, and other elements, early meaning making cues advance learning to read and write, including decoding skills (Beers & Henderson, 1977; Chomsky, 1979; Yaden & Templeton, 1986; Yaden, Rowe, & MacGillivray, 2000). Even less apparent in this research is any consideration of the extensive, multidisciplinary discussions of these issues, dating back some 75 years, across linguistics, psychology, sociolinguistics and behaviorism. Scholars across different fields (Bissex, 1980; Dyson, 1995, 2013, 2016; Ferreiro & Teberosky, 1982; Halliday, 1975, 2010; Harste, 2021; McGee & Richgels, 1990; Olson, 1977; Purcell-Gates, 1995, 2007; Purcell-Gates, Jacobson, & Degener, 2004; Scribner & Cole 1981; Teale, & Sulzby, 1986) have observed that from birth, learners have an extraordinary capacity for learning written as well as oral language—without any apparent instruction. Their discussions draw upon the rich history of scholarship in oral language development—including work by Lenneberg (1967), who argued that language development, including reading, has a genetic basis; or Peirce (e.g., Peirce, Hartshorne, & Weiss, 1932, 1933, 1935; Peirce & Burks, 1958), whose approaches to reading informed sociolinguistics and socio-semiotic perspectives. As Noam Chomsky (1965) suggested with his influential notion of a Language Acquisition Device, learners have an innate capacity for language learning:

> ...a child cannot help constructing a particular sort of transformational grammar to account for the data presented to him, any more than he can control his perception of solid objects or his attention to line and angle. Thus it may well be that the general features of language structure reflect, not so much the course of one's experience, but rather the general character of one's capacity to acquire knowledge—in the traditional sense, one's innate ideas and innate principles. (p. 59)

Arguably, in a similar vein, Stanislas Dehaene (2009) suggested that research in neurology pointed to a form of cultural adaptability akin to an ability to recycle or engage in forms of cultural learning.

Learning by Observation. Observational studies of young learners suggest that reading development proceeds both alongside oral language development as well as independently. Young learners use their innate prowess as they engage with print and related representations for a range of purposes (e.g., functional, communicative, imaginative). Reflecting their developing understanding of norms, and evolving facility with meaning making processes (e.g., seeking coherence; predicting and connecting ideas), young learners explore and enlist various conventions, including forms of utterances and graphic representations, as they read, write, and draw (see Bissex, 1980; Dyson, 1995, 2013, 2016; Ferreiro & Teberosky 1982; Halliday, 1975, 2010; Harste, 2021). Numerous observational studies note how reading and writing development begins at birth, and evolves within families and everyday settings. As Dyson (2001) notes, written language exposure actually introduces new sociocultural contexts for children:

> Learning about written language is thus not just about learning a new code for representing meanings. It is about entering new social dialogues in an expanding life world. As such, written language learning is inevitably a part of learning about social and ideological worlds and about the place of a child's own relationships and experiences in those worlds. (p. 138).

This spontaneous or minimally guided learning occurs as young learners interact with symbols, images, or print, creating multimodal responses to engage with their world. Perry (2023), drawing upon semiotics, noted that the practice of engaging through sign-systems is "...the primary or central characteristic of life, whether human or organic" (p. 1); her perspective gives printed language a "natural" status equivalent to oral language. But the link between oral and written language is even more salient, as it is the practical work of all literacies—engaging with reading/print communities in partnership with oral language development. Granted, what may be missing from such discussions are studies that more fully consider whether these skills are best acquired in a natural quest for meaning making—i.e., the result of learners' natural prowess—or are more efficiently taught as an independent enterprise within a school curriculum. Also missing are studies examining how teaching and learning might build upon, rather than displace, these innate reading propensities.

A Communicative Perspective. Athey (1971), in her extensive review of different models of language development and reading, emphasized that reading should be examined not as "a bundle of skills, but a system of social communication" (p. 11; see also Davis, 1971). She outlined the need for a sociolinguistic perspective in studies attempting to unravel what naturally develops and what might be taught. In a similar vein, Seigel (2006) noted that the evidence from these studies supports the idea of emergent literacy—a notion which emphasizes that these early efforts should not be regarded as "pre-literate" but rather as early, literate attempts at sense-making:

> ...when children wrote signs (famously DO NAT DSTRB, GNYS AT WRK [Bissex, 1980]) or read familiar storybooks, the results could not be interpreted as unsuccessful imitations of adult writing and reading, but as reflections of children's growing facility with the full array of knowledge required to mean through written language. (p. 66)

The Interdependence of Oral and Written Language. In the afterword to Adams' influential (1990) treatise, *Beginning to Read*, Dorothy Strickland and Bernice Cullinan discussed the natural versus unnatural distinction. They suggested the primacy given to phonics by Adams assumes that children learn only what they are taught and, in the case of phonics, that they master skills separately rather than in combination. Instead, they argued, reading is more developmental, and reading abilities emerge interdependently as skills and strategies integrate—especially in rich literate environments, where the abilities of readers and understandings of reading expand. From this developmental perspective, they questioned the characterization of learners as readers and non-readers. Moreover, they challenged the focus on phonics as a decontextualized and isolated linguistic practice:

> We feel it is misleading to categorize a child as either a reader or a non-reader with no in between. We prefer to trust the evidence that Adams provides about her own children as well as the careful observations of numerous researchers (Cochran-Smith, 1984; Bissex, 1980; Baghban, 1984) whose work suggests that literacy development starts early and is ongoing. Rather than classifying children as readers and non-readers, we believe it is more accurate to consider their literacy development as being on a continuum of increasing competence.
>
> ... The research that Adams cites often assumes that linguistic awareness is a precondition to reading and writing. Most of the studies show a relation between knowledge of letter names and literacy development are correlational. The researchers use measures that diagnose a child's linguistic

> awareness—the result of which is not important in itself as much as it is a reflection of a broader knowledge about reading and language (Anderson, Hiebert, Scott & Wilkinson, 1985; Nurss, 1980). Moreover, this information does not provide a base to sort out any kind of temporal sequence nor does it imply that the best way for children to acquire linguistic awareness is through direct instruction. It may be that development in literacy *causes* growth in linguistic awareness. Ignoring recent observations about growth in literacy may lead us to lose sight of the fact that it is story reading, talking about stories and print, and attempts at writing that may influence the acquisition of phonics rather than the other way around. (Strickland & Cullinan, writing in Adams, 1990, pp. 427-428)

William Teale (1982), drawing upon his extensive observations of young readers and writers, argued that using terms such as natural and unnatural when defining learning to read and write fails to acknowledge how learning to read can, and often does, develop as an interplay between learners and their environments. That environment might be in a home, a community center, a day care, or even a school setting. Efforts to differentiate natural from unnatural, Teale explained, often missed the transactional nature of learning to read, ignored the mutually constitutive nature of teaching and learning, and failed to recognize the "natural" propensities of learners:

> Frequently the adult assumes that the typical literacy curriculum with its progression from part to whole and its hierarchy of skills represents a model of how children learn to read and write. The belief is that literacy development is a case of building competencies in certain cognitive operations with letters, words, sentences and texts, competencies which can be applied in a variety of situations. A critical mistake here is that the motives, goals, and conditions have been abstracted away from the activity in the belief that this enables the student to "get down to" working on the essential processes of reading and writing. But, ... these features are critical aspects of the reading and writing themselves. By organizing instruction which omits them, the teacher ignores how literacy is practiced (and therefore learned) and thereby creates a situation in which the teaching is an inappropriate model for the learning. Some children are able to maintain the whole and learn despite the teacher; others accept the teaching model as a way of learning and become its victims. (p. 567).

Teale's response to those who argue that learning to read is unnatural might well be something like: "It's only unnatural if you arrange the conditions to make it so." According to Teale, if you let learning to read follow its course in making a difference in the daily lives of children, where it can be nurtured by purposes and motives, it will appear to be much more a part of the natural course of events.

Yaden, Reinking and Smagorinsky (2021), in their discussions of the Science of Reading, also considered this tendency in research to use binaries or opposing views. They were particularly concerned with the use of the nature versus nurture binary to dismiss views of reading development. Citing a Vygotskian perspective, they argued (as Teale did) for a transactional view:

> Vygotsky (1987, 1997) argued that human development is a function of the intersection of nature and nurture. He continually stressed that although germane to the developing personality, materialist explanations alone (i.e., biological, neurological, physiological, stimulus–response mechanisms) of human behavior were never sufficient to explain the higher, culturally mediated psychological functions, such as attitudes, ideologies, methods of abstract reasoning, memory, emotions, voluntary attention, or will. To Vygotsky and the cultural-historical approach that he and his colleagues founded (Cole, 1996), the nature/nurture debate was not an either/or question but a both/and proposition. (p. S125).

Situated Language Use—Both Oral and Written. This tension between oral and written language as it pertains to what is or is not natural hearkens back to the second claim in this series, about how we define reading. If reading is identifying and understanding words available in one's oral language repertoire, then it can be easily divorced from meaning making. Such an intentionally narrow definition of reading also prevents scholars from taking into account what we know of reading development—including the synergies between reading, various forms of representations (e.g., drawings), writing, and oral language that educators have gleaned from observation. Consequently, those who emphasize this unnatural character make scant mention of the power of writing or other forms of representation as vehicles for learning to read (see Tierney & Shanahan, 1991). For example, it is noteworthy that despite some mention of research on invented spellings by Carol Chomsky, her work with writing as integral to reading development receives no mention. In particular, they exclude reference to her assertion that the natural goal of early readers is to make sense of print:

> Children who have been writing for months are in a very favorable position when they undertake learning to read. They have at their command considerable phonetic information about English, practice in phonetic segmentation, and experience with alphabetic representation.... They have, in addition, an expectation of going ahead on their own. They are prepared to make sense, and their purpose is to derive a message from the print, not just pronounce the words. (Chomsky, 1979, pp. 51-52)

Those who view reading as natural, by contrast, align with the perspective that meaning making with print (for a range of functions) arises as young learners encounter the world. In essence, this is tied to the notion that learners engage with reading their world from the outset—exploring the nature and role of print as they encounter and learn the prompts of signs. As Meek (1982) suggested, based upon her extensive experience with young learners:

> The biggest mistake that we make is in giving the five-year-old the notion that you learn to read by a series of exercises, like scales in music, and then you are rewarded with a 'real' book or 'real' reading in another form. (p.11)

Meek's view aligns with Jerome Bruner's (1990) discussion of meaning making; he argues that the quest for meaning, explanation, and coherence drives all of our interactions with the natural, social, and cultural worlds in which we live.

Our Revised Version of the Claim

Our own sentiments align with those of both Bruner and Meek. We don't propose a wired in reading acquisition device that parallels the consensus view of a built-in language acquisition device (Chomsky, 1965). However, we do believe that all humans are wired to engage in sense-making in all their encounters with the natural, social, and cultural worlds in which they live. They seek coherence in their explanations of everything. From this perspective, learning to read is no more or less natural than learning how to cross a street, ride a bike, do multiplication, categorize dinosaurs, or find support for claims you make when developing arguments. Moreover, it is consistent with what Freire (1972) had in mind when he discussed the need for humans to read both the word and the world.

Our current working hypothesis, in trying to understand why so many scholars regard learning to read as unnatural, is that they really want to divide reading into two phases: a) Identifying and understanding words; and b) Understanding connected discourse. Again, we return to the Rayner et al. (2001) definition from the third claim that we fact-checked. Recall their distinction between reading and literacy. Reading, for them, is phase A—that is, getting the words mapped onto students' oral language lexicon. At that point, all the language, knowledge, and contextual resources that readers bring to the printed page can kick in to aid in the discourse comprehension phase. Phase A is arbitrary and unnatural; phase B is highly natural, or at least as natural as everything else we do. Put another way, with this approach, the only meaning making in reading is understanding words; the meaning making that comes later in discourse comprehension is just like meaning making for oral language, or for any other artifacts or phenomena we encounter in everyday experience.

If reading is defined as the translation of print into sounds (to identify words tied to the alphabetic principle; see Claim 2), then the case for learning to read as an unnatural activity (at least for some learners) may have some support. It is likely, however, that you will find exceptions. While most children will require explicit instruction to master the cipher, some young children learn to read without the need for explicit intervention—and do so in ways that parallel learning to speak. By contrast, if you define learning to read as achieving a range of functions through engagement with symbols of various types (linguistic and non-linguistic), then you will likely suggest that learning to read occurs naturally—from an innate propensity to enlist and expand one's use of symbols (letters in the alphabet among them) as one expresses oneself or interprets the world. In other words, if you take a step back and look at reading through the lens of writing development, print awareness, or reading the signs that we encounter as we engage with people, places, and our environment—then what counts as reading includes much more than reading print.

For us, learning to read may not be specifically wired in the same way we have come to accept the specificity of the wiring for learning one's oral language. But, as nearly as we can fathom, it is as natural or unnatural as learning anything else we learn in our quest to make meaning and achieve coherence about all of life's phenomena. Learning to read print, in this sense, is integrated with—and a natural outcome of—learning to make sense of the world.

CLAIM 7

Balanced Literacy and/or Whole Language is responsible for the low or falling NAEP scores we have witnessed in the U.S. in the past decade.

The Evidence Marshalled in Support of the Claim

Using scores from the National Assessment of Educational Progress (NAEP), or any other wide-scale assessment, to make a claim about why the U.S. education system (or that of any other English-speaking country) is failing its students is not a new practice—especially coming from policy pundits with an axe to grind. Historically, questionable claims regarding the rise and fall of test results have fueled conversations, more speculative than certain, about the quality of schooling and student learning outcomes. And the SoR movement is no exception.

For example, in a February 2023 opinion column for *The New York Times*, Nicholas Kristoff enlisted familiar arguments to suggest a connection between the teaching of phonics and better test results. As he stated:

> Two-thirds of fourth graders in the United States are not proficient in reading.
>
> Reading may be the most important skill we can give children. It's the pilot light of that fire.
>
> Yet we fail to ignite that pilot light, so today some one in five adults in the United States struggles with basic literacy, and after more than 25 years of campaigns and fads, American children are still struggling to read. Eighth graders today are actually a hair worse at reading than their counterparts were in 1998. (paras. 3-5)

The column segued into a case for teaching reading through systematic phonics. A month or so later, in March of 2023, a similar argument was made by the Editorial Board of *The Washington Post* (WP Editorial Board, 2023)—citing tests score changes in Mississippi as evidence of the virtues of phonics. This particular case, commonly referred to as the Mississippi Miracle, has often been used to demonstrate the power of legislative action to contribute to positive change in teaching practices. Indeed, the National Council on Teacher Quality (Ellis et al., 2023) touted the state of Mississippi as "a top state in the NCTQ review" (p. 24), arguing:

> … this dedication to teacher preparation is achieving results for students: Between 2013 and 2019, the state saw fourth grade NAEP scores rise dramatically, including for historically marginalized groups such as Black and Hispanic students. Even after the pandemic, Mississippi maintained its gains in reading in 2022, while many other states declined. (p. 24)

Likewise, in Australia, SoR claims and the Mississippi miracle have been touted to advance alarmist inferences of a crisis, justify a purging of past practices, and to insist that systematic phonics offer a panacea. Media, such as the Australian Broadcasting Corporation (ABC; e.g., Duffy, 2024), and policy lobby groups, such as the Grattan Institute (Hunter, Stobart, & Haywood, 2024), have suggested that declining reading performances propel the need to reform curriculum and teacher education to align with a systematic phonics emphasis. As authors of a report by the Grattan Institute suggested:

> Australia has an unacceptably high number of children and adolescents who fail to reach minimum proficiency standards in reading. According to 2023 NAPLAN results, about one in three Australian students are not meeting grade-level expectations in reading. Australia has too many 'instructional casualties'—students who should read proficiently, but haven't been taught well.
>
> At the same time, not enough Australian students are excelling in reading. According to PISA (the OECD's Programme for International Student Assessment), in 2022 only 12 per cent of Australian students were high performers in reading, compared to 22 per cent in Singapore. (Hunter, Stobart, & Haywood, 2024, p. 8)

Our Reading of the Evidence and the Claim

Can and should such test results be used to support causal connections between past and present practices and outcomes—especially if the timelines for practices and the results do not always align? We concur with a number of our colleagues: The use of national and international test results to judge the effectiveness of approaches to teaching reading constitute a commonplace problem. As Bowers (2020) argued, it is a bridge too far for a government to attribute improvement in national and international test results to their advocacy and demands for phonics instruction—or, for that matter, for any type of instruction. These claims often draw faulty inferences about patterns and trends in test scores; misinterpret performance levels (e.g., basic versus proficient versus advanced); and ignore the correlational nature of the evidence. These arguments also ignore the limits of the measures themselves. Even if we did accept the dubious practice of elevating correlations to causal connections between practices and outcomes, we would be forced to also acknowledge that on other outcomes—such as the enjoyment of reading—the evidence favors those countries that have been largely spared from reforms and mandates requiring the teaching of phonics (Goldstein, 2023).

Reinking, Hruby and Risko (2023) noted that NAEP data has remained largely unchanged: "What is particularly remarkable is that...plotting reading scores on the NAEP across decades results in essentially a flat line, although with a slight upward movement since the outset" (pp. 113-114.). In an endnote, they add that this flat trajectory reflects "...the average scores for Grade 4 students, which is most relevant to early reading, but graphs for students in Grades 8 and 12 are similarly flat" (p. 126). Other countries have witnessed similar trends, as seen in discussions of increased national testing regimens and international comparative measures such as PIRLS (the Progress in International Reading Literacy Study). For example, educational authorities in England applauded their country's rise in 2021 PIRLS rankings, from 8th to 4th place. Despite no change in their overall score from the preceding 2016 PIRLS results, they ascribed such improvements to an emphasis in phonics instruction (e.g., Weale & Adams, 2023). (Media accounts in New Zealand, by contrast, have suggested that high performance on PIRLS can be ascribed to support for motivating young readers—e.g., by nurturing their self-confidence and love of reading; see RNZ, 2023).

As Reinking, Hruby, and Risko (2023) also noted, the manner of reporting NAEP results by proficiency levels (advanced, proficient, basic) contributes to the problem. As they showed (see Figure 7) and explained:

Proficiency levels created a custom-made crisis. Using the 2019 NAEP reading scores, a typical argument goes something like this: "Only 34% of fourth-grade students nationally scored at or above the proficient level in reading." That sounds alarming, suggesting that only about a third of readers are proficient. Some might even interpret this to mean that two thirds of students are hardly reading at all. But, if "basic" means something closer to "average," which it does, and readers in that group are combined with "proficient" or above... approximately two thirds of all fourth-grade students are reading at or near grade level, with slight increases over the year. There was a statistically significant drop by 1 point in 2019; although that drop is worth watching, it is not a trend indicating a crisis. (p. 115)

Figure 7

Percentage of Fourth-Grade Students Scoring Basic Level or Above on Reading on the National Assessment of Educational Progress (NAEP), 1992–2019 (Reinking, Hruby, & Risko, 2023)

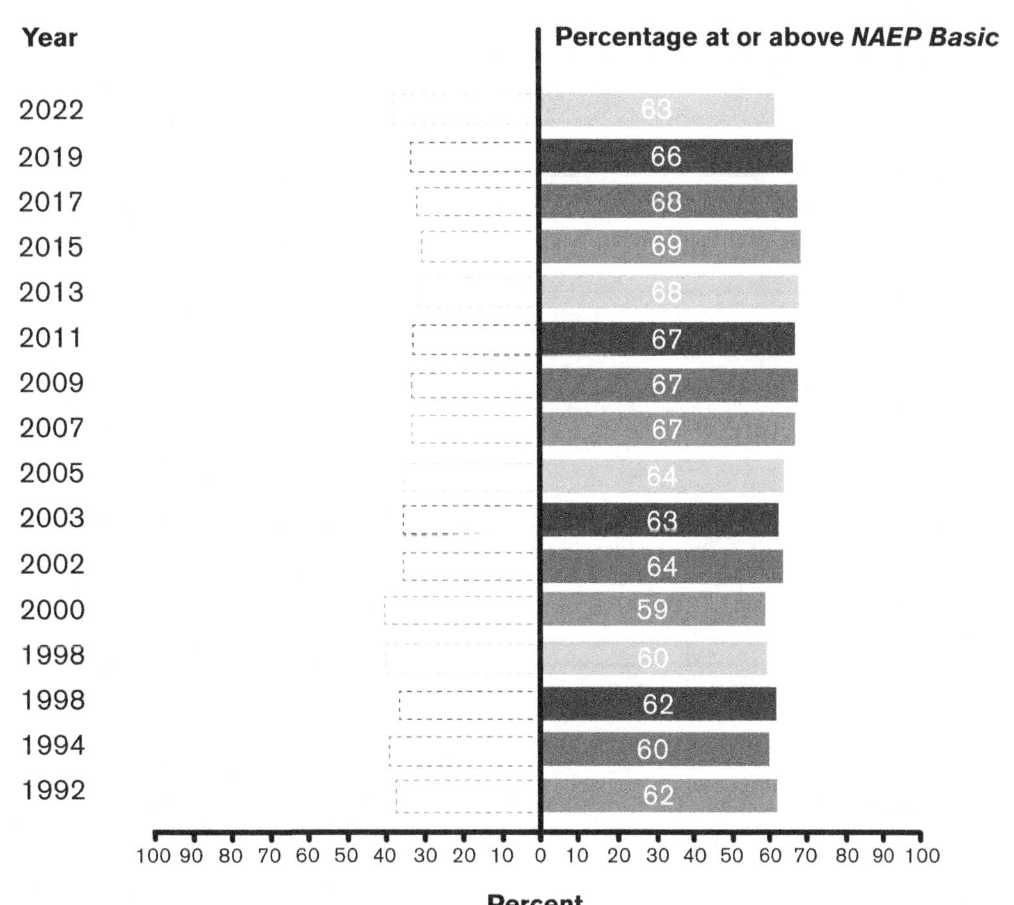

Similar evidentiary paths and arguments have been pursued in Australia. For example, data from Australia's National Assessment Program–Literacy and Numeracy (NAPLAN) have been used to discredit approaches to teaching reading and teacher education. As shown in Figures 8 and 9, the results bring to the fore differences across student populations, such as Indigenous and non-Indigenous groups. Yet the results should not be misread as trends over time; for instance, the test performance of Indigenous students may signal a need to improve the tests themselves—in other words, a need to recognize that the tests enlisted may not afford a valid measure of Indigenous students' literacies.

Figure 8

NAPLAN Mean Results by Student Year, 2008-2022 (ACARA, 2022)

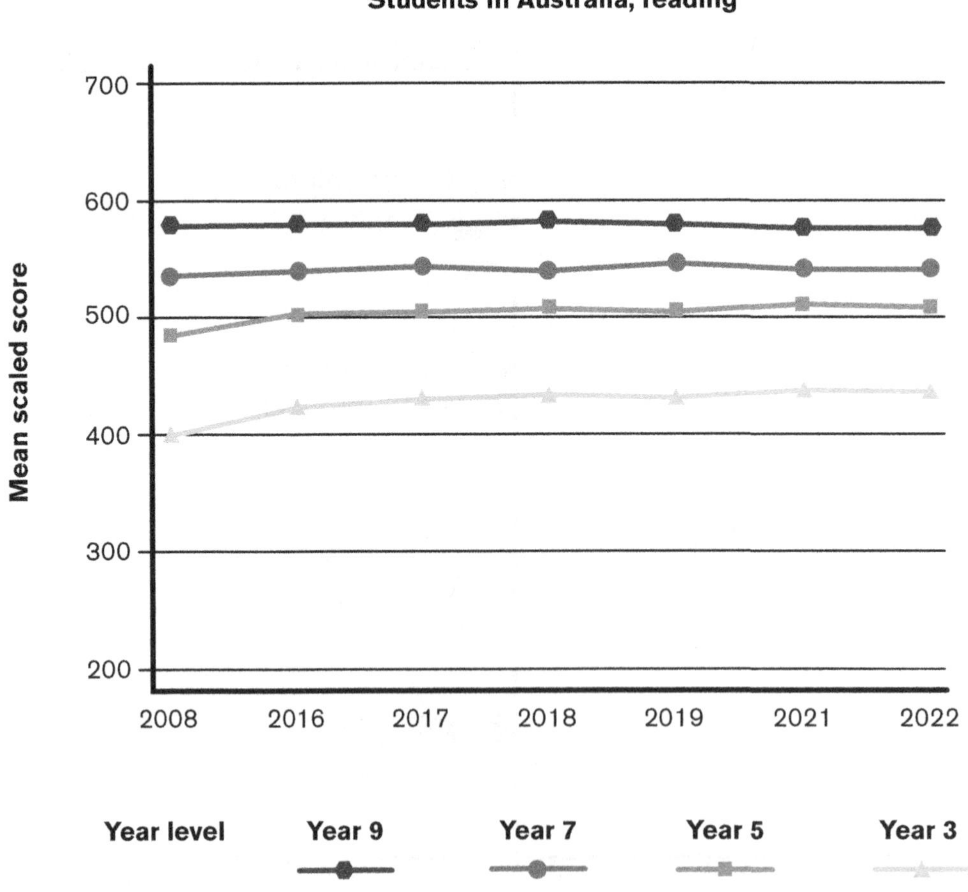

Figure 9

NAPLAN Mean Results for Year 3 Students Indigenous & Non-Indigenous, 2008-2022 (ACARA, 2022)

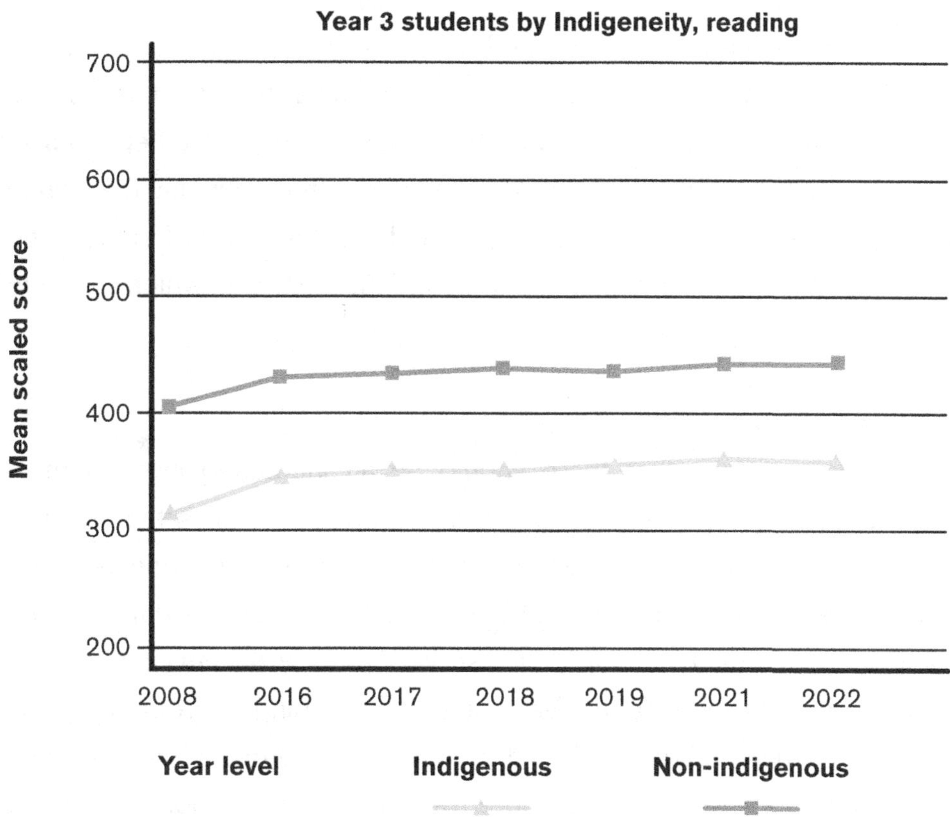

Nevertheless, the NAPLAN results reinforce concerns about a widening gap between Indigenous and non-Indigenous students. As Natasha Bita (2022), the education editor of *The Australian*, commented:

> Fresh NAPLAN data exposes a growing gap in achievement between students from wealthy and poor families, as well as girls and boys, with at least a third of Indigenous teenagers functionally illiterate. (para. 2)

Despite the longstanding nature of these gaps, and the range of factors that have been identified as contributors to such results (e.g., economic factors resulting in major disparities in school funding; the application of a one-size-fits-all, Eurocentric curriculum), some SoR advocates continue to claim that such differences have arisen from curricular emphases (e.g., that emphasize Whole Language and, as a result, fail to teach phonics). As Bita (2022) suggested:

> ...nearly 9 per cent of all year 9 students—taught to read using the "look and guess" whole-language technique popular a decade ago—are still struggling to read and write, with boys falling behind faster than girls. (para. 5)

On a global scale, the same trend can be seen in the interpretation of PISA results (Programme for International Student Assessment). Claims are made that crises have arisen—even when fluctuations and differences in performance (between benchmarked countries) might be minimal (i.e., when other factors are taken into consideration, such as the range of scores, the sampling of students, the timing of the tests, and the manner in which students are prepared; see Figure 10).

Our Revised Version of the Claim

We do not deny that there should be an increased investment in reading instruction; however, it should not be based on claims that dismiss past efforts and suggest new directions without stronger evidence. Aligning the timing of educational developments with test performance data is quite speculative; it is well-nigh impossible to ascribe causality with any confidence. At best, such data provide a justification for probing more deeply, by conducting experimental research that can evaluate the causal relationships between programs and outcomes. Moreover, this practice ignores (perhaps conveniently) those economic and other factors have been shown to be influential. Yet in the United States and elsewhere, educators, the public, and politicians and policy makers continue to be presented with such evidence to support or dismiss educational developments.

A recent manifestation of this tendency involves the heralding of developments in Mississippi. The alleged Mississippi Miracle—celebrated by the governor of Mississippi, *The Washington Post*, and the National Council on Teacher Quality (NCTQ)—was touted as an example of how phonics instruction would lead to dramatic NAEP score increases. Unfortunately, closer examinations of the data and Mississippi education policy have raised concerns that the data may not be as strong as claimed (especially over the long term). The alleged increases in reading performances may have arisen not from an emphasis upon phonics, but rather from policies directed at

Figure 10

PISA Mean Reading Literacy Scores and Distribution of Student Performance by Country (Based upon De Bortoli, Underwood, & Thomson, 2023)

Country	Mean Score	SE	Confidence Interval	Difference between 10th & 90th percentiles	Distribution of scores
Singapore	543	1.9	538-546	271	
Ireland	516	2.3	511-520	227	
Japan	516	3.2	509-522	249	
Korea	515	3.6	508-522	262	
Chinese Taipei	515	3.3	508-521	269	
Canada	507	2.0	503-510	278	
United States	504	4.3	495-512	292	
New Zealand	501	2.1	496-505	287	
Hong Kong (China)	500	2.8	494-505	255	
Australia	498	2.0	494-501	288	
United Kingdom	494	2.4	489-499	269	
Finland	490	2.3	485-494	270	
Denmark	489	2.6	483-493	238	
Poland	489	2.7	483-494	272	
Czech Republic	489	2.2	484-493	256	
Sweden	487	2.5	482-491	290	
Italy	482	2.7	476-486	240	
Germany	480	3.6	472-486	276	
Portugal	477	2.7	471-481	243	
Norway	477	2.5	471-481	295	
OECD Average	476	0.5	474-476	262	
Spain	474	1.7	471-477	250	
France	474	3.1	467-479	277	
Israel	474	3.5	466-480	323	
Hungary	473	2.8	467-478	264	
Viet Nam	462	3.9	454-469	197	
Greece	438	2.8	432-443	245	
Iceland	436	2.1	431-439	271	

200 300 400 500 600 700

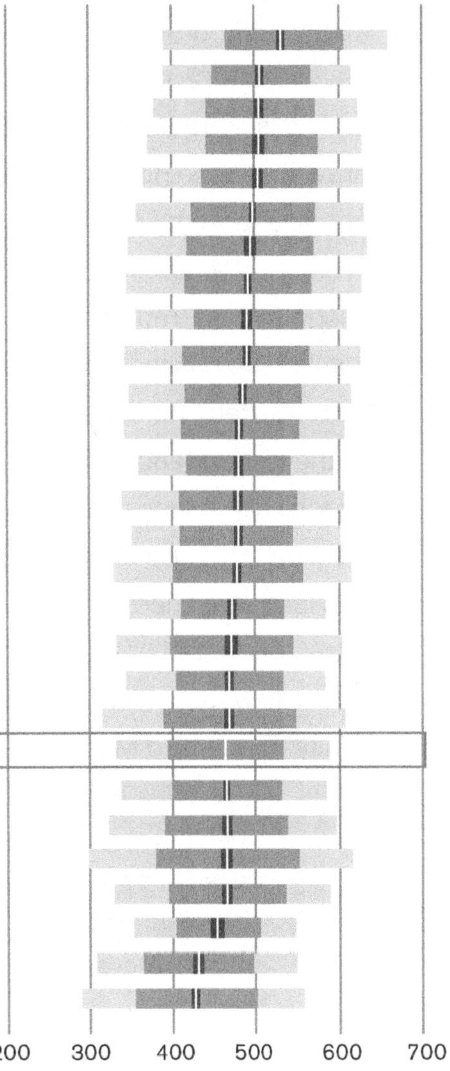

teaching to the test and from the exclusion of certain students from being tested. Indeed, further examinations expose what might be considered more tempered claims for improvements in reading performance, as well as uncertainty about the antecedents of such results—questioning the influence of the shift to phonics, and the extent to which such initiatives are replicable (Drum, 2023; Westall & Cummings, 2023).

In reviewing the Mississippi results, *LA Times* business columnist Michael Hiltzik (2023) and education bloggers Bob Somerby (2023) and Kevin Drum (2023) reported what they deem to be a statistical illusion—one that mischaracterizes Mississippi fourth-grade students' unprecedented growth in reading performance as correlated with the state's emphasis on phonics (and, by extension, the Governor's support of Mississippi's Literacy Promotion Act). According to Somerby and Drum, the results are not just suspect; they represent a cover-up. The miracle growth suggested in the results, they assert, arises from the exclusion of the lowest 10% of students from the data. As Somerby and Drum reveal, if the data are examined in terms of the performance of Mississippi students across the elementary grades—specifically, if those students forced to repeat the third grade were included in the pool—the gains espoused would disappear. Claims that the achievement gap had lessened would be likewise be countered if a closer examination were conducted of select minorities. African American and Mexican American students were not faring any better than in prior years; indeed, the gap between White, Black, and Mexican American students was widening. Essentially, they argue, the reforms had no effect. As Hiltzik (2023) noted in his review:

> ...whatever gains had shown up in Mississippi's fourth-grade scores had vanished by the eighth grade, when all students notched exactly the same scores in 2022 as they had in 2013. A teaching program whose gains evaporate over a four-year span doesn't much warrant the label "miracle." (para. 27)

Despite efforts to counter such concerns by individuals and advocacy groups (e.g., Collins, 2022), there is sufficient uncertainty to warrant questioning the claims being made, and their generalizability. The jury is still out on the long-term nature of changes in Mississippi, and how and why the scores of some Mississippi students may have climbed the way they did. If it were as simple as changing curriculum standards, then why didn't states that made similar changes yield similar results? What is clear, however, is that assigning causal connections between curriculum and the results of widely-used tests, such as DIBELS or NAEP, is based on spurious reasoning. Moreover, efforts to even consider the evidence of any causal relationship may suffer from a credibility problem, stemming from the measures themselves. NAEP, like many of the national assessments in various countries, offers a broad measure that should not be viewed as sampling the diverse literacies of the readers. Indeed, the NAEP does not test for knowledges and skills in which minority students might excel. Tests such as DIBELS likewise approach the testing of comprehension in a very narrow fashion—using the Maze procedure, which has been shown to be insensitive to comprehension beyond the boundaries of single sentences (Shanahan, Tobin, & Kamil, 1982).

We advocate a more cautious approach, one in which the trends observed in national (such as NAEP or NAPLAN) or even international (such as PISA or PIRLS) assessments are regarded as warning signs, as causes for alarm or surprise, that will trigger more careful and longer-term studies by the broader research community—research that, by design, would have the capacity to evaluate causal relationships. As current policy pundits and reporters have done, we ask more of these assessments than they were designed to accomplish, as they spread unwarranted—and potentially harmful—claims about both the positive (phonics first will solve our woes) and negative (Balanced Literacy is the culprit) effects of curricular change.

CLAIM 8

Evidence from neuroscience research substantiates the efficacy of focus on phonics-first instruction.

The Evidence Marshalled in Support of the Claim

A neuroscientific basis for learning to read has been a focus for over 100 years as physicians and psychologists and have sought to understand dyslexia, aphasia, and various language processing issues. These investigations have ranged from crude measures (such as measuring the circumference of the brain) to studies of eye movements and, more recently, enlisting magnetic resonance imaging (MRI) to map brain activity. By correlating the results of these measures with processes such as language comprehension, language production, and reading, scholars have offered hypotheses and explanations about the neurological basis of language development and how brain activity interfaces with reading processes and development. As Maryanne Wolf (2008), based on her explorations of the Science of Reading, suggested:

> The more we know about the development of the reading brain and the dyslexic brain, the better we are able, in our interventions, to target more specifically the particular parts or connections that are not developing in some children. Interventions in dyslexia—just as in reading that is developing typically—must explicitly address every component system of reading intensely and imaginatively, until some level of automaticity and comprehension is attained (p. 227)

Of particular relevance to reading and writing within neuroscience research is the work of neuropsychiatrist Samuel Orton and his colleague, educator and psychologist Anne Gillingham (see Gillingham & Stillman, 1946; Orton, 1937; 1966). Drawing on their own observations, eye movement work attributed to ophthalmologist Louis Émile Javal (e.g., Javal, 1905; see also Wade & Tatler, 2009), and work by educational psychologist Grace Fernald (1943), Orton and Gillingham suggested that many reading difficulties involve a habitual shortcoming in brain activity—specifically, in left hemispherical engagements—that, in turn, might be related to the limitations of approaches to reading (e.g., the "look say" method). Enlisting synthetic phonics in approaches to reading development, they postulated, might compensate for what they deemed to be an overdependency on the right versus the left hemisphere, and help and support the brain development they saw as lacking. The Orton-Gillingham multisensory pedagogical approach—grounded in Orton's (1937) neurological work on language processing and reading difficulties, and later built upon by Gillingham and Stillman (1946)—has over time remained a prominent method of dealing with issues of dyslexia (see Orton, 1966). Despite questions that might be raised about the "science" of Orton's hypothesis linking brain development and pedagogy (e.g., in terms of pinpointing brain activity to the act of reading, or demonstrating how brain activity is prone to the influences of pedagogy), Orton's work continues to undergird SoR claims that neuroscience research supports a phonics-first approach to reading.

Providing partial support for Orton's hypothesis, functional magnetic resonance imaging (fMRI) has led some neuroscientists and educators to suggest that reading development (i.e., phonological coding and syntactic and semantic processing) tends to be associated with certain regions of the brain—and that activation of those regions might advance learning to read (as defined by those elements). For example, among children identified as dyslexic, often-cited Sally Shaywitz and Bennett Shaywitz (e.g., Shaywitz & Shaywitz, 2020; Shaywitz & Shaywitz, 2005; 2008) have demonstrated a preponderance of development in the frontal lobe and the right, as opposed to the left, hemisphere of the brain. They suggest that a large proportion of struggling readers, while they have intact systems, lack development in the left hemisphere associated with language processes—and, as a result, are disadvantaged in terms of the automaticity and fluency required to succeed as readers. The claim is that these shortcomings contribute to a failure to identify words, as suggested by Figures 11 and 12.

Figure 11

Dyslexia: Going from Text to Meaning
Adapted from Shaywitz and Shaywitz (2020)

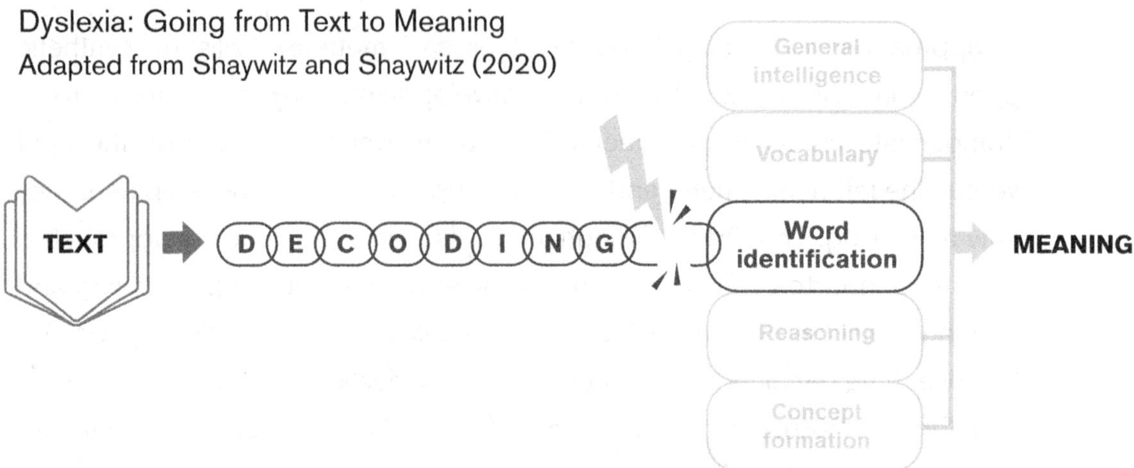

A phonological weakness blocks decoding, which in turn interferes with word identification. This prevents a dyslexic reader from applying his higher-level skils to get at a word's meaning. But even if he can't identify the word specifically, he can apply these higher-level skills to the context around the unknown word to guess at its meaning.

Figure 12

Word Retrieval in Typical and Dyslexic Readers
Adapted from Shaywitz and Shaywitz (2020)

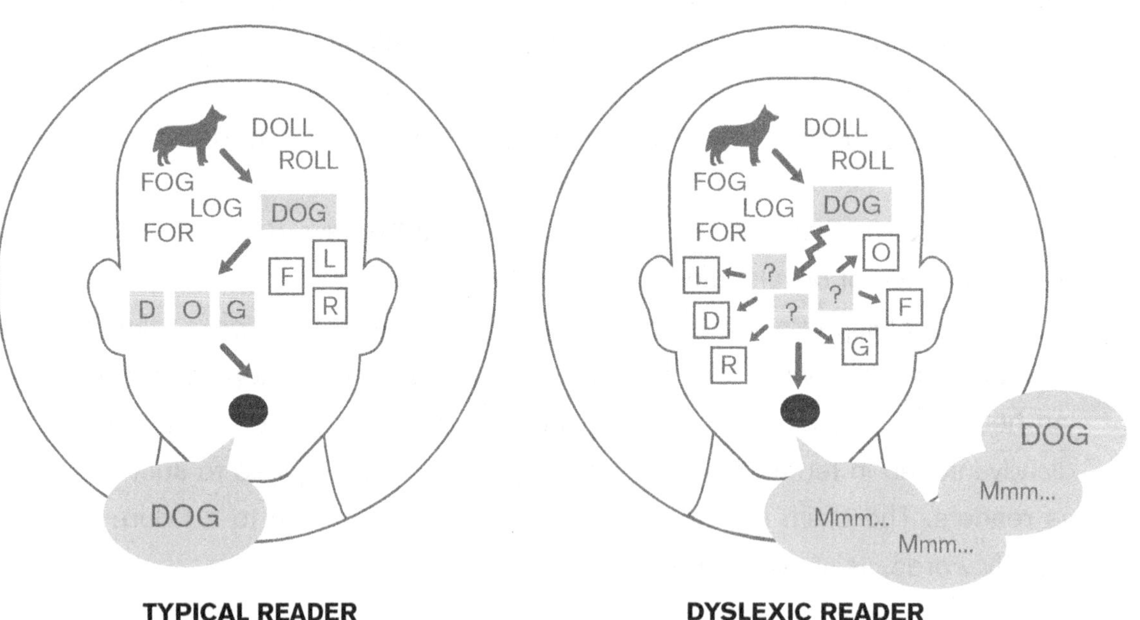

It is this fundamental dofficulty in retrieving the tiny individual sounds of spoken language that lies at the heart of dyslexia and explains the dyslexic's problem in word retrieval.

Shaywitz, S. E. & Shaywitz, J., (2020) Overcoming dyslexia. (Second edition). New York: Alfred A. Knopf; ISBN: 9780385350327

Shaywitz and Shaywitz ascribe this skewed development (i.e., an overreliance on the right hemisphere, and what they suggest is a less efficient left hemisphere) to environmental influences, including a lack of opportunity to engage with learning words (e.g., through an engagement with phonics). The notion of the key role played by the left regions of the brain is coupled with two views: 1) Activation (or lack thereof) of certain parts of the brain (while reading) may be symptomatic of a failure of brain development; and 2) The simultaneous engagement of various areas of the brain is possibly significant as well (see Figure 13).

Figure 13

Activated Neural Systems in Nonimpaired and Dyslexic Readers
Adapted from Shaywitz and Shaywitz (2020)

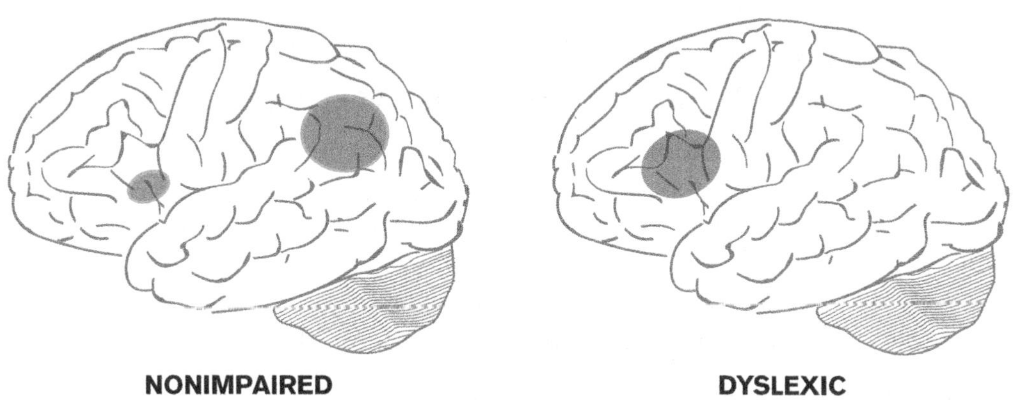

At left, nonimpaired readers activate neural systems that are mostly in the back of the left side of the brain (shaded areas); at right, dyslexic readers underactivate these reading systems in the back of the brain and tend to overactivate frontal areas.

Shaywitz, S. E. & Shaywitz, J., (2020) Overcoming dyslexia. (Second edition). New York: Alfred A. Knopf; ISBN: 0780385350327

A frequent if aspirational goal of many neurological researchers, such as Shaywitz and Shaywitz or Wolf, is to connect neurological activity to reading development and pedagogy. Yet without more sophisticated devices for tracking readers' brain activity, and further research studies exploring instructional possibilities, this may well more speculative than assured. As neurologists note, the fMRI affords tentative implications but significant constraints, including its failure to assess brain activity over time, its failure to register brain activity that has occurred, and the lack of resolution found in the images. Researchers also highlight variability in responses of different readers, such that pinpointing a one-to-one relationship and generalizing across learners is problematic. Recent discussions have noted the limitations of generalizing, across learners, brain activity in specific regions (i.e., those involved in certain functions of language processing) (Crinion et al., 2013; Maisog et al., 2008). To summarize, the limitations of brain scans have included:

1. The tools enlisted for brain scans afford a snapshot of brain activity—reflecting an instant, not an extended period of time;
2. Efforts to localize specific areas of the brain where activation occurs is variable across readers—and even may vary across the same readers;
3. Attributing signals within specific regions to reading behaviors and not to other factors is problematic;
4. Efforts to enlist magnetic resonance devices are difficult with very young learners.

In her pursuit of what Shaywitz (2003) refers to as "the holy grail" (p. 87)—identifying the neurological underpinnings of dyslexia—she emphasizes the variability of dyslexia and the need for considerably more research on teaching, learning, and development. Her discussions are coupled with recommendations for parents and educators, such as considering the range of factors that might contribute to some readers' struggles. It is noteworthy that she points to the importance of reading connected text—not just words—and describes how learning occurs via interactions with more than just phonetic cues.

While there is some optimism that additional research and more refined observation devices will yield more clarity on the relationship between brain activity and reading development, there is an admission that we are not there yet. In their discussion of dyslexia and the brain, the International Dyslexia Association (IDA, 2020) summarized such future hopes:

> The role of the brain in developmental dyslexia has been studied in the context of brain anatomy, brain chemistry, and brain function—and in combination with interventions to improve reading and information about genetic influences. Together with results of behavioral studies, this information will help researchers to identify the causes of dyslexia, continue to explore early identification of dyslexia, and determine the best avenues for its treatment. (p. 3)

In his book *Reading in the Brain: The New Science of How We Read,* Stanislas Dehaene (2009) discusses developments in neuroscience on a number of fronts—highlighting the extraordinary advances made by researchers studying the nature of brain activity and development in relation to reading. He describes how studies suggest an extensive flow of activity across regions of the brain when readers are exploring the meaning of text. He also discusses the learning brain's plasticity from birth, as it "recycles" to address cultural systems such as reading and writing. However, he notes:

> The insight into how literacy changes the brain is profoundly transforming our vision of education and learning disabilities. New remediation programs are being conceived that should, in time, cope with the debilitating incapacity to decipher words known as dyslexia. (p. 2)

Dehaene offers suggestions, based upon correlational data, and some speculations as to how teaching and learning might proceed—including critiques of Whole Language as an "approach" to learning words. Yet he refrains from offering firm suggestions based upon what he recognizes to be the limitations of the science, such as the lack of an adequate convergence of findings, and a void in instructional studies available to substantiate speculative instructional implications. He even suggests that the practical wisdom of teaching and teachers still has a role in shaping everyday practice, at least perhaps, until more definitive research findings are available:

> My own impression is that neuroscience is still far from being prescriptive. A wide gap separates the theoretical knowledge accumulated in the laboratory from practice in the classroom. Applications raise problems that are often better addressed by teachers than by the theory-based expectations of scientists. (p. 218)

Our Reading of the Evidence and the Claim

It is clear that the scholars whose work we have reviewed are aware of the "aspirational" potential of neurological insights to guide pedagogy. Although advocates of teaching phonics often might concede some of the aforementioned limitations, they dismiss them as more circumstantial than substantive. Their arguments combine anecdotes about learners who have benefitted from phonics; alternatively, they make reference to evidence of the benefits of teaching phonics from neuroscience research (e.g., Dehaene, 2009; 2011; Shaywitz & Shaywitz, 2020; Shaywitz, 2003; Shaywitz et al., 1996; Simos et al., 2002). In terms of the latter, they tout select fMRI findings from a small number of neuroscientists who claim to have evidence of neural pathways that lead from phonemic analysis to word naming to comprehension of meaning. This may be due in part to the fact that, despite the somewhat speculative use of fMRI results among researchers, the notion of reading research supported by identifiers such as neuroscience or the science of reading has appeal. It suggests a biological connection to reading (including, perhaps, reading difficulties). Of particular importance to SoR advocates, it appears to provide evidence of brain activity reflecting a neural pathway from orthography to meaning mediated by phonology.

Given the questionable reliability of such results and other factors that might be in play, claims that enlist select neuroscience studies to argue for the primacy of phonics may be difficult to substantiate or even verify. For example, as Compton-Lilly et al. (2023) report, reading processes involve multiple networks distributed across various regions of the brain (see Table 6); as such, phonics is not exceptional, but one of many information sources and factors related to reading that have been shown to register brain activity. Additionally, at a base level, fMRIs or brain scans have been shown to lack reliability (e.g., when the same stimuli mimicking the same conditions yield different results). Therefore, to match the results from neuroscience to propositions for the primary role of phonics for functional purposes seems spurious—more curious than convincing.

Table 6 Reading Processes Distributed across the Brain (Compton-Lilly et al., 2023)

Sources of information	Definition	Neural regions involved
Phonetics	The sounds in a language	Temporal lobe, auditory cortex
Orthographics	Conventions of written language	Occipital-temporal ventral cortex
Semantics	Word meanings and general knowledge	Temporal-parietal and frontal cortex
Syntax	The arrangement of words and phrases in a sentence	Left frontal cortex

For some, substantiation of the important role of phonics—to the exclusion of other approaches—derived from select neuroscience observations may be "a bridge too far." As Strauss, Goodman, and Paulson (2009) have argued, these arguments fail to reckon with other findings. As they stated:

> The functional MRI studies which claimed to show that the brain uses letter-sound relationships as it reads, and that reading is essentially matching letters with sounds, were based on an inadequate understanding of human brain function. The studies indeed demonstrated that a sufficiently advanced machine can reveal brain sites where letter-sound processes occur. But they were misinterpreted to imply that nothing else of significance to reading is going on when the reader transacts with a whole, meaningful text (p. 032)

If other neuroscience studies of learning and development are considered, then all learning, including learning to read, appears more complex than triggering the phonological processing areas of the brain. Other fMRI studies have identified additional factors that trigger changes in the brain's response, demonstrating the engagement of the whole brain in conjunction with social and cultural contexts and socio-emotional responses (e.g., Immordino-Yang & Gotlieb, 2017). With the advent and growth of culturally-based studies of neuroprocessing (e.g., neuroanthropology), studies have highlighted the limitations of distilling or separating brain activity in certain regions, as well as the extent to which neuroscience can offer discrete and unfettered conclusions about the relationships between brain activity and external engagements. Cultural neuroscience in particular has drawn attention to how routine cultural practices as well as what might be considered socio-emotional engagements interface with human brain development and learning (e.g., Chiao & Immordino-Yang, 2013; Han, et al., 2013; Immordino-Yang & Gotlieb, 2017; Immordino-Yang & Yang, 2017; Immordino-Yang, et al., 2009; Lee et al., 2020; Zhou & Fischer, 2013). In addition to influencing brain function, culture changes the structure of the brain (e.g., Domínguez et al., 2009). This work illustrates how culture operates in tandem with other influences—in a fashion that not only shapes pre-existing patterns of neural activity, but also may determine whether a pattern is present at all.

Neuroscience research has also identified how experience with different tasks impacts brain functioning. Recent fMRI studies by Immordino-Yang and her colleagues have documented how meaning making engages the whole brain rather than isolated regions, interconnecting emotion, cognition, and executive functioning. In their imaging studies of teens' responses to stories of struggle and resilience, abstract meaning making was associated with activity in a network of the brain—what they term the default mode network—that supports reflective and imaginative modes of processing, often with cultural, ethical, and identity-related implications (Gotlieb et al., 2022; Gotlieb, Yang, & Immordino-Yang, 2022; 2021; Immordino-Yang, Christodoulou, & Singh, 2012; Yang et al., 2018). Among adolescents, activation of this network in response to stories was found to predict memory of the stories and growth in brain structures five years later (Immordino-Yang & Knecht, 2020). Although these areas of research are still in their infancy, such studies do highlight the need to temper claims that neuroscience substantiates a discrete and independent pathway to learning to read through phonics. At minimum, as Gotlieb et al. (2022) note, fMRI studies suggest a tension between neuroscience research findings and approaches to education. As they state: "The tension, then, in effective literacy curriculum design and delivery is around how best to navigate and support both [foundational skills and broader literacy] aspects of children's learning" (p. 83).

Our Revised Version of the Claim

Neurologist and linguist Stephen Strauss (2014) noted that the select findings of by some phonics advocates fail to reckon with the limitations of extrapolating from brain imaging studies. As he suggested:

> ...being able to image brain regions where sounding out letters takes place does not mean that sounding out letters is the key to successful reading. It just means that we have a technology that can identify where the brain accomplishes the conversion of letters to sounds. For sure, we have learned something about the technology, that it has a certain degree of cognitive resolution, so to speak. What it tells us about reading remains an open question. ...magnetic resonance technology is powerful enough to find brain regions that carry out otherwise useless and meaningless tasks, like identifying a font as not conventionally familiar. For all we know, sounding out letters is just as useless and meaningless. Its status as a central principle in a model of reading and dyslexia needs to first be established on the basis of the empirical evidence from reading research. In other words, the high-tech evidence cannot be interpreted in the absence of a theory of reading.
>
> The medicalizers claim that giving dyslexic readers hours and hours of intensive direct phonics instruction can literally repair their damaged brains. ...No; they merely observed that the subjects of their studies learned what they were taught. (pp. 41-42)

At the very least, and until more definitive neurological (and pedagogical!) evidence is available, we should be somewhat skeptical about connections drawn between the biology of the brain and learning to read. Studies of the brain may not provide evidence of a clear relationship between phonics and learning to read or, by extension, overcoming reading difficulties. As educational psychologist Julian Elliott (2020) noted in his discussion of neuroscience and dyslexia:

> Confusion seems particularly evident in this discipline, where beguiling references to brain scans and the brightly colored pictures of brain activation seem to reduce the critical faculties of many. Many fail to understand that the contribution of neuroscience to the practical task of assessment and intervention of reading disability is still rudimentary, and scientific understandings continue to be undermined by methodological difficulties and the selective use of evidence.

> … neuroscientific research on dyslexia is frequently characterized by "distortions, simplifications, and misrepresentations" (Worthy, Godfrey, Tily, Daly-Lesch, & Salmerón, 2019, p. 314). An absence of criticality reflects a form of neuroseduction, whereby neuroscientific accounts increase the likelihood that one will be persuaded by explanations or conclusions that are not justified by the facts. Principal among these for dyslexia, perhaps, is the erroneous belief that brain imaging can be employed for the purpose of differential assessment and intervention rather than this being an aspiration for the future that may ultimately "be proven to be unfeasible" (Ozernov-Palchik, Yu, Wang, & Gaab, 2016, p. 52). (p. S66)

In exploring the use of neuroscience in discussions of the Science of Reading, Yaden, Reinking and Smagorinsky (2021) raised some of these same issues. As they note, detractors of neuroscience in the SoR debates have expressed major concerns, including: 1) The extent to which fMRI's yield images that can or should be viewed as discrete images of learning responses associated with teaching specific foundational skills (i.e., apart from other responses to reading); 2) The reliability of such research, especially considering the difficulty of replicating data from brain scans; and 3) The extent to which data from brain scans can serve as evidence or the basis for educational practices. As they stated:

> Many researchers in neurobiology (e.g., Elliott et al., 2020; Hickok, 2014; Lyon, 2017) have voiced alarming concerns about the validity and preciseness of brain imaging techniques such as functional magnetic resonance imaging (fMRI) to detect reliable biomarkers in processes such as reading and in the diagnosis of other mental activity. (p. 123)

Yaden and colleagues (2021) particularly highlight the concerns, expressed by neuroscientists themselves, regarding the problems with replicability—most notably inconsistencies in results from scans for the same individual. They emphasize the flaws in moving from brain scans to pedagogy; as they describe, inferences are "uncritically derived from these constructed, multicolored pictures and extrapolated to classroom practices that fit with theories about the relation between neurobiology and action in the world or, in our case, processes of and subsequent instruction in reading" (p. S122). Reiterating concerns voiced by Elliott and colleagues (2020)—that "commonly used task-fMRI measures lack the minimal reliability standards necessary" (p. 803) to identify abnormal brain activity—they raise serious caveats to interpreting any imaging study as applicable to classroom applications.

Even those claiming major breakthroughs admit that a cloud hangs over connections between neurological studies and reading processes and pedagogies. While major gains have been made in learning about brain activity during reading, the findings are more suggestive than certain. To date, they are limited by the state of neurological science, the complications associated with generalizing across individuals, and the lack of instructional studies supporting their ties to specific approaches to teaching and learning.

As for us, we remain both hopeful and skeptical about the capacity of neuroscience to inform curriculum and pedagogy. Breakthroughs are certainly welcome. And, other things being equal, we should expect a degree of resonance between basic brain research and pedagogy. When it comes to classroom practice, perhaps we should regard neuroscience with hopeful skepticism as we explore research on teaching and learning to assess the relevance and carryover of findings from brain research. But before we invest in changes in policy, we owe it to students, parents, and the broader society to test those hypotheses in the crucible of the classroom by employing a full range of methodological, both quantitative and qualitative, tools, along the lines of the suggestions we made in the introduction to this fact-checking exercise.

CLAIM 9

Sociocultural dimensions of reading and literacy are not crucial to explain either reading expertise or its development.

The Evidence Marshalled in Support of the Claim

Despite some mention of issues around equity, ethnic differences, and language, most scholars and pundits aligned with the SoR give scant attention to the sociocultural dimensions of literacy. Instead, this entire domain is simply defined as irrelevant to (i.e., not affecting) the reading process. Our review of Claim 3, which focused on a definition of reading, provides the best perspective on how and why contextual features of learning in general—and reading in particular—are excluded from accounts of the skilled reading process as well as reading development. As a reminder, in the November, 2001 issue of *Psychological Science in the Public Interest*, Rayner and his colleagues offered this intentionally narrow definition of reading:

> In focusing on reading's distinguishing features, we define learning to read as the acquisition of knowledge that results in the child being able to identify and understand printed words that he or she knows on the basis of spoken language. (p. 34)

This is followed by a clear and concise statement concerning contextual factors:

> To see the value of the narrower definition, it is useful to make a distinction between literacy and reading. Literacy dispositions toward learning include a variety of educational outcomes— interests in reading and writing, and knowledge of subject-matter domains—that go beyond reading. These dimensions of literacy entail the achievement of a broad range of skills embedded in cultural and technological contexts. An extended functional definition is useful in helping to make clear the wide range of literacy tasks a society might present to its members. For example, literacy may be defined as including computer literacy, historical literacy, and scientific literacy, among others. Such a functional definition takes literacy as referring to a level of achievement, an extension of basic skill to reasoning and discourse in a domain (Rayner, et al., p 34)

In essence, what Rayner et al. accomplished was to exclude almost all things sociocultural from their definition of reading—assigning contextual factors to what they labeled the domain of literacy. Beyond reading, literacy covered "extended functional definitions," which might entail "reasoning and discourse." This is a clever move if one desires to keep a tight rein on what is meant by reading. But notice that it does not absolve educators from dealing with these elements and issues; all it does is to shift the responsibility to other curricular areas. In this definition, reasoning, discourse, (presumably) knowledge, and functional applications of reading likely fall to disciplinary curricula, such as literature, science, or history—but do not concern the reading teacher.

Our Reading of the Evidence and the Claim

In 2018, the National Academies of Sciences, Engineering and Medicine (NASEM) published a follow-up to the National Research Council's 1999 classic report, *How People Learn*. In the updated volume, *How People Learn II,* the authoring panel established a new norm for framing learning:

> ... all learning is a social process shaped by and infused with a system of cultural meaning... Human development, from birth throughout life, takes place through processes of progressively more complex reciprocal interactions between the human individual (an active, biopsychological organism) and that individual's immediate physical and social environments. Through these dynamic interactions, culture influences even the biological aspects of learning. (pp. 27-28).

It is difficult to understand how the Rayner et al. definition could possibly meet this new standard—defining learning, including learning to read, as an inherently social, cultural, and contextual process. Addressing inequities, especially the needs of struggling readers, is sometimes declared as the raison d'être for SoR approaches to reading. Yet by giving so little consideration to sociocultural factors, such views lead to universal generalizations (i.e., across ethnic groups) and standardized recommendations for instruction.

As we have argued, advocates of a narrow definition of reading prefer to keep sociocultural elements at bay—whether it be the situated nature of learning and cognition, consideration of issues of diversity and multiculturalism, or the dynamics of classrooms themselves—and out of the reading process. As Maryanne Wolf

(2008) acknowledges, her treatment of cultural and historical perspectives is lacking (p. 17). Despite professing views that lean toward transactional and cognitive perspectives—those that embrace definitions of reading that go beyond the page—her orientation and focus ultimately land on the mastery of grapho-phonemic correspondence for beginning readers, at least as the first step toward meaning. As we have suggested, these perspectives are in sharp contrast to what the authors of *How People Learn II* (NASEM, 2018) noted:

> all learners grow and learn in culturally defined ways in culturally defined contexts. While humans share basic brain structures and processes, as well as fundamental experiences such as relationships with family, age-related stages, and many more, each of these phenomena are shaped by an individual's precise experiences. Learning does not happen in the same way for all people because cultural influences are influential from the beginning of life. These ideas about the intertwining of learning and culture have been reinforced by research on many facets of learning and development. (p. 2).

Adding to this, the authors of the NASEM report also underscored the need to understand and acknowledge "the constellation of influences that affect individual learning" (p. 2):

> Each learner develops a unique array of knowledge and cognitive resources in the course of life that are molded by the interplay of that learner's cultural, social, cognitive, and biological contexts. Understanding the developmental, cultural, contextual, and historical diversity of learners is central to understanding how people learn. (pp. 2-3).

Selective Attention to Cultural Dimensions. Nevertheless, there remains a tendency among SoR and phonics advocates to defer meaning making to attaining accurate and automatic word identification via mastery of grapho-phonemic relationships. What is particularly vexing is that some of the discussions of beginning reading by SoR scholars include lengthy exposés on the history of print, as well as developmental reading research that references the cultural, social, and other dimensions of reading. Books by Seidenberg (2017) and Wolf (2008, 2018), for instance, trace the history of print and its evolution across time and place—by relating these developments to sociocultural considerations. In their discussions of reading, however, they seem to discard any mention of these sociocultural elements, focusing almost exclusively on orthographic factors in learning to read. It is as if they pivot from approaches that draw on sociocultural views of reading development—only to segue into touting the necessity of grapho-phonemic correspondence as the exclusive goal of beginning reading for English speakers.

These accounts also give scant attention to engaging with print and other symbolic representations. In doing so, they largely ignore the extent to which reading is about making sense of one's world and the world of others—and participating in those worlds for various purposes, including survival and sustaining relationships. The chasm in this approach ignores the innate linguistic talents of learners, such as the pragmatic discernments of learners who, as they read their worlds, piece together coherent and feasible understandings of the role of print within them. We wonder if the shortcomings of phonics approaches (i.e., in terms of carryover to comprehension development) is rooted in this failure to graft the approach to sociocultural considerations, such as the interests and backgrounds of learners. While SoR advocates would suggest that a limited focus ensures word-level mastery for beginning readers, those concerned about the ramifications of a widening sociocultural chasm would argue instead that the goals of teaching reading should extend beyond word learning to the ways in which readers comprehend and engage with broader worlds. As noted earlier, the results of a number of longitudinal studies suggest that a focus on phonics does indeed propel the learning of letter-sound relationships and readers' abilities to pronounce pseudo-words. However, these results also suggest that this approach fails to enhance reading comprehension, and offers little to support young readers' abilities to read for meaning (Tierney & Sheehy, 2005).

As noted in Claim 1, the U.K.'s Rose Report (2006) likewise gave cultural issues limited attention. In an arguably apologetic tone, brief mention is made of readers' cultural backgrounds and teaching English as a second language. As the report states:

> Children's backgrounds will obviously shape their experiences and should be taken into account, for example, by recognising cultural events, such as religious festivals and traditional stories. These can provide powerful learning opportunities to boost speaking, listening, reading and writing in English. (p. 24)

Reports emanating from the U.S. (e.g., Adams, 1990; Snow, Burns, & Griffin, 1998) similarly make occasional references to the importance of relevant content in reading instruction, but their discussions are minimal. Discerning the influence of sociopolitical considerations—or viewing diversity as a goal, or as a means of enhancing and complementing beginning readers' experiences—is rarely examined in detail. Furthermore, when discussions of diversity do arise, they seem to position difference as synonymous with deficit. This lack of attention given to sociocultural considerations seems antithetical to discussions of learning and reading.

While the SoR instructional focus on decoding may frame reading as distinct from sociocultural considerations (Rayner et al., 2001), our contention is that doing so is ill-advised and unnecessary limiting. SoR advocates claim their focus is on neural, perceptual, and psychological factors; however, any research-based description of reading processes and reading development that does not account for the social, cultural, historical, and other contextual elements of reading cannot and should not claim to call itself "a science of reading." We contend that sociocultural considerations are integral to individual and societal development, and should serve as foundational educational tenets—forming a key lens in educational research, theory, and practice.

Missing Research Perspectives. We are concerned that the Science of Reading, by privileging phonics as the key starting point for learning to read, may advance an approach limited in its potential reach, relevance, and outcomes. The SoR focus on teaching decoding can contribute to a shortfall in supporting readers' development, and ignores an entire body of sociocultural research and findings about literacy development. Certainly, carefully controlled studies of early readers involving manipulated circumstances are relevant to our understanding. But they should not be viewed as superior to the thick descriptions of learning to read and its precursors that have been undertaken by scholars such as Dyson (1982, 1989); Ferreiro and Teberosky (1982); Halliday (1975); Harste, Woodward, and Burke (1984); Purcell-Gates (1995, 2007), and her work with Jacobson and Degener (2004); and Teale and Sulzby (1986). These researchers have illuminated the many social, cultural, and contextual dimensions of reading and writing as foundational to understanding reading development, including word reading. As Carol Lee (2020), in discussing the documentary film *Babies* (Balmès, 2010), suggested:

> This film clearly shows that each of these infants works to accomplish the fundamental life tasks I have articulated, but in very different ways, with very different kinds of social supports, and toward very different social goals. They are physiologically predisposed to explore in order to accomplish these fundamental tasks (to stand, to grasp, to walk, to use language, to get what they want, to establish relationships with others, to explore their material and social worlds) through their participation in the practices of their diverse cultural niches (Rogoff, 2003; Super & Harkness, 1986).
>
> It is the dynamic interplay between physiological processes rooted in our biology and our participation in cultural practices that creates the ecology of human development. (p. 40)

Ann Haas Dyson (1987), in her extensive observations of young children in classrooms, has also noted how important written language is to the functions of everyday social purposes and activities:

> ...written language is a social tool that functions in varied ways in our society. As children grow up, they learn about this tool—its purposes, its features, its processing demands—as they encounter meaningful activities. Even in communities where literacy assumes a relatively minor role, children are not isolated from written language (Heath, 1983). The adults who live with children write notes, jot down phone numbers, and needed grocery items, fill out forms and checks and children take to pen and paper. They participate in literacy activities with more skilled others, explore and play with print's functions in varied ways in our society. As they grow up, they learn about this tool—its purposes, its features, its processing demands and uses as a means of expression. From the beginning, then, literacy is woven into the familiar fabric of social life. (p. 6)

Extending these examinations to digital worlds, scholars have also noted how young learners, as they interact with digital devices, are involved in a range of sociocultural engagements—with others on and off screen as well as with the multilayered and dynamic images and symbols encountered in digital environments. As Deuze, Blank and Speers (2012) noted, "the social arrangements of media both stretch existing ways of doing things and making sense of the world across cultural and spatial boundaries, while at the same time functioning to articulate and demarcate local communities and identities" (p. 9). Understanding life in a virtual world, they argue, requires moving beyond the immediate sociocognitive, semiotic, and embodied underpinnings of meaning making articulated in earlier research to a more complex explorations of living with and across multiple worlds.

Extending Sociocultural Considerations to Ecopedagogy. We argue that sociocultural considerations are seminal to studies of reading development; they are not simply ancillary matters that can be deferred. They also, we suggest, heighten consciousness in a way that can inform approaches to research. In her discussions of Indigenous methodologies, New Zealand M ori scholar Linda Tuhiwai Smith (2005) has suggested that a culturally-informed research approach is "a transformative project that is active in pursuit of social and institutional change, that makes space for indigenous knowledge, and that has a critical view of power relations and inequality" (p. 89). Sociocultural considerations, in addressing the specific needs of local circumstances and the diverse interests and backgrounds of learners, should therefore facilitate more ethical approaches to working with and for communities, and enable "indigenous communities to theorize their own lives" (p. 90).

Sociocultural considerations also reframe the roles of teachers and approaches to teaching. To capture the fundamental commitment to diversity and the idea that cultural, social, and historical affordances shape learning—and teaching—at every turn, we posit that teachers, in their facilitative and supportive roles, should assume the roles of cultural workers and ecopedagogues (a term emanating from Paulo Freire and various other scholars; see Grigorov & Fleuri, 2012; Misiaszek, 2020; and the definition below).

Ecopedagogy (from Misiaszek, 2020)

> Ecopedagogy is essentially literacy education for reading and rereading human acts of environmental violence with its roots in popular education, as they are reinventions of the pedagogies of the Brazilian pedagogue and philosopher Paulo Freire. Ecopedagogies are grounded in critical thinking and transformability, with the ultimate goal being to construct learning with increased social and environmental justice. Rooted in critical theories and originating from popular education models of Latin America, ecopedagogy is centered on better understanding the connections between human acts of environmental violence and social violence that cause injustices/oppressions, domination over the rest of Nature, and planetary unsustainability. Teaching to understand the social aspects of environmental issues, from local-to-global perspectives and knowledges, as well as through the scholarship of multiple disciplines, is essential to determine actions for lasting changes toward environmental well-being and planetary sustainability. (p. 1)

As teachers engage with learners in culturally-responsive ways, enlisting their skills as educators, they partner with learners and communities in a fashion akin to community builders—developing allyships in support of learners' literacy developments and their communities. They adopt critically reflexive dispositions, always seeking to be informed, with humility and respect, by the communities and learners with whom they negotiate curricula. As Māori scholar Graham Hingangaroa Smith (2000) has suggested, culturally-responsive teaching and research entails engaging in ways that are mutually supportive of diverse cultures—not in a fashion that dismisses cultural differences or reelevates colonial dispositions of the past. This, as Lester-Irabinna Rigney (2021) has advocated, develops spaces of learning that are aligned with the rights of learners—where their unique voices are heard, and their ways of knowing, rooted in and seeded from their cultures, are supported.

As cultural workers and ecopedagogues, teachers also assume a role of mentorship, introducing learners to cultural and social practices as they help them to read and represent their worlds (as has been done in some societies for tens of thousands of years). Such engagements in "reading and writing the world" mirror the observations of Dyson (1995) and McEneaney (2006) in school settings, as well as articulations of participatory culture in digital settings (Jenkins et al., 2009). As Jenkins et al. (2009) define it, participatory culture involves

> ...relatively low barriers to artistic expression and civic engagement, strong support for creating and sharing creations, and some type of informal mentorship whereby experienced participants pass along knowledge to novices. In a participatory culture, members also believe their contributions matter and feel some degree of social connection with one another (at the least, members care about others' opinions of what they have created) (p. xi).

Jenkins et al. (2009) also emphasize how "participatory culture shifts the focus of literacy from one of individual expression to community involvement. The new literacies almost all involve social skills developed through collaboration and networking" (p. xiii). As such, learnings are place-based and people-oriented in participatory settings; students read and write their worlds as they encounter different forms of transactions (and co-constructions) and engage with colleagues and collaborators.

Our advocacy for the teacher as a cultural worker and an ecopedagogue builds upon notions of respect for diversity and culturally-relevant schools—those that "provide educational self-determination, honor and respect the student's home culture" (Ladson-Billings, 1994, pp. 135–137; see also Ladson-Billings, 1995). Such an orientation aligns with emerging findings from studies of effective schools, which point to customized testing and teaching practices, developed collaboratively by teachers, as key factors in school success (Taylor et al., 2000: Taylor et al., 2002). It also requires that we view educators as being akin to cosmopolitans; as Allan Luke (2004) has argued: "What is needed is a teacher whose very stock and trade is to deal educationally with cultural 'others', with the kinds of transnational and local diversity that are now a matter of course" (p. 1439). This befits the forms of engagement that Mike Rose (1995) gleaned from his study of effective teachers in different U.S. communities. As he stated:

> As one teaches, one's knowledge plays out in social space…teaching well means knowing one's students well and being able to read them quickly and, in turn, making decisions to slow down or speed up, to stay with a point or return to it later, to underscore certain connections, to use or forgo a particular illustration. This decision-making operates as much by feel as by reason; it involves hunch, intuition, at best, quick guess.
>
> There is another dimension to the ability to make judgments about instruction. The teachers we observed operate with knowledge of individual student's lives, of local history and economy, and of sociocultural traditions and practices. They gain this knowledge in any number of ways: living in the communities in which they work, getting involved in local institutions and projects, drawing on personal and cultural histories that resemble the histories of the children they teach, educating themselves about the communities and cultures of the students before them, connecting with parents and involving parents in schooling, and seeing students as resources and learning from them. (p. 419)

This kind of culturally-responsive teaching requires a greater and more genuine respect for the plurality of assets all students bring with them to school. It also entails other shifts—from viewing teachers as sages to teachers as allies; from espousing singularity to plurality in crafting practices; from approaching curriculum as generic and standardized to instead approaching it as particular and generative; and from framing cultural differences as barriers to embracing them as assets to be leveraged in building a classroom culture of respect. As Purcell-Gates & Tierney (2008), based in part upon Purcell-Gates' extensive work linking reading development to communities, suggested:

> Teachers must be aware of what the children come to school knowing, and not knowing, and then must be allowed to tailor beginning reading instruction that will make a difference for all children in the context of real reading and writing activities. Teaching models that strip down reading and writing to technical skills outside of meaningful practice may show what looks like good results on skills tests, but these gains are quickly lost after grade two. Children learn to read and write better when teachers respond to them based upon knowledge of them as individuals and as members of cultural communities. (p. 5)

This approach repositions teaching reading as a method of creating a space in which learners explore meaning making with culturally diverse tools and partners. It is what we would expect to find in Kris Gutiérrez's (2008) notion of a "third space"—a learning environment wherein students explore on their own terms and with their own practices. Such an approach builds upon or advances learners' abilities and opportunities to draw on their cultural repertoires of experiences and possible strategies—catering to rather than squelching practices that enrich learners' situational and linguistic diversity.

Our Revised Version of the Claim

As core studies of reading comprehension have established, the background experiences of readers are the key determinants of meaning making. As we read, we take on roles that supersede as well as intersect with a range of other factors. Yet sociocultural considerations are often dismissed in the name of seeking broad consensus on some common ground. Consider the case of members of the Development Panel, selected by the Governing Board of the National Assessment of Educational Progress (NAEP), who revised the framework for the NAEP reading assessment (NAGB, 2021). Consistent with advances in theory and research on learning (NASEM, 2018), the Panel encountered open resistance from the Governing Board when they introduced sociocultural considerations into framework. As Forzani et al. (2022) document, efforts to update the framework were ultimately rejected by a small minority of the Board, "resulting in missed opportunities to advance NAEP reading in ways that would have emphasized equity and the role of sociocultural context in reading while also better accounting for the role of prior knowledge in reading" (p. 158). In several states, pushback on sociocultural issues and diversity have similarly undergirded debates over critical race theory, woke culture, and the censorship of books (Bethea, 2023; Delgado & Stefancic, 2023; Jago, 2022; Lukianoff & Schlott, 2023; Romano, 2020; SLJ, 2023).

We favor approaches that instead build upon or advance learners' use of their cultural repertoire of experiences and possible strategies. Unfortunately, many of our curricular approaches often give restricted recognition to the value and power of learners' situational and linguistic diversity. Discussions of synthetic phonics are not exceptional, and materials (e.g., projects, words, texts) are not aligned with learners' worlds (i.e., their language experiences and linguistic repertoires). By contrast, as García and Kleifgen (2020) note, a translanguaging literacies approach:

> .... holds much promise to provide minoritized bilingual students, especially those who are emergent bilinguals, with ways to deepen understandings of texts, generate more diverse texts, enjoy more confianza as literate beings, and experience a deeper critical multilingual awareness. (p. 568)

Although the SoR focus on teaching decoding may appear to be neutral with respect to matters of equity and diversity, it is not. Questioning the racialized implications of SoR policies and frameworks in the context of U.S. schools, Richard Milner (2020) suggested:

> Acknowledging the importance of students' language and literacy skill development in their very early years of life, educators may set Black students up for failure when they refuse to recognize or do not have the frames to identify language and literacy assets, strengths, skills, dispositions, mindsets, and practices that these students already possess and bring into a classroom. With an empirical and analytic framework that only sees what is missing, what is "wrong" with these students, Black students' experiences in schools become dehumanizing from the very start of school. (p. S250)

In keeping with these perspectives, we think both the evidence about learning, including learning to read (e.g., Lee, 2020; NASEM, 2018), as well as the moral imperative to ensure curricular and pedagogical equity and relevance, point us toward sociocultural views of reading research, theory, and practice. The mistake, we think, of the SoR reform initiatives is that in their zeal to ensure a secure hold on the science of word reading and understanding, they have lost their grip on the other equally-scientific endeavors—namely, the vast body of research that tells us that learning is enhanced when matters of diversity, equity, relevance, ecological validity, and cultural plurality are front and center in our enactment of curriculum and teaching. Time to rebalance!

CLAIM 10

Teacher education programs are not preparing teachers in the Science of Reading.

The Evidence Marshalled in Support of the Claim

In his closing remarks following a panel discussion with Kymyona Burk, Emily Hanford, and Donna Hejtmanek, Mark Seidenberg remarked: "I do not blame teachers. I go out of my way not to blame teachers, but I will blame those who taught them" (Tommy G. Thompson Center on Public Leadership, 2023; this stance was similarly voiced in Seidenberg's 2017 book, Language at the Speed of Sight).

Teacher education programs have been the focus of a great deal of criticism, even blame, for failing to address the findings, often referred to as the settled science, about key elements of teaching beginning reading (e.g., phonics and phonemic awareness), and meeting the needs of struggling readers—especially those that might be identified as dyslexic. At times, these critiques lay the blame for these alleged omissions on the prevailing Whole Language or Balanced Literacy views that teachers receive in their teacher preparation programs (Buckingham & Meeks, 2019; Moats, 2014).

In the United States, the National Council on Teacher Quality—guided by an advisory panel of expert teacher educators and researchers—has evaluated teacher education programs with a rubric derived from scientific studies of reading to determine whether scientifically-based principles and practices are being taught. In their most recent effort (Ellis, et al., 2023), NCTQ researchers obtained and evaluated copies of syllabi and other material from undergraduate and graduate teacher education programs (relying, at times, on the Freedom of Information Act to obtain materials) to measure the alignment of those programs with principles and practices stemming from their reading of the scientifically based reading research. More specifically, they assessed whether programs teach future teachers to:

> ...understand and know how to explicitly and systematically teach the five components of scientifically based reading instruction, including: (1)

> developing students' awareness of the sounds made by spoken words (phonemic awareness); (2) systematically mapping those speech sounds onto letters and letter combinations (phonics); (3) providing students extended practice reading words with learned letter-sound combinations so they learn to read words with automaticity, without a lot of effort, at a good rate, and with expression (fluency)—allowing them to devote their mental energy to the meaning of the text; (4) building word knowledge using student-friendly definitions and engaging practice opportunities (vocabulary), a skill closely associated with the final component; (5) ensuring students have the skills, knowledge, and strategies to understand what is being read to them and eventually what they will read themselves (comprehension). (Ellis et al., 2023, p. 5)

The program review was based upon a large set of submissions in response to a solicitation from NCTQ across the 50 states and the District of Columbia—693 programs in total. Overseeing the analyses was a panel of "experts" on the Science of Reading, who helped to establish the criteria used in the rubric and the training program for the analysts. The trained analysts were charged with discerning whether program material featured the desired emphasis on key components (e.g., in terms of time and content covered), along with a de-emphasis on practices deemed contrary to those core elements (e.g., use of the cueing system, running records, guided reading, balanced reading, etc.). NCTQ assigned letter grades (A-F) to each university program, based on scores obtained by applying their rubrics—and made recommendations for remedial action for low-scoring programs.

Most programs reviewed received low marks, with programs at many highly regarded universities and schools of education receiving failing or near failing marks. Operating on the assumptions that the science is settled, and their rubrics reflect that science, NCTQ concluded that the majority of teacher education programs are falling short; they lack the required emphasis on key components of scientific research and placing too much emphasis on scientifically discredited components (e.g., three-cueing; balanced components). The logic behind such a review was to pair scientific methods (an evaluation based upon criteria allegedly derived from research) with a public airing of the data to convince low-scoring and arguably recalcitrant programs to mend their ways and adhere to the NCTQ standards for evidence-based components of effective early reading instruction. The Council advocated for increased accountability measures for teacher education and licensure programs; recommended the development of reading licensure tests; and urged state and university leaders to use their own "bully pulpits" to promote these desired changes.

This type of report is not unique to U.S. contexts; a similar review was pursued in Australia, where the suggested evidenced-based approaches were those that emphasized phonics (Teacher Education Expert Panel, 2023). Similar to the U.S., in both Australia and the U.K., media and government officials have criticized teacher education programs for inadequately preparing educators to teach reading in the early years with an emphasis upon phonics (see Hanford, 2018; 2019b; Harris & Grace, 2023; MacPhee, Handsfield, & Paugh, 2021; Wilson, 2021).

Critics of current teacher education programs infer from these data that teacher education programs are failing to adequately prepare teachers in the Science of Reading (e.g., in terms of both the linguistic knowledge required to meet the needs of beginning readers, as well as the teaching practices that might be pursued to support students). Some studies suggest that teachers may claim adequate knowledge on the teaching of phonics, but close examination of the specifics of their knowledge may suggest otherwise (Arrow, Braid, & Chapman, 2019; Bell, Ziegler, & McCallum, 2004; Malatesha Joshi, Binks, & Graham et al., 2009; Malatesha Joshi, Binks, & Hougen et al., 2009; Bos et al., 2001; Cunningham et al., 2004; Tortorelli, Lupo, & Wheatley, 2021). In terms of teachers' preparation for teaching phonics, they report that a combination of preservice programs and ongoing professional development contribute to their practices. As Meeks and Kemp (2017) concluded from a survey of Australian teacher education:

> Although preservice teachers generally rated themselves as prepared to teach early reading, most demonstrated minimal to very poor knowledge of the components of early reading, indicating a substantial discrepancy between the general confidence of preservice teachers to teach, and their limited content knowledge of beginning reading skills. (p. 1.)

Our Reading of the Evidence and the Claim

Our reading of the claim and evidence leads us to conclude that the research used as the basis for evaluating teacher education programs fails to meet the standards for evidence-based practice that such arguments claim to support. The critiques coming from NCTQ and other sources (e.g., Moats, 2014; Hanford, 2019; Seidenberg, 2013) attempt to link teachers' knowledge of effective practices and the linguistic principles behind those practices to classroom practices; they further assume that what teacher education students do once they get into their own classroom is a direct reflection of the influence of the teacher preparation programs that they experience. A further assumption behind the NCTQ critique (and many prior critiques) is that if teachers can receive the right, relevant technical knowledge, they will more or less automatically apply related and implied research-based practices effectively in their classrooms.

The history of teacher education suggests, to the contrary, that the content of university methods courses is far down the list of factors that shape what beginning teachers do in their classrooms. Even more important, research on teacher learning and professional development suggests that simple transmission models of teacher change (disseminating the fruits of scientific knowledge will usher in new paradigms and practices) are woefully naïve and inadequate (Richardson, 1992; Pearson & Cervetti, 2006 in Snow, et al., 2006). Changes in declarative knowledge (WHAT teachers know) is but one facet in the process of nurturing changes in practice; it is also necessary to address HOW (procedural knowledge) as well as WHY and WHEN (conditional knowledge) to employ certain practices. Even when new information is accompanied by monitoring and sanctions (either rewards or penalties), teachers often resist changes that do not comport with their existing views about what students need to succeed Callahan, et al., 2009).

The NCTQ work fails to consider the important understandings about teacher education and learning embodied in the long history of key constructs, such as Shulman's pedagogical content knowledge (Shulman, 1987) Ball's variation of content knowledge for teaching (Ball et al., 2008), Ladson-Billing's (2020) culturally relevant pedagogy, or notion of learning communities (Lave and Wenger, 1991; Rogoff et al., 2001; Wenger, 1998), This is unfortunate because contextualizing their goals within the rich literature on teacher learning would have offered some basis for judging the likelihood that any efforts at changing the knowledge base for teaching reading would stand a chance of succeeding.

Nor did they choose to consult, or even consider, the considerable and growing reviews of literacy teacher education—both historical and from recent years—enlisting various meta-analyses in their efforts to glean a clearer illumination of trustworthy trends. This work is highly relevant to the NCTQ enterprise since it is a direct, explicit critique of the NCTQ portfolio as well as other efforts that, on the face of it, appear to be driven by key features of the SoR. For example, Hoffman, Hikida, and Sailors (2020) explore the manner in which teacher preparation has been examined by the NCTQ . Drawing upon research syntheses of a large and dynamic database of research on literacy teacher preparation, known as the Critical, Interactive, Transparent, and Evolving review of literature on Initial Teacher Education in Literacy (CITE-ITEL), Hoffman et al. question the conclusions reached and recommendations offered—Hoffman et al. The online database comprises over 600 empirical studies published between 1999 and 2019; the syntheses cited by Hoffman et al. (2020) reviewed research published between 2000 and 2018 (Fowler-Amato et al., 2019). Hoffman et al. (2020) point to major gaps in the scope of the review of teacher preparation offered by SoR advocates. Noting how studies have been excluded from discussions of the SoR, they suggest that the conclusions and recommendations offered through a SoR lens should be viewed reservedly. In turn, they argue for substantially more research—such as studies that extend to sociocultural considerations and those that include a more formative approach to teaching practices (i.e., that do not presume a research base for the practices that SoR advocates suggest are either counterproductive or essential).

In a study that complements and extends the research by Hoffman et al. and others, Tortorelli, Lupo & Wheatley (2021) pursue a focused study of code-related preparation of teachers in various countries (largely the U.S. and Australia). Reviewing a large data set of studies representing a wide range of programs, they scrutinize the focus, methodology, and findings of a select subset of 27 studies—comprised overall of 5,226 preservice teacher participants from 180 programs. These also represented a mix of examinations—such as technical knowledge of linguistic awareness, and pedagogical knowledge[1] derived from a range of circumstances. The reflections on the review neither confirmed or disconfirmed deficits in teacher knowledge and raised questions about the relevance. As they suggested in the overview of their research:

> We identified 27 studies examining preservice general elementary preparation in code-related instruction, including phonological/phonemic awareness, phonics/decoding, spelling/orthography, and morphology, published between 2001 and 2020. We analyzed the studies to determine (a) how preservice knowledge of code-related instruction has been studied, (b) how preservice teachers' literacy knowledge was defined and assessed in these studies, and (c) primary findings across studies and implications for teacher preparation and future research. We found that the research base largely relied on quantitative multiple-choice assessments that privileged linguistic content knowledge over pedagogical and situated knowledge. The body of research was constrained by narrow definitions of science and knowledge, repetition across studies in methods and data sources, limited samples that overlooked diversity in preservice teachers and elementary contexts, and methodological problems. (p. 317)

They concluded that we need more robust research to evaluate "...the claim that increased linguistic knowledge improves the quality of code-related instruction" (p. 319).

As they stated:

> Overall, our findings contextualize and complicate claims that code-related skills are being neglected in teacher preparation programs. We found that the research base privileges technical, linguistic content knowledge over pedagogical knowledge of how to teach code-related skills and situated practice in engaging and supporting real students. .... We agree that much work needs to be done in teacher preparation programs to better prepare

1 Fewer than 50% of the studies examined pedagogical knowledge. In those studies, examining technical knowledge, the connections to classroom practices were rarely researched.

> teachers to teach code-related instruction in adaptable and equitable ways. However, this work requires more complex solutions than simply teaching more linguistic knowledge to preservice teachers. Instead, we call for collaborations among researchers, teacher educators, and advocates to support all students in learning code-related skills. (p. S334)

Teacher education efforts are being dismissed on the basis that they are misdirected and obstructionist, with little exploration of the earnest efforts of teachers and teacher education programs to meet the needs of learners with different needs[2]. While programs are being discredited and past teacher development initiatives discounted, the commitment of teachers to address the individual needs of students (in relation to phonics and other facets key to ongoing reading development) are questioned. As Jenny Gore (2023) noted in her discussion of the Strong Beginnings Report in Australia (Teacher Education Expert Panel, 2023):

> This specification of core content comes from the Australian Education Research Organisation (a government created, independent education evidence body). It has no particular expertise in research on teacher education. The approach taken is narrow and overlooks swathes of high quality research ...
>
> What's missed in education debates—which invariably pitch teaching practices against each other—is that what matters most is the underlying quality of the teaching. The report assumes new graduate teachers deliver poor teaching and their university education is to blame. This premise has been challenged by recent studies, which show new teachers teach just as well as those with years of experience.
>
> The new regulations recommended by the panel treat teacher educators as if they aren't already motivated to improve the student experience and outcomes, understand and incorporate the latest educational research, or engage in good practice. (Gore, 2023, paras. 27-28)

---

2 In the 1970s, considerable attention was focused upon identifying the relationship and role of teacher variable in the teaching of reading. In the 1980s and 1990s, initiatives such as the Holmes Group focused upon teacher education improvements through enhanced teamwork within the university and in schools. Tutoring programs for reading—and, likewise in recent years, the influence of coaches—have been subjected to major research. Programs that some advocates have dismissed, such as Reading Recovery, have a history of extraordinary teacher preparation efforts. Both technical and pedagogical deliberations are fine-tuned as teachers are observed and afforded feedback as they engage with students under the close scrutiny of other teachers and Reading Recovery trainers.

Or, as Harrison (2006) noted in response to an earlier report by the National Council on Teacher Quality (Walsh, Glaser, & Wilcox, 2006) entitled, What Education Schools Aren't Teaching about Reading and What Elementary Teachers Aren't Learning, much of the public discourse surrounding literacy research in the U.S. is filtered through the lens of "necessary illusions"—one of which, he notes, is that teacher education is fundamentally flawed, and needs to be radically overhauled (or even abandoned).

With a measure of reserve by some SoR advocates (e.g., Seidenberg, 2023c) the overhaul has gained considerable momentum in efforts to realign teacher education to ensure that teachers know code-based instruction and possess the linguistic knowledge (e.g., grapho-phonemic understandings) needed to enhance the word learning of young readers. For example, Louisa Moats and her colleagues have been responsible for development of Language Essentials for Teachers of Reading and Spelling (LETRS), a professional development program intended to enhance in-service K-3 teachers' linguistic knowledge (Moats, 2023; Schwartz, 2022). Likewise, in Australia, SoR advocates have argued for a revamping of teacher education programs to prepare teachers with the knowledge they need to teach phonics. In turn they have recommended programs they have authored (e.g., Buckingham, 2023).

Our Revised Version of the Claim

If the NCTQ scholars, or scholars who align themselves with some version of the SoR, want to use teacher education, either pre- or in-service, as a vehicle for promoting enduring changes in classroom practice, they need to contextualize their policy efforts and research syntheses in a more substantive understanding of the rich lines of theory and research on teacher education, teacher learning, and teacher change. Implicit in their recommendations seems to be erroneous theory of action, which assumes that (a) if you provide teachers with the right knowledge and (b) provide incentives and/or sanctions for holding themselves and their students to practices emanating from that knowledge, change will happen. Teacher learning, teacher change, and teacher education are a lot more complicated than that (Cochran-Smith & Reagan, 2021, 2022; Darling-Hammond & Bransford, 2005).

There exists a far more extensive research base on teachers and literacy teacher education than that which is considered in SoR discussions. The research enlisted in the critiques of reading teacher education—used as the basis of calls for reform—does not meet the standards of the research that Science of Reading advocates have often touted as essential in mining the pedagogical research for reliably effective classroom practices. Given a very different set of conclusions from the elaborate reviews of Hoffman et al. (2020) and Tortorelli, et al. (2021) we recommend that all scholars wanting to evaluate the presence or absence of teacher education programs need to bring a broader set of lenses to the effort. Missing from SoR arguments are considerations from various ongoing discussions of teacher education (e.g., Britzman, 2003; Cochran-Smith & Reagan, 2021, 2022; Darling-Hammond & Bransford, 2005: National Council for Accreditation of Teacher Education, 2010; National Education Policy Center, 2022; Richardson, 1998; Zeichner, 2020).

The pool of studies of teacher education drawn upon by the SoR advocates appear to be limited in terms of their discussions of how, when and where teaching practices are shaped. For example, Sanden and her colleagues questioned the scope of the surveys in terms of when and how teachers were prepared (Sanden et al., 2022). Based upon a survey of practicing teachers in Illinois, Sanden et al. suggested a combination of contributions to their practices, preservice programs, professional development or in-service programs, and curricular materials. Befitting Britzman's (2003) discussion of practice begetting practice, Sanden et al. suggested that the teachers also emphasized how their practices contribute to and evolve from feedback from teaching and student learning.

Still to be addressed more fully are questions pertaining to the nature of teacher knowledge, including how teacher knowledge develops, how teaching practices change and how both knowledge and practices might be enlisted to support student reading development. Some studies do suggest a correlation between student learning and changes in teacher knowledge and improvements in practices through preparation or in-service support (e.g., coaching), but a clear picture of the relationship does not exist (Atteberry

& Bryk, 2011: Cassidy, et al. 2010; Kraft, Blazar & Hogan, 2018; Neuman S. B., Wright, 2010; Metzler & Woessmann, 2010; Palincsar et al., 2020; Rivkin, Hanushek, Kain, 2005; Rockoff, 2004; Sailors & Price, 2015). Further illumination is needed of other approaches to the professional development of reading teachers. For example, "behind the glass" training of teachers enlisted in Reading Recovery merit examination (e.g., Compton-Lilly, 2011) likewise, the role of collaborative engagements of teachers (e.g., Green et al. 2012: Green et al., 2015; Johnson, 1997; Taylor, Pressley & Pearson, 2002) and the systems that contribute to or detract from meeting the needs of students through the support of ancillaries, teacher aides and especially special education staff and school psychologists (e.g., Allington & Franzen, 1989).

Then there is the matter of explicit instruction—a common recommendation, especially when phonics is the instructional activity. SoR admonishments to teach "explicitly" teaching should also be unpacked. Our reading of the research on variations of explicit teaching reveals mixed views on its enlistment without consideration of the nature of learning being pursued. There is a long continuum of possibilities, ranging from direct instruction of the sort involved in the implementation of Distar in the 1960s (see Stockard, et al., 2018) to occasional scaffolding of largely independent work (see Raphael & Au, 1998). For example, nuanced explorations of the gradual release of responsibility by Pearson and his colleagues (Pearson et al, 2019; Dole, et al, 2019) together with reciprocal teaching (e.g., Palincsar & Brown 1984) might inform such discussions. Further, consideration of complex learning theories pertain—that is discussions of cognitive flexibility (e.g., Spiro et al. 1988; Wittgenstein, 1953) tied to situated learning wherein learning is developed from multiple engagements in the activity of reading. As Brown et al. (1989) noted:

> The activity in which knowledge is developed and deployed, it is now argued, is not separable from or ancillary to learning and cognition. Nor is it neutral. Rather, it is an integral part of what is learned. Situations might be said to co-produce knowledge through activity. P. 42.

Increasingly, relevant to such considerations are case studies of learning enlisting conversational analyses and sociolinguistic research examining classroom interactions (e.g., Bloome et al., 2005; Bloome et al., 2008; Bloome and Green, 2015; Feltovich et al. 1988; Garcia & Kleifgen, 2019; Gutiérrez et al., 1999: Johnston, 2004; Saville-Troike, 2003) and the research on the constraints and affordances of varying discussion routines (Murphy et al., 2009). Studies of teaching need to move beyond judging teacher education on the basis of course syllabi and surveys; scholars should be examining teaching in the context of classrooms, student teacher interactions and learning. Judging teacher education should extend beyond a consideration of inputs to outputs including what teachers have learned and do and their influences.

Certainly, building upon our discussion of sociocultural considerations in Claim 9, we would also recommend that research on teacher education extend to matters of diversity, equity, and contextualization. To address issues of equity in education requires us to reckon with the issues raised by Milner (2020)—that is, to scrutinize the ideology undergirding the SoR for beginning reading and consider whether teachers and teacher education are engaging with or sidelining diversity. Do our approaches ignore our diversities by disconnecting teaching and learning from an appreciation and recognition of culturally-based and idiosyncratic identities? Unfortunately, if considered through the lens of the populations that teachers intend to serve, studies should examine how minorities positioned to better support their learning. Minorities should not be outsiders as they encounter teaching approaches, texts, and tests that are alien to their worlds.

Concluding Statement

Now that we have navigated 10 claims frequently encountered in the public discourse about the Science of Reading (SoR), what's next? Where should you—and we—go from here? As we said at the outset of this book, we hope our airing of these claims moves us in the direction of reaching consensus and finding common ground, with a more modest and evidence-based set of claims that emanate from a full(er) reading of the science(s) of reading. We'll get to that search for common ground. But first, a few reminders of the nature of our journey—particularly its limitations.

The Science of Reading is not the Whole Story

We all need to acknowledge that the question of what the SoR does and does not tell us about early reading development and pedagogy is one step in the journey toward universal literacy. There is so much more to the reading puzzle that must be addressed in any society that aspires to help all its citizens develop the literacy expertise they will need to lead engaged, productive, discerning, and personally satisfying lives.

Influences from New Cultural Practices. Even a cursory examination of recent developments in our digital age reveals a host of new and not fully understood matters. For instance:

- The spread of multimedia has exploded traditional notions of what counts as text. Very soon, print on paper will no longer be the dominant form of text.
- The democratization of information on the internet has raised the ante with regard to the need for schools and society to nurture the development of critical dispositions toward digital information. The need for knowledge and reasoning to evaluate the validity and trustworthiness of ideas we encounter every day, hour, and minute while we are online grows more urgent with every election cycle, and every attempt to mask the truth. To foster literacy in these new settings as a tool of liberation rather than domination, we need to build our capacity to promote healthy skepticism and critical stances toward the claims and evidence we encounter everywhere we look in our cultures.

- Youth are leading the way in the evolution of online and multimedia literacies. Adults and scholars around the world need to catch up with them.

As Selfe and Hawisher (2004) noted some 20 years ago:

> ...if literacy educators continue to define literacy in terms of alphabetic practices only, in ways that ignore, exclude, or devalue new-media texts, they not only abdicate a professional responsibility to describe the ways in which humans are now communicating and making meaning, but they also run the risk of their curriculum no longer holding relevance for students who are communicating in increasingly expansive networked environments. (pp. 234-235)

Other Curricular Matters. By limiting our focus to the claims of others about reading development and pedagogy (i.e., those that have captured the popular press and social media), we have, albeit unintentionally, omitted, or at least underrepresented, other important facets of reading curriculum and pedagogy—all of which deserve at least as much attention as the development of word-level expertise. These all-important elements—which just did not arise in our fact-checking—include:

- The key role of knowledge and meaning vocabulary, both as cause and consequence of comprehension, in shaping reading expertise and our capacity to use the insights gained in reading to address issues and take action in the natural and cultural worlds in which we live. Knowledge and the words we use to name that knowledge are doubly important when we venture into disciplines that define schooling across the age span. The natural and social sciences, the humanities (especially history and literature), and the arts all render knowledge ever more salient in the literacies needed to fathom their content and discourse.
- The critical role of language, again as both cause and consequence of comprehension. This includes three facets of language: a) Everyday language; b) Academic language, or the language that helps students learn to "talk like a book;" and c) The role of first language, in the case of bilingual or multilingual students, in shaping second or additional language reading and writing.

- The central role of talk in so many aspects of learning to read: Talk about text (both content and structure); talk about words (i.e., semantic networks, morphological families, and contextually-nuanced meanings); and talk about solving problems (e.g., for both unknown words and obscure passage meanings) and apply what we learn from reading to everyday problems.
- The set of processes that have been variously labeled—for example, as conative factors, or, more recently, literate dispositions (Aukerman & Chambers Schuldt, 2021). These include motivation, engagement, interest, self-efficacy, agency, identity, growth mindset, disposition, social-emotional learning, and empathy—all of which shape acts of literacy.
- Asset-based and culturally-sustaining pedagogical practices that allow all students to "see themselves" and their cultural practices in the curriculum, providing "hooks" for students to make personal connections to the texts and ideas they encounter.
- The role of writing in enhancing reading development, both at the word level (e.g., spelling and meaning vocabulary) and at the text level (e.g., the comprehension and critique of text-based ideas, explanations, and arguments).
- The pervasive role of text in both reading and writing, as it reflects both language and knowledge; introduces knowledge of genre, text structure, and other pragmatic features of written language; and extends to imaginal and multimedia text. Texts provide both scaffolds and challenges for readers at every stage of development.
- Assessments—both large-scale, summative assessments, used to evaluate broad trends over time, as well as internal (to schools and classrooms), formative assessments, used to provide feedback about the day-to-day progress of students and the relevance and impact of daily curricular experiences—matter. We know that, for better or worse, assessment drives instruction. We should strive for better.

If we were writing a monograph about the elements of a comprehensive reading/literacy curriculum, all these matters would have been in the foreground of our presentation. Remembering that school improvement involves teacher learning as well as student learning, our plan for outlining a comprehensive curriculum would have insisted that teacher learning be as research-based as student learning. That would mean recognizing the importance of teachers' voices and leadership in planning and implementing professional development (Bryk et al; 2010; Callahan, Griffo, & Pearson, 2009; Taylor, Pressley, & Pearson, 2002). Such a monograph would also have revealed the irony of delivering research-based knowledge about pedagogy for K-12 students in a manner that defies all we know about adult and professional learning.

Broader Societal Constraints. Complicating matters further are the societal phenomena that affect all aspects of literacy expertise, at every stage of development (i.e., from preschool to nursing home). Our individual and joint experiences as literacy professionals tell us that we won't solve the reading problem (which we take to be the unconscionable gaps in achievement between rich and poor, minority and majority, Indigenous and non-Indigenous, and privileged and marginalized groups) in any country across the Americas, the United Kingdom, Europe, Africa, or Asia and Oceania until and unless we solve a host of other inequities. The right to read entails the right to the finest teachers with the broadest cultural repertoires, and to the very best, most scientifically-grounded and culturally-sustaining curriculum we can muster. However, it also entails many other rights: Good health care; preschool learning opportunities; decent and affordable housing; satisfying jobs; safe neighborhoods; equitable school funding; and fair justice systems. We won't get to any of these rights without fundamental reforms that redistribute wealth, income, and privilege.

The Science of Reading is an Important Story

Even so, in acknowledging the importance of these disclaimers, we also acknowledge just how significant the momentum has been for the SoR. It is even more important when policy is involved, as it clearly is in today's political landscape. As we've witnessed:

- More than 40 states in the U.S. have passed SoR-based laws that limit the choices that districts, schools, and teachers can make;

- Phonics is the core component of the U.K.'s reading strategy, and a version of the SoR is gaining traction in some Canadian provinces;
- Specific approaches to the teaching of the code are being prescribed for both public schools and teacher preparation programs in Australia; and
- Similar forces are at work in New Zealand, especially in critiques of Reading Recovery.

Indeed, it was the scope and impact of the SoR meme—across social media, the popular press, and ultimately policymaking bodies, such as legislative halls and school boardrooms—that prompted us to pursue this "fact-check." Our goal has been to illuminate the claims, the evidence offered to support the claims, and the reasoning used to link the two. For each claim, as you recall, we began with what we intended to be a sympathetic reading—our best attempt to lay out the arguments provided by SoR scholars and advocates to justify the claim. We followed this with our admittedly critical reading of the claim and evidence—providing, as best we were able, other evidence that we felt had been overlooked. Finally, we ended our treatment of each claim with an updated version of the claim that we, from our vantage point, could accept—especially in terms of guiding policy and practice.

The Science (of Reading) is Not Settled

Our most important conclusion from this effort is that the science of reading is not settled. This is mainly due to the fact that science is an inherently-unsettled, ever-provisional, always self-improving enterprise. But we also reach this conclusion because, in the case of reading, the evidence should have guided us, as a field, to more modest claims than those that have been provided.

Based on our analyses in this book, we further conclude that we are engaged in an unwarranted rush to judgment in our policymaking efforts. Many of the laws and policy initiatives, however well-meaning they may be, go well-beyond the warrants provided by the available evidence. They should be reined in such cases—so that districts, schools, and teachers can choose from the full range of evidence-based practices warranted by the research.

While we have no desire to diminish the professionalism of teachers, we also have no desire to turn (or return) to any version of an "anything goes" approach, in which individual teachers have the sole authority, responsibility, and prerogative to determine what's best for students in their care. As noble a homily as it is, the notion that "teaching is what happens when you close the classroom door" should, in the name of equity, be strongly resisted by all parties engaged in policy conversations, especially teachers and their organizations. Better to replace it with the homily, "teaching is what happens when you open the classroom door to bring knowledge of learning, development, and teaching—along with the hopes and concerns of children, their families, ***and*** the professional expertise of your peers—into the classroom." That is the ideal in any profession, be it medicine, law, the clergy, or teaching. Namely:

- To know as much as we can; and
- To serve the interests and needs of our clientele.

More specifically, the bargain we as teachers make for the prerogative granted by society should be to possess—and use—the very best, valid, and research-based knowledge we can about learning, development, and teaching. That goes for all disciplines in the school curriculum, not just reading.

A Rush to Judgment. The other side of the coin is that if policy-making bodies—at the federal, state/provincial, or local level—aspire to develop and/or work with research-based curricula, they must abide by two key principles: 1) Examine the full range of relevant research when establishing goals to pursue and standards that districts, schools, and teachers should meet; and 2) Resist policies that are more restrictive than the full body of relevant evidence warrants. Currently, however, we see several areas where policy-making bodies have yet to facilitate such research-based curricula and pedagogy, by errors of omission or, alternatively, through errors of commission. Some key omissions:

- Where are the policy levers to ensure that students have the tools they need to understand and evaluate the trustworthiness of information available across public and social media?
- Where are the incentives to promote the capacity to comprehend, critique, and compose arguments that link claims and evidence through reasoning?

- Where are the mandates to ensure that all students receive curricular opportunities to use their cultural assets in learning from the school curriculum?

Some errors of commission:

- When a district limits its teachers to a single "systematic" approach to teaching phonics (e.g., sequential decoding or word family phonics). In the face of evidence supporting a range of systematic approaches, this oversteps the bounds of the available science.
- When a district or a state adopts a year-long, print-free program to teach phonemic awareness (PA) to all kindergarteners. This again oversteps the boundaries of the science of reading. A research-based approach to PA would have: a) Linked PA instruction to letter-sound instruction (e.g., work with the sound of "t" when introducing the letter); b) Limited the total amount of time to under 20 hours of PA activityacross a school year, and c) Given a free pass to kids who acquired PA incidentally while learning to spell on their own.
- When a district adopts a series that provides nothing but decodable texts for students to read, they disregard the accumulating body of evidence showing that decodable texts are no more effective than (and, at times, not as effective as) a collection of garden-variety texts from the array of available children's literature.
- When a state passes a law forbidding the use of a range of contextual cues to unlock unknown words—in deference to only orthographic and phonological cues—it privileges, in the face of mixed evidence, some relevant research (e.g., Landi et al., 2006) over other relevant research (e.g., Scanlon & Anderson, 2020). This may be to the possible detriment of some students, for whom early reliance on context may eventually lead to, or even facilitate, later preference for direct letter-sound matching. A wiser state would ask for more scientific research to clarify the matter.

In countries like the U.S., Australia, and Canada, federal systems of education give states and provinces most of the prerogative in how they enact educational policy. When such authorities do make excessively restrictive policies, they should admit that values, beliefs, and/or cultural traditions—not evidence—are the foundations of those policies. Honest declarations of political interests are preferable to false claims of scientific rigor. Moreover, whether we like it or not, there will be decisions about the curriculum—decisions that some individuals or collective will have to make—for which the research bases are silent, ambiguous, or insufficiently rigorous and robust to merit firm policy recommendations. Better to admit an underlying appeal to belief, tradition, or a working theory, than to engage in a pretense that research was the guiding force.

In these cases—when existing research cannot provide a clear pathway—what standard shall we choose to guide us? What do we do until trustworthy and definitive evidence from randomized trials is available? Our view is that we use the best available evidence we have—from natural experiments, close ethnographies, case studies, and the wisdom of practice p. In the final analysis, in exchange for the teaching profession's commitment to know as much as it can know, we must respect the prerogative of teachers to adapt and modify research-based practices to meet the constraints and affordances of the situations in which they teach. This disclaimer is all the more important when research guidance is, at best, weak.

Provisional Conclusions

Now to some guidance from us. What have we learned in this deep dive? We have struggled with how to position and name our ideas about how to move forward. Books and monographs such as this often end with recommendations—and each of us, both separately and together, have offered more than our fair share over the years. But "recommendation" seemed too strong a term for analysts who have just declared that science is a modest, provisional, eternally-evolving, seldom-settled endeavor. Alternatively, we considered the term "extrapolations," in recognition of the idea that the statements we make are our interpretations, not necessarily summaries or syntheses of the work of others. But besides sounding ponderous, we were not really sure what that meant. Also in the running were "thoughts"—as in "thoughts about the Science of Reading"—but that seemed too timid, even for provisionalists like us. We finally settled on "conclusions," to emphasize the end, for now, of this leg of our journey. Here they are.

Conclusion 1: Accept the principle that science is never settled. As we argued in the introduction to this book, and again in the previous section, the first thing all of us (especially researchers) who touch or are touched by the reading research enterprise must do is to accept the premise—and the reality—*that the science of reading* (indeed, the science of anything) *is never settled.* Science, by its nature and commitment to modesty, is always provisional; ever-ready to be tweaked, revised, or replaced by the next theoretical insight or empirical finding. Settled science, as Reinking, Hruby, and Risko (2023) have argued, is an oxymoron.

Conclusion 1.1. We should examine reading and its development through many scholarly lenses. It is not so much that the use of one research tool is or is not settled. Rather, the complexity of the phenomena we examine through a scientific lens demands a diverse, flexible, and complementary set of tools. As we argued in the introduction, we always need to employ the full range of methodological and epistemological perspectives available to us—shifting from one to another as purposes and questions change, or, even more likely, tussling with the differences of interpretation that arise when we examine any phenomenon through different lenses. We must be ready for a variety of outcomes when multiple perspectives are in play, ranging from consensus to complementarity to conflict.

Conclusion 1.2. Research findings need to be situated (i.e., adapted to individuals, settings, and purposes). Application is always situated, not generic. As we have argued in more than one claim, teachers, like doctors, must use both generic and situated knowledge. We want teachers, just as we want doctors, to be equipped with the most relevant and up-to-date knowledge of the very best practices to use in serving their clientele. And, lacking any specific information about an individual patient (in medicine) or student (in education)—as the saying goes, "all other things being equal"—we expect professionals to use their knowledge of what works best in general to treat or nurture individuals. However, when professionals possess particular knowledge about any of us as individuals, including our social and cultural histories, settings, and experiences, we expect them to use that "situated" knowledge to revise, modify, or adapt generic treatment or practice. Individual differences are real (Afflerbach, 2016; Connor et al., 2009); we need to remember that as we persuade teachers to apply the ideal of evidence-based practice as they shape instruction for students in their care.

Conclusion 1.3. The Science(s) of Reading must be modest in its claims—especially with regard to application. The overall degree of confidence we place in the reading research enterprise and our role within it should be tempered by the knowledge that science itself is a modest enterprise. We should accept and take pride in that reality, especially as we contemplate overgeneralizations from research to practice. Doctors are taught to be vigilant about variations from the norm, expecting that any case encountered is likely to be an exception to the rule. That perspective is equally important in educational practice. We must embrace the complexities of reading, both for expert and novice readers. And we must be prepared to reconsider our positions when new and more trustworthy evidence becomes available. In those instances, we would do well to remember Anthony Fauci's public updates on the Covid-19 pandemic (as well as those of many other scientists). When his updates contradicted his earlier analyses or recommendations, he indicated, in response to the sometimes-frustrated reactions of reporters, that his approach was to *follow the evidence*—wherever it took us. New evidence often leads to revised explanations and adapted recommendations. That's the spirit we need in the science(s) of reading.

Conclusion 1.4. Let's not ask research to carry burdens it is not designed to carry. The best example of such unfair burdens is asking basic research about the reading process to reveal direct implications for classroom practice. Basic research in reading—of the very sort we see coming from eye-movement studies, fMRI scans, and tightly-orchestrated laboratory studies—are great at revealing the neurological processes involved in reading and responding to texts of various sorts. But you do not recommend phonics for all six-year-olds because the area of the brain in which phonological processing is located activates when adults decode nonsense syllables. If you want to know whether phonics works, you compare it with viable alternative approaches in an ongoing line of classroom-based research and development that might lead eventually to randomized trials. And randomized trials may not be the last word: There are, for instance, many examples in which the common usage of a drug or a procedure after federal approval has yielded dangerous side effects—effects that did not arise during the experimental phase of testing (thalidomide and fentanyl come to mind). Other prominent examples include the failure of medical experiments to include sufficiently broad samples of participants (e.g., excluding minority participants) to assess the generalizability of findings.

A close second in terms of unfair burdens is asking classroom ethnographies to reveal evidence that generalizes to all classrooms. The thick descriptions of classrooms from the ethnographic tradition are great at revealing, up close and personal, what makes some classrooms tick. Why do some classrooms hum, while others devolve into chaos, and still others wither in boredom? Nevertheless, you don't pass a law requiring a particular approach to discussion for all schools in Alberta because one gifted teacher in Calgary was masterful at engaging all her students in rich talk about text. Instead, you expand ever-outward—to see how far her approach might travel and perhaps conduct further studies of the efficacy of the approach or its modifications.

Third, you don't use NAEP or PISA data to answer causal questions about the relative effectiveness of different movements—like Balanced Literacy (whatever that is) or SoR-based curricula (whatever that is)—by comparing the achievement of different states or countries to one another over time. Instead, you use the outcomes of those wide-scale assessments to seed hypotheses about important policy questions, for which relevant research studies should be developed and implemented.

All three examples are important for two reasons: 1) Too many enthusiastic advocates try to force one or another of these genres of scholarship into exactly that role—of causal explanation—and 2) All three of these genres of scholarship are wonderful at generating questions, and even hypotheses, that deserve testing—with appropriate research designs. A corollary of this conclusion is that in the final analysis, questions of curricular and instructional efficacy ought to be settled in the crucible of the classroom. As Shanahan (2020) noted in the first special issue of *Reading Research Quarterly* devoted to the SoR, the science of reading instruction ought to be as salient and well-funded as the science of basic reading processes.

Conclusion 1.5. Claims about settled science notwithstanding, there are major gaps in our knowledge about reading development. Time to address them. On this matter, we prefer to be suggestive rather than definitive—largely because we think this is a matter for the literacy/reading research community, not just us, to hammer out (see Conclusion 3, below, for our thoughts regarding professional collaboration). Currently, there also exist some useful recommendations in other research syntheses (e.g., Pearson et al, 2020) that should be consulted as part of any broad effort to define a new research agenda. We think the following questions and others—about research and implementing research-based practice—deserve more attention.

- Has the three-cueing system really been discredited? If so, then why is a set for variability in reading and solving words so important? Why do approaches that include multiple cues for word-reading and word-solving outperform those with fewer cues available?
- Is reading development better captured by an assembly-line model (i.e., one building block at a time until the repertoire has been completed) or an orchestration model (i.e., at every stage of development, articulating and harmonizing all of the word- and text-level processes to achieve understanding)?
- Can an emphasis on processes, such as comprehension and composition, enhance growth on decoding and word learning? There is some evidence for such interactions (Cervetti, et al, 2020; Seidenberg, 2023); a closer look is needed.
- Is comprehension best supported by an emphasis on a single element (such as decoding, language, knowledge, strategy instruction, self-efficacy, or motivation), or, alternatively, a comprehensive approach—that attempts to orchestrate all of these elements?

- What roles do text features play at each stage of development from novice to expert reader? Is there a viable role for decodable text, one that our research up to now has not been able to validate? Recent examinations of the impact of decodable and garden variety texts on early reading by Hiebert and her colleagues (Hiebert & Tortorelli, 2022; Pugh, et al., 2023) suggest that relative effects are mixed, with some results pointing to a place for a range of texts in early reading programs. And at all grade levels, are there aspects of text complexity that our work up to this point missed, or underestimated?
- Has the Simple View of Reading (SVR) outlived its usefulness? As helpful as it has been over the last 40+ years, is it time to admit that the Simple View is not so simple after all? Even its ardent supporters are in the business of modifying it on a regular basis; moreover, we have alternatives, such as the Active View of Reading and the Direct and Inferential Mediation (DIME) models, that build on, complicate, and complement the SVR. Perhaps it is time to move on.
- What can we do to ensure that hypotheses about pedagogy undergo thorough testing in schools and classrooms before they make their way into the policy world? We agree with Shanahan (2020) that the science of reading instruction deserves as much attention as the science of basic reading processes.
- What knowledge about reading, literacy, and learning do teachers need at various stages of their careers, and how can we best nurture it? A mammoth undertaking, surely, and one that we, as a profession, have been grappling with for the best part of a century. But we still manage to find ways to disregard most of what we know about the research on adult and professional learning when we try to "deliver" information to teachers about research-based practices. The National Academy of Education rekindled an effort to specify a developmental trajectory almost 20 years ago (Darling-Hammond & Bransford, 2006; Snow et al, 2006); time to return to that effort.We can do better. We must.
- Finally, how do all of these other questions interact with language proficiency, in L1, L2, and across languages? In a number of jurisdictions, a large percentage of students have a home language other than English.

For example, in California 1.1 million English learner (EL) students are enrolled in TK-12. Across the State, 60% of young children have a home language other than English. Not surprisingly, groups such as the California Association for Bilingual Education question the reverence of some legislators and policymakers for the SoR and what they deem the lack of support given teachers as they navigate the diversity of language and cultural backgrounds in their classrooms. Members of the Association lament the extent to which a one size fits all approach, derived from the SoR, is under consideration. We do not disagree with their concerns. Alas, we have said very little about emergent bilinguals in this monograph. Part of the reason, of course, is that it has not been as major a claim in the social and popular media as the claims we have addressed. Although we make mention of translanguaging as an important insight and promising practice, we treat the topic minimally. We know that the situation for these learners deserve a much fuller discussion as a cultural assets of all learners. A child's mother tongue may be their most important cultural asset; finding ways to privilege it as an asset in an English-only classroom is a sobering challenge. Some scholars have claimed that the SoR is as applicable to emergent bilinguals as it is to English-only speakers (Goldenberg, 2020). Others, ourselves included, would say that the science of cultural assets is as applicable to English-only speakers as it is to emergent bilinguals. Discussions of the SOR for all learners (and especially multilingual learners) need substantially more development.

As we indicated, this short list is intended to be suggestive of issues that some collaboratively-constituted panel, task force, or committee might examine as part of a more fulsome consideration of the state of our knowledge.

Conclusion 2: At all levels, including pre-K, students deserve a comprehensive curriculum. Single-factor solutions to multi-faceted problems are predisposed to failure. Whether you call it balanced, comprehensive, structured, or well-orchestrated, we should leave nothing to chance.

Conclusion 2.1. A comprehensive curriculum requires a full reading of all the science(s) of reading. The broadest goal is to ensure that students can construct meaning with the texts we ask them to read—hence, all the component, or enabling, skills and processes included in the curriculum should be focused on achieving that broad and overarching goal. Teaching the code has been a consistent message in the research cited by researchers and policymakers aligned with the popular version of the SoR, as well as those advocating versions of comprehensive literacy. Yet equally consistent in these syntheses has been the qualification that the code cannot, and should not, stand alone. The rest of the curriculum should be informed by the most up-to-date knowledge. At minimum, a comprehensive curriculum should be informed by these literatures:

- **Models** of Reading, Literacy, and Learning shape literacy pedagogy. Especially important are models that help us as teachers learn about:
    - The nature of meaning making;
    - The nature and development of the cipher that links print and speech;
    - Language (especially talk about text, language, and words);
    - Knowledge; and
    - Social, cultural, and contextual experiences and settings that shape reading.
- **Disciplinary Literacy.** Wed first-hand inquiries (i.e., experiential) with second-hand inquiries (e.g., through reading texts) to explore how the worlds we live in work—preferably through project-based learning. In Freire's words, we must learn to read both the word and the world.
- **Literate Dispositions.** Motivation, engagement, interest, self-efficacy, agency, identity, growth mindset, dispositions, social-emotional learning, and empathy all shape acts of literacy.
- **Asset-Based and Culturally-Sustaining Pedagogies** that enhance literacy development. Why? Because…
    - We all need to see, find, and expand ourselves in the curriculum.
    - We need to unearth and name systemic racism, especially that which we cannot see ourselves.

Key to reading/literacy development is the engagement of student's meaning making from the outset—by connecting to and building from their worlds. Learning to read should bridge from opportunities to represent thinking in talk, image, and text. Learning about the code be embedded in and emerge from such engagements.

Conclusion 2.2. Novice readers should acquire a full repertoire of word-level skills as a part of the meaning making process. The repertoire includes word-reading, orthograhic mapping, word-solving skills, and the disposition to orchestrate them in tandem with language and knowledge in making meaning. As we detailed in our reading of Claim 1, versions of the claim that the code deserves a prominent curricular home have emerged from the endless analyses of the data (from previous and new syntheses). Looking across several of the claims we have evaluated, it is clear to us that embracing this responsibility is an enduring and recurrent theme. It was a conclusion of each of these syntheses:

- Chall's 1967 *Learning to Read: The Great Debate*
- Anderson and his colleagues' 1985 *Becoming a Nation of Readers*, sanctioned by the National Academy of Education
- Adams' 1990 *Beginning to Read: Thinking and Learning about Print*, sponsored by the U.S. Department of Education
- Snow and her colleagues' 1998 *Preventing Reading Difficulties in Young Children*, sponsored by the National Academy of Sciences
- The 2000 Report of the National Reading Panel and the National Institute for Child and Human Development, *Teaching Children to Read*
- The 2010 Report of the National Early Literacy Panel and the National Institute for Child and Human Development, *Developing Early Literacy*

The idea that students need to become good codebreakers has never been controversial. Whole Language advocates, for instance, want students to develop a repertoire of tools (including grapho-phonemic) that will help them unlock words they might encounter. The controversy has arisen from arguments over the curriculum and pedagogy needed to internalize code-breaking and other knowledge, skills, and dispositions. At the center of this debate lies the question: Must we teach what must be learned? Implying, of course, that we might be able to orchestrate learning environments in which children will discover the cipher for themselves, as a natural byproduct of reading for meaning. Mark Seidenberg, a strong advocate of explicit code teaching (e.g., Seidenberg, 2017), recognizes that many students engage in what he terms statistical, or implicit learning (e.g., Seidenberg, 2023a)—by drawing inferences about the underlying rules, patterns, or heuristics that operate across data sets they encounter while reading.

For now, we are provisionally siding with what might be termed, in legal parlance, a strict originalist approach—in which we assert that the syntheses mean what they say. Our close, text-based reading of the evidence, as we argued for in Claim 1, suggests that systematic (rather than opportunistic) programs show a consistent advantage in terms of developing word-level skills (with less consistent effects on comprehension), as long as they also attend to a range of other curricular matters (e.g., comprehension, language, motivation, and agency). Any assertion that the approaches also need to be synthetic (e.g., sequential decoding) or structured is reaching further than the evidence permits. The approaches could be synthetic, but they needn't be.

At this point, it would seem consistent with the evidence to implement programs that help students develop and use a full complementary repertoire of ways of reading and unlocking words, whether it be Linnea Ehri's (2005) combined approaches to reading words (e.g., sequential decoding; decoding by analogy, sight, and context); Scanlon et al.'s (2024) Interactive Strategies Approach; or even the phonics-on-the-fly portfolio of practices that Taylor and her colleagues (2002) found so predictive of achievement. Readers need a full toolbox, supported by teachers who are keeping tabs on their development and switch from one resource to another as they help students develop what Gough and Hillinger (1980) called, "cryptoanalytic intent" (p. 188).

Word reading, especially the facile sort that is accurate, automatic, and fluent, cannot be achieved without a repertoire of word-solving skills that help students figure out the pronunciation and meaning of words they cannot immediately recognize and/or understand. As we demonstrated in Claim 4, nowhere in the entire repertoire of reading skills and practices are variability and flexibility more important than in addressing these "clunks" in the reading process. As Gibson and Levin (1975) argued at a theoretical level, and others (Scanlon & Anderson, 2020; Chapman & Tunmer, 2011) have demonstrated empirically, readers must learn to expect variability in the consistency between English orthography and phonology and deploy a flexible set of strategies that nimbly shift between the orthographic, phonological, semantic, and syntactic cues in the texts they encounter. The interactive nature of skill development and the orchestrated use of skills should be uppermost in our thinking, planning, and delivery of word-level curricular practices.

Conclusion 2.3. Accept responsibility for ensuring that all readers, including novice readers, acquire the knowledge, language, skills, and dispositions they need to become learners who can use reading, writing, and language to learn about—and live productive lives within—the natural, social, and cultural worlds they inhabit.
With a goal this broad and deep, we are asking much of the educational system and its teachers. Yet no teacher would accept less for any of the students under their tutelage. It is why we teach, and it is why citizens invest in and support their schools. At the curricular level, this means that the curriculum to support reading acquisition ought to be connected to, perhaps even integrated with, the curriculum for learning other language arts, as well as for learning in the disciplines (i.e., within the sciences, the social sciences, and the arts and humanities). It is our way of maximizing the likelihood that students will gain access to the knowledge, language, and inquiry skills they will need to live productive lives—and enhance their reading development. This recommendation is grounded in both research and the moral imperatives of education. We know, from diverse and continuously-expanding bodies of theory and research (Cervetti et al., 2020; Duke & Cartwright, 2021; Kim, 2017; Scarborough, 2001), that language development is as important to reading development as the acquisition of the cipher—the code that allows readers to map written onto oral language. We also know that when reading (and writing, by the way) are situated within these broader goals of knowledge and language development, students have a space in which to apply, refine, and hone their ever-developing reading skills.

Conclusion 3. The field needs a complete "reset" on how to manage differences, controversy, and deeply-held beliefs in our quest for common ground.

Conclusion 3.1. We need to replace false debates with real debates. We need to stop speaking for others, asserting confidently what we take to be their position (often in caricature, as a straw man), and offering our critique (not of their position, but of our rendition of their position). Let us speak only for ourselves, bring our data to the table, and stay there—until all possible avenues of research-based consensus have been explored and exhausted. Let's stay long enough to figure out what we do agree on, and build from there. Above all, let's avoid what we see so much of in some Western societies nowadays—particularly in politics, and especially on culturally divisive issues: Engaging in confirmation bias, by limiting our input to messages from those who think just like us.

False debates often sow distrust and misinformation among parents, schools, and policy makers—thereby alienating teachers and cutting off opportunities for productive discussion (see Gabriel, 2020; Gabriel & Strauss, 2013; Pearson, 2004; Pearson, Madda, & Raphael, 2023; Reinking, Hruby, & Risko, 2023). We do not discount the importance of debate; we simply argue that critics on both sides should commit to a genuinely scientific and collaborative dialogical examination of research that informs these complex issues. Real debates might lead to a hierarchy of consensus. For example:

- We begin with a search for consensus—to identify research-based policies upon which we can agree. The list will be longer than we think. As we said in our concluding section for Claim 1, we are sometimes surprised that the debate continues, even when alleged antagonists express agreement (e.g., the debate between Bowers, Fletcher and colleagues, and others about the instructional surround for phonics; see p. 41).
- We unearth disagreements and sort them into categories, such as:
    - Unsettled questions for which we can imagine a short-term line of research leading to resolution.

  - Unsettled questions for which the current or even short-term line of research—due to ambiguous, unclear, or conflicting results—is unlikely to lead to resolution.
  - Unsettled questions for which evidence is irrelevant—most likely because they are rooted in moral and ethical issues about the nature of schooling in societies. Political resolution seems the only option
- The panels reconvene periodically (Five-year intervals seem right) to revisit the unsettled issues in light of more recent research.

None of these tough conversations will work, however, unless our discourse becomes more civil. In the preface to this monograph, we expressed our shock and dismay at the bad behavior we have witnessed in some of the interactions, especially in social media. Critique, supported by evidence, is welcome. But name-calling, impugning motives, and other tools of the ad hominem disposition, are not. And, of course, disrespect for those with whom we disagree is equally as problematic in legislative halls and political discourse, where it has become so prevalent that it is viewed as a threat to democracy worldwide.

Conclusion 3.2. It is time for what might be considered "learning nests," and perhaps another National Reading Panel. Better yet, an International Reading Panel. Still better: A panel selected to represent the full range of basic and applied research and full range of constituents whose lives are shaped by the panel's outcomes. As a field, we constitute a panel that ensures a voice for all constituents, with either relevant knowledge or high stakes in the quality of reading curricula. Experts in reading research will surely provide an important nucleus to such a panel, but also included would be researchers representing all of the fields previously identified in Conclusion 2.1 (on a comprehensive curriculum). It would also include parents, teachers, policymakers, and teacher educators, all representing the groups whose lives will be shaped by the panel's recommendations. Models exist for just these sorts of broadly-representative groups. In the U.S., these include the National Assessment of Educational Progress (NAEP) Framework panels, or, with some modification, the Institute of Education Sciences (IES) What Works Clearinghouse (WWC) panels. At the local level, we would also encourage "learning nests"—gatherings wherein colleagues might discuss teaching and learning pathways, share the data and research they've engaged in in their own classrooms, and plan their own design studies (i.e., in which they study their students' needs and development to better tailor and refine their curricular practices).

Closing

We hope that our examination of these claims contributes to a respectful consideration of the issues related to learning to read. Beyond the fact-checking, there may not be agreement with everyone on all issues; in fact, we are not always sure we agree with one another with some of our recommendations for moving forward. That's healthy. But the two of us do try to model what we hope becomes a professional ethic: Staying at the table, in the conversation, until every ounce of consensus and goodwill has been expended. Even if the two of us don't agree on everything, we're staying at the same table! We hope these discussions help to open a conversation, consistent with one of the views expressed in Johns' (2023) conclusion to his history of the Science of Reading:

> We should look much further and more deeply, not only at the science of reading, but at the reading of science—or rather, at the act of reading in science. One way to resolve the alleged crises of the scientific enterprise may lie in an understanding of those practices. (p. 427)

References

Adams, M. J. (1998). The three-cueing system. In J. Osborn & F. Lehr (Eds.), *Literacy for all: Issues in teaching and learning* (pp. 73-99). Guilford Press.

--- (1990). *Beginning to read: Thinking and learning about print.* MIT Press.

Adesope, O. O., Lavin, T., Thompson, T., & Ungerleider, C. (2011). Pedagogical strategies for teaching literacy to ESL immigrant students: A meta-analysis. *British Journal of Educational Psychology*, 81(4), 629-653. https://doi.org/10.1111/j.2044-8279.2010.02015.x

Afflerbach, P. (Ed.). (2016). *Handbook of individual differences in reading: Reader, text, and context.* Routledge. https://doi.org/10.4324/9780203075562

Alexander, P. A. (2020). What research has revealed about readers' struggles with comprehension in the digital age: Moving beyond the phonics versus whole language debate. *Reading Research Quarterly, 55*(1), S89-S97. https://doi.org/10.1002/rrq.331

Allington, R. (2007). NEPC Review: Whole language high jinks: How to tell when 'scientifically-based reading instruction' isn't. Boulder and Tempe: Education and the Public Interest Center & Education Policy Research Unit. National Education Policy Center. https://nepc.colorado.edu/thinktank/review-whole-language-high-jinks-how-tell-when-scientifically-based-reading-instruction-is

Allington, R. L., & McGill-Franzen, A. (1989). School response to reading failure: Instruction for Chapter 1 and Special Education students in grades two, four, and eight. *The Elementary School Journal, 89*(5), 529-542. https://doi.org/10.1086/461590

Altwerger, B., Edelsky, C., & Flores, B. M. (1987). Whole language: What's new? *The Reading Teacher, 41*(2), 144-154.

Anderson, R. C., Hiebert, E. H., Scott, J. A., & Wilkinson, I. A. G. (1985). *Becoming a nation of readers: The report of the Commission on Reading.* National Academy of Education, National Institute of Education, & Center for the Study of Reading.

Arrow, A. W., Braid, C., & Chapman, J. W. (2019). Explicit linguistic knowledge is necessary, but not sufficient, for the provision of explicit early literacy instruction. *Annals of Dyslexia, 69*(1), 99-113. https://doi.org/10.1007/s11881-018-00168-0

Athey, I. J. (1971). Synthesis of papers on language development and reading. *Reading Research Quarterly, 7*(1), 9-15. https://doi.org/10.2307/747056

Atteberry, A., & Bryk, A. S. (2011). Analyzing teacher participation in literacy coaching activities. *The Elementary School Journal, 112*(2), 356-382. https://doi.org/10.1086/661994

Aukerman, M., & Chambers Schuldt, L. (2021). What matters most? Toward a robust and socially just science of reading. *Reading Research Quarterly, 56*(S1), S85-S103. https://doi.org/10.1002/rrq.406

Australian Curriculum, Assessment and Reporting Authority (ACARA). (2022). *NAPLAN: National Report for 2022*. ACARA. https://nap.edu.au/docs/default-source/default-document-library/2022-naplan-national-report.pdf

Balmès, T. (Director). (2010). *Babies* [Film]. StudioCanal Productions.

Beers, J. W., & Henderson, E. H. (1977). A study of developing orthographic concepts among first graders. *Research in the Teaching of English, 11*(2), 133-148.

Bell, S. M., Ziegler, M., & McCallum, R. S. (2004). What adult educators know compared with what they say they know about providing research-based reading instruction. *Journal of Adolescent & Adult Literacy, 47*(7), 542-563.

Bethea, C. (2023, Feb 7). Why some Florida schools are removing books from their libraries. *The New Yorker*. https://www.newyorker.com/news/letter-from-the-south/why-some-florida-schools-are-removing-books-from-their-libraries

Bissex, G. L. (1980). *Gnys at wrk: A child learns to write and read.* Harvard University Press.

Bita, N. (2023, May 17). Girls beat boys in reading standard, ACER PIRLS test shows. *The Australian*. https://www.theaustralian.com.au/nation/national-reading-test-proves-poorest-kids-are-falling-behind/news-story/3417635b1b729ca992ad8ba3bbc-7c7d5

--- (2022, Oct 31). Teen boys at record low for literacy. *The Australian*. https://www.theaustralian.com.au/nation/boys-literacy-plummets-in-naplan-results-but-phonicsled-recovery-in-early-years/news-story/4fbc1b58f1c634cf3d4c20a8e8e34b52

Bloome, D., Carter, S.P., Christian, B. M., Otto, S., & Shuart-Faris, N. (2005). Discourse analysis and the study of classroom language and literacy events: *A microethnographic perspective*. Lawrence Erlbaum Associates. https://doi.org/10.4324/9781410611215

Bloome, D., Carter, S.P., Christian, B. M., Otto, S., & Shuart-Faris, N., Madrid, S., & Smith, M. (2008). *Discourse analysis in classrooms: Approaches to language and literacy research* (with Goldman, S., & Macbeth, D., Contributors). Teachers College Press.

Bond, G.L., & Dykstra, R. (1967). Cooperative Research Program in First-Grade Reading Instruction. *Reading Research Quarterly, 2*(4), 5–142. https://doi.org/10.2307/746948

Bos, C., Mather, N., Dickson, S., Podhajski, B., & Chard, D. (2001). Perceptions and knowledge of preservice and inservice educators about early reading instruction. *Annals of Dyslexia*, 51(1), 97-120. https://doi.org/10.1007/s11881-001-0007-0

Boulton, D. & Perfetti, C. (2005, Sept 30). An interview: Dr. Charles Perfetti – Word recognition and comprehension. *Children of the Code* [Website]. Learning Stewards. https://childrenofthecode.org/interviews/perfetti.htm

Boulton, D. & Shaywitz, C. (2004, Apr 28). An interview: Dr. Sally Shaywitz – The brain and dyslexia – What brain imaging can and can't tell us about reading difficulties. *Children of the Code* [Website]. Learning Stewards. https://childrenofthecode.org/interviews/shaywitz.htm

Bowers, J. S. (2020). Reconsidering the evidence that systematic phonics is more effective than alternative methods of reading instruction. *Educational Psychology Review, 32*(3), 681-705. https://doi.org/10.1007/s10648-019-09515-y

Britzman, D. P. (2003). *Practice makes practice: A critical study of learning to teach* (Rev. ed.). State University of New York Press.

Brooks, G. (2023). Disputing recent attempts to reject the evidence in favour of systematic phonics instruction. *Review of Education, 11*(2), e3408. https://doi.org/10.1002/rev3.3408

Brown, J. S., Collins, A., & Duguid, P. (1989). Situated cognition and the culture of learning. *Educational Researcher, 18*(1), 32-42. https://doi.org/10.3102/0013189X018001032

Bruner, J. (1990). *Acts of meaning.* Harvard University Press.

Bryk, A. S., Sebring, P. B., Allensworth, E., Luppescu, S., & Easton, J. Q. (2010). *Organizing schools for improvement: Lessons from Chicago.* University of Chicago Press.

Buckingham, J. (2023, Jun 23). Don't discard comprehension strategies [Blog post]. *Five from Five.* MultiLit. https://fivefromfive.com.au/blog/dont-discard-comprehension-strategies/

--- (2020). Systematic phonics instruction belongs in evidence-based reading programs: A response to Bowers. *The Educational and Developmental Psychologist, 37*(2), 105-113. https://doi.org/10.1017/edp.2020.12

--- (2019a). *Reading Recovery: A failed investment* [Policy Paper No. 15]. The Centre for Independent Studies and MultiLit. Available from https://fivefromfive.com.au/wp-content/uploads/2022/07/PP15-RE-BRAND.pdf

--- (2019b). Putting the record straight about research on reading. The Centre for Independent Studies and MultiLit. Available from https://fivefromfive.com.au/wp-content/uploads/2022/07/Setting-the-Record-Straight.pdf

--- (2016). *Focus on phonics: Why Australia should adopt the Year 1 Phonics Screening Check* [Research Report No. 22]. The Centre for Independent Studies and MultiLit. Available from https://fivefromfive.com.au/wp-content/uploads/2022/07/Phonics-Check.pdf

Buckingham, J., & Meeks, L. (2019). *Short-changed: Preparation to teach reading in initial teacher education* [Research Report]. MultiLit. Retrieved from https://fivefromfive.com.au/wp-content/uploads/2022/07/ITE-REPORT-FINAL-WEB-R1.pdf

Buckingham, J., Wheldall, K., & Beaman-Wheldall, R. (2013). Why Jaydon can't read: The triumph of ideology over evidence in teaching reading. *Policy, 29*(3), 21-32.

Bullock, A. (1975). *A language for life.* (The Bullock report). Her Majesty's Stationary Office (HMSO).

Burns, M. K., Duke, N. K., & Cartwright, K. B. (2023). Evaluating components of the Active View of Reading as intervention targets: Implications for social justice. *School Psychology, 38*(1), 30–41. https://doi.org/10.1037/spq0000519

Callahan, M., Griffo, V. B., & Pearson, P. D. (2009). Teacher knowledge and teaching reading. In F. Falk-Ross, S. Szabo, M. B. Sampson, & M. M. Foote (Eds.), *Literacy issues during changing times: A call to action,* 30th yearbook of the College Reading Association (pp. 37-62). College Reading Association.

Camilli, G., Kim, S. H., & Vargas, S. (2008). A response to Steubing et al., "Effects of systematic phonics instruction are practically significant:" The origins of the National Reading Panel. *Education Policy Analysis Archives, 16*(15). https://doi.org/10.14507/epaa.v16n16.2008

Camilli, G., Vargas, S., & Yurecko, M. (2003). Teaching children to read: The fragile link between science and federal education policy. *Education Policy Analysis Archives, 11*(15), 15. https://doi.org/10.14507/epaa.v11n15.2003

Camilli, G., Wolfe, P. M., & Smith, M. L. (2006). Meta-analysis and reading policy: Perspectives on *Teaching Children to Read. The Elementary School Journal, 107*(1), 27–36. https://doi.org/10.1086/509525

Cassidy, J., Garrett, S., Maxfield, P., & Patchett, C. (2010). Literacy coaching: Yesterday, today, and tomorrow. In J. Cassidy, S. D. Garrett, & M. Sailors (Eds.), *Literacy coaching: Research and practice* (pp. 15–27). Center for Educational Development, Evaluation, and Research.

Castles, A. Rastle, K. & Nation, K. (2018). Ending the reading wars: Reading acquisition from novice to expert. *Psychological Science in the Public Interest, 19*(1), 5–51. https://journals.sagepub.com/doi/pdf/10.1177/1529100618772271

Catts, H. W. (2018). The simple view of reading: Advancements and false impressions. *Remedial and Special Education, 39*(5), 317-323. https://doi.org/10.1177/0741932518767563

Calkins, L. (2019). No one gets to own the term Science of Reading. Teachers College Reading and Writing Project, Columbia University. https://members.readingandwritingproject.org/news/no-one-gets-to-own-the-term-the-science-of-reading

Calkins, L., & Teachers College Reading and Writing Project (TCRWP) Colleagues. (2022). *Comprehensive Overview: Units, tools, and methods for teaching reading, writing, and phonics: A workshop curriculum, Grades K-8.* Heinemann.

Central Advisory Council for Education (CACE). (1967). *Children and their primary schools.* (The Plowden Report). Her Majesty's Stationary Office (HMSO).

Cervetti, G. N., Pearson, P. D., Palincsar, A. S., Afflerbach, P., Kendeou, P., Biancarosa, G., Higgs, J., Fitzgerald, M. S., & Berman, A. I. (2020). How the Reading for Understanding Initiative's research complicates the simple view of reading invoked in the science of reading. *Reading Research Quarterly, 55*(1), S161-S172. https://doi.org/10.1002/rrq.343

Chall, J. S. (1983). *Stages of reading development.* McGraw-Hill.
--- (1967). *Learning to read: The great debate.* McGraw-Hill.

Chapman, J. W., & Tunmer, W. E. (2015, July 8). The literacy performance of ex-Reading Recovery students between two and four years following participation on the program: Is this intervention effective for students with early reading difficulties? Paper presented at the 39th Annual Conference of the *International Academy for Research in Learning Disabilities* (IARLD), Vancouver, Canada.
--- (2011). Reading recovery®: Does it work? *Perspectives on Language and Literacy, 37*(4), 21-24.

Chiao, J. Y., & Immordino-Yang, M. H. (2013). Modularity and the cultural mind: Contributions of cultural neuroscience to cognitive theory. *Perspectives on Psychological Science, 8*(1), 56-61. https://doi.org/10.1177/1745691612469032

Chomsky, C. (1979). Approaching reading through invented spellings. In L. B. Resnick & P. A Weaver (Eds.), *Theory and practice of early reading, Vol. 2.* Lawrence Erlbaum.

Chomsky, N. (1965). *Aspects of the theory of syntax.* The M.I.T. Press. Available from http://www.jstor.org/stable/j.ctt17kk81z

Clay, M. M. (1998). *By different paths to common outcomes.* Stenhouse Publishers.
--- (1993). *Reading recovery: A guide book for teachers in training.* Heinemann.

Cochran-Smith, M., & Reagan, E. M. (2022). Centering equity in teacher education evaluation: From principles to transformative enactment. *Journal of Teacher Education, 73*(5), 449-462. https://doi.org/10.1177/00224871221123728
--- (2021). *"Best practices" for evaluating teacher preparation programs.* National Academy of Education Committee on Evaluating and Improving Teacher Preparation Programs. National Academy of Education. Retrieved from https://files.eric.ed.gov/fulltext/ED615385.pdf

Collins, T. (2022, Jan 6). Student retention and third grade reading: It's about the adults. Thomas B. Fordham Institute. https://fordhaminstitute.org/national/commentary/student-retention-and-third-grade-reading-its-about-adults

Compton-Lilly, C. (2011). By the book and behind-the-glass: Teacher self-regulation in one reading intervention. *Language Arts, 88*(6), 429-438.

Compton-Lilly, C., Spence, L. K., Thomas, P. L., & Decker, S. L. (2023). Stories grounded in decades of research: What we truly know about the teaching of reading. *The Reading Teacher, 77*(3): 273-422. https://doi.org/10.1002/trtr.2258

Connor, C. M., Piasta, S. B., Fishman, B., Glasney, S., Schatschneider, C., Crowe, E., Underwood, P., & Morrison, F. J. (2009). Individualizing student instruction precisely: Effects of Child X instruction interactions on first graders' literacy development. *Child Development, 80*(1), 77-100. https://doi.org/10.1111/j.1467-8624.2008.01247.x

Crinion, J., Holland, A. L., Copland, D. A., Thompson, C. K., & Hillis, A. E. (2013). Neuroimaging in aphasia treatment research: Quantifying brain lesions after stroke. *NeuroImage, 73,* 208-214. https://doi.org/10.1016/j.neuroimage.2012.07.044

Cromley, J. G., & Azevedo, R. (2007). Testing and refining the direct and inferential mediation model of reading comprehension. *Journal of Educational Psychology, 99*(2), 311-325. https://doi.org/10.1037/0022-0663.99.2.311

Cunningham, A. E., Perry, K. E., Stanovich, K. E., & Stanovich, P. J. (2004). Disciplinary knowledge of K-3 teachers and their knowledge calibration in the domain of early literacy. *Annals of Dyslexia, 54*(1), 139-167. https://doi.org/10.1007/s11881-004-0007-y

Curtis, E., Jones, R., Tipene-Leach, D., Walker, C., Loring, B., Paine, S., & Reid, P. (2019). Why cultural safety rather than cultural competency is required to achieve health equity: A literature review and recommended definition. *International Journal for Equity in Health, 18*(1), 174-174. https://doi.org/10.1186/s12939-019-1082-3

Darling-Hammond, L., & Bransford, J. (2005). *Preparing teachers for a changing world: What teachers should learn and be able to do.* Jossey-Bass.

Davis, F. B. (Ed.). (1971). *The literature of research in reading with emphasis on models: Final report.* Graduate School of Education, Rutgers University, and the National Center for Educational Research and Development. https://files.eric.ed.gov/fulltext/ED059023.pdf

De Bortoli, L., Underwood, C., & Thomson, S. (2023). PISA 2022. *Reporting Australia's results, Volume I: Student performance and equity in education.* Australian Council for Educational Research. https://doi.org/10.37517/978-1-74286-725-0

Dehaene, S. (2011). The massive impact of literacy on the brain and its consequences for education. Pontifical Academy of Sciences. *Human Neuroplasticity and Education, 117,* 19–32, 237–238.
--- (2009). *Reading in the brain: The new science of how we read.* Penguin Books.

DeJulio, S., Massey, D. D., Stahl, N., & King, J. (2024). Terminologically speaking, the reading wars. *Reading Psychology*, 1-27. https://doi.org/10.1080/02702711.2024.2309342

Delgado, R., Stefancic, J. (2023). *Critical race theory: An introduction* (4th ed.). New York University Press.

Deuze, M., Blank, P., & Speers, L. (2012). A life lived in media. *Digital Humanities Quarterly, 6*(1), 37. Retrieved from http://digitalhumanities.org:8081/dhq/vol/6/1/000110/000110.html

Dole, J. A., Duffy, G. G., & Pearson, P. D. (2019). Epilogue: Reflections on the gradual release of responsibility model: Where we've been and where we're going. In M. B. McVee, E. Ortlieb, J. Reichenberg, & P. D. Pearson (Eds.), T*he gradual release of responsibility in literacy research and practice* (pp. 245-263). Emerald Publishing Limited. https://doi.org/10.1108/S2048-045820190000010016

Domínguez D., J. F., Lewis, E. D., Turner, R., & Egan, G. F. (2009). The brain in culture and culture in the brain: A review of core issues in neuroanthropology. In J. Y. Chiao (Ed.), *Progress in brain research, Vol 178* (pp. 43-64). Elsevier Science & Technology. https://doi.org/10.1016/S0079-6123(09)17804-4

Drum, K. (2023, Jun 24). How miraculous is Mississippi? [Blog post]. Jabberwocking [Blog]. Kevin Drum. https://jabberwocking.com/how-miraculous-is-mississippi/

Duffy, C. (2024, Feb 11). One-third of Australian children can't read properly as teaching methods cause 'preventable tragedy,' Grattan Institute says. *The Australian Broadcasting Corporation (ABC) News.* https://www.abc.net.au/news/2024-02-11/grattan-institute-reading-report/103446606

Duke, N. K., & Cartwright, K. B. (2021). The science of reading progresses: Communicating advances beyond the simple view of reading. *Reading Research Quarterly, 56*(1), S25-S44. https://doi.org/10.1002/rrq.411

Durkin, D. (1966). *Children who read early: Two longitudinal studies.* Teachers College Press.

Dyson, A. H. (Ed.). (2016). *Child cultures, schooling, and literacy: Global perspectives on composing unique lives.* Routledge. https://doi.org/10.4324/9781315736518

--- (2001). Writing and children's symbolic repertoires: Development unhinged. In S. B. Neuman & D. K. Dickinson (Eds.), *Handbook of early literacy research*, Vol. 1 (pp. 126-141). Guilford Press.

--- (1995). Writing children: Reinventing the development of childhood literacy. *Written Communication, 12*(1), 4-46. https://doi.org/10.1177/0741088395012001002

--- (1989). *Multiple worlds of child writers: Friends learning to write.* Teachers College, Columbia University.

--- (1987). Unintentional helping in the primary grades: Writing in the children's world (Report No. 12). University of California, Berkeley, Center for the Study of Writing. Retrieved from https://files.eric.ed.gov/fulltext/ED282227.pdf

--- (1982). Reading, writing, and language: Young children solving the written language puzzle. *Language Arts, 59*(8), 829-839.

Ehri, L. C. (2021, June 22). White Paper: How beginning reading instruction teaches word reading skill. *The Reading Forum.* https://thereadingforum.com/wp-content/uploads/2021/06/White-Paper-final-Beginning-Reading-Instruction.docx.pdf

--- (2020). The science of learning to read words: A case for systematic phonics instruction. *Reading Research Quarterly, 55*(S1), S45-S60. https://doi.org/10.1002/rrq.334

--- (2014). Orthographic mapping in the acquisition of sight word reading, spelling memory, and vocabulary learning. *Scientific Studies of Reading, 18*(1), 5-21. https://doi.org/10.1080/10888438.2013.819356

--- (2005). Learning to read words: Theory, findings, and issues. *Scientific Studies of Reading, 9*(2), 167-188. https://doi.org/10.1207/s1532799xssr0902_4

Ehri, L. C., Nunes, S. R., Stahl, S. A., & Willows, D. M. (2001). Systematic phonics instruction helps students learn to read: Evidence from the National Reading Panel's meta-analysis. *Review of Educational Research, 71*(3), 393-447. https://doi.org/10.3102/00346543071003393

Elliott, J. G. (2020). It's time to be scientific about dyslexia. *Reading Research Quarterly, 55*(S1), S61-S75. https://doi.org/10.1002/rrq.333

Elliott, M. L., Knodt, A. R., Ireland, D., Morris, M. L., Poulton, R., Ramrakha, S., Sison, M. L., Moffitt, T. E., Caspi, A., & Hariri, A. R. (2020). What is the test-retest reliability of common task-functional MRI measures? New empirical evidence and a meta-analysis. *Psychological Science, 31*(7), 792-806. https://doi.org/10.1177/0956797620916786

Ellis, C., Holston, S., Drake, G., Putman, H., Swisher, A., & Peske, H. (2023). Teacher prep review: Strengthening elementary reading instruction. National Council on Teacher Quality. https://www.nctq.org/dmsView/Teacher_Prep_Review_Strengthening_Elementary_Reading_Instruction

Ercikan, K., & Roth, W.-M. (Eds.). (2009). *Generalizing from educational research: Beyond qualitative and quantitative polarization.* Routledge. https://doi.org/10.4324/9780203885376

Feltovich, P. J., Spiro, R. J., & Coulson, R. L. (1988). *The nature of conceptual understanding in biomedicine: The deep structure of complex ideas and the development of misconceptions* [Technical Report No. 440]. U of Illinois Center for the Study of Reading & Bolt, Beranek and Newman, Inc. Retrieved from https://files.eric.ed.gov/fulltext/ED302820.pdf

Fernald, G. (1943). *Remedial techniques in basic school subjects.* McGraw-Hill.

Ferreiro, E., & Teberosky, A. (1982). *Literacy before schooling.* Heinemann Educational Books.

Fletcher, J. M., Savage, R., & Vaughn, S. (2021). A commentary on Bowers (2020) and the role of phonics instruction in reading. *Educational Psychology Review, 33*(3), 1249-1274. https://doi.org/10.1007/s10648-020-09580-8

Foorman, B. R., Francis, D. J., Fletcher, J. M., Schatschneider, C., & Mehta, P. (1998). The role of instruction in learning to read: Preventing reading failure in at-risk children. *Journal of Educational Psychology, 90*(1), 37-55. https://doi.org/10.1037/0022-0663.90.1.37

Foorman, B., Beyler, N., Borradaile, K., Coyne, M., Denton, C. A., Dimino, J., Furgeson, J., Hayes, L., Henke, J., Justice, L., Keating, B., Lewis, W., Sattar, S., Streke, A., Wagner, R., & Wissel, S. (2016). *Foundational skills to support reading for understanding in Kindergarten through 3rd grade* (NCEE 2016-4008). National Center for Education Evaluation and Regional Assistance (NCEE), Institute of Education Sciences, U.S. Department of Education. https://ies.ed.gov/ncee/wwc/Docs/practiceGuide/wwc_foundationalreading_040717.pdf

Forzani, E., Afflerbach, P., Aguirre, S., Brynelson, N., Cervetti, G., Cho, B., Coiro, J., García, G. E., Guthrie, J. T., Hinchman, K., Lee, C. D., Pacheco, M., Pearson, P. D., Ross, A., Skerrett, A., & Uccelli, P. (2022). Advances and missed opportunities in the development of the 2026 NAEP reading framework. *Literacy Research, 71*(1), 153-189. https://doi.org/10.1177/23813377221112388

Fountas, I. C., & Pinnell, G. S. (1996). *Guided Reading. Good first teaching for all children.* Heinemann.

Fowler-Amato, M., Hikida, M., O'Neil, E., & Taylor, L. (2019). An introduction to the CITE-ITEL database: Access, dialogue, and possibility. *Contemporary Issues in Technology and Teacher Education, 19*(2), 156-170. https://citejournal.org/volume-19/issue-2-19/english-language-arts/an-introduction-to-the-cite-itel-database-access-dialogue-and-possibility/

Francis, D. J., Kulesz, P. A., & Benoit, J. S. (2018). Extending the simple view of reading to account for variation within readers and across texts: The complete view of reading (CVRi). *Remedial and Special Education, 39*(5), 274-288. https://doi.org/10.1177/0741932518772904

Freire, P. (1972). *Pedagogy of the oppressed.* New York: Herder and Herder.

Gabriel, R. E. (2020). Converting to privatization: A discourse analysis of dyslexia policy narratives. *American Educational Research Journal, 57*(1), 305-338. https://doi.org/10.3102/0002831219861945

Gabriel, R., & Strauss, V. (2013, Aug 21). How the 'reading wars' are being reignited. *The Washington Post.* https://www.washingtonpost.com/news/answer-sheet/wp/2013/08/21/how-the-reading-wars-are-being-reignited/

Galuschka, K., Ise, E., Krick, K., & Schulte-Körne, G. (2014). Effectiveness of treatment approaches for children and adolescents with reading disabilities: A meta-analysis of randomized controlled trials. *PloS One, 9*(2), e89900-e89900. https://doi.org/10.1371/journal.pone.0089900

Gamse, B.C., Jacob, R.T., Horst, M., Boulay, B., & Unlu, F. (2008). *Reading first impact study: Final report* (NCEE 2009-4038). National Center for Education Evaluation and Regional Assistance, Institute of Education Sciences, U.S. Department of Education. Retrieved from https://files.eric.ed.gov/fulltext/ED503344.pdf

García, J. R., & Cain, K. (2014). Decoding and reading comprehension: A meta-analysis to identify which reader and assessment characteristics influence the strength of the relationship in english. *Review of Educational Research, 84*(1), 74-111. https://doi.org/10.3102/0034654313499616

García, O., & Kleifgen, J. A. (2020). Translanguaging and literacies. *Reading Research Quarterly, 55(*4), 553-571. https://doi.org/10.1002/rrq.286

Gay, G. (2000). *Culturally responsive teaching: Theory, research, and practice.* Teachers College Press.

Gibson, E. J., & Levin, H. (1975). *The psychology of reading.* MIT Press.

Gillingham, A., & Stillman, B. (1946). *Remedial training for children with specific disability in reading, spelling and penmanship.* Sackett & Wilhelms.

Goldenberg, C. (2020). Reading wars, reading science, and English learners. *Reading Research Quarterly, 55*(S1), S131-S144.

Goldstein, D. (2023, Jun 21). What the new, low test scores for 13-year-olds say about U.S. Education now. *The New York Times.* https://www.nytimes.com/2023/06/21/us/naep-test-results-education.html?searchResultPosition=2

Goodman, K. S. (1969). Analysis of oral reading miscues: Applied psycholinguistics. *Reading Research Quarterly, 5*(1), 9-30. https://doi.org/10.2307/747158
--- (1968). *The psycholinguistic nature of the reading process.* Wayne State University Press.
--- (1967). Reading: A psycholinguistic guessing game. *Journal of the Reading Specialist, 6*(4), 126–135. https://doi.org/10.1080/19388076709556976
--- (1965). A linguistic study of cues and miscues in reading. *Elementary English, 42*(6), 639-643.

Goodman, Y. M., Burke, C. L. & Sherman, B. (1980). *Reading strategies: Focus on comprehension.* Holt, Rinehart, and Winston.

Goodman, K.S., & Goodman, Y.M. (1982). A Whole Language comprehension-centered view of reading development. In L. Reed & S. Ward (Eds.), *Basic skills issues and choices: Approaches to basic skills instruction,* Vol. 2 (pp. 125-134). Cemrel. https://files.eric.ed.gov/fulltext/ED218649.pdf
--- (1979). Learning to read is natural. In L. B. Resnick & P. A. Weaver (Eds.), *Theory and practice in early reading* (pp. 137-155). Lawrence Erlbaum.
--- (1976, April). *Learning to read is natural* [Conference presentation]. Paper presented at the conference on Theory and Practice of Beginning Reading Instruction, University of Pittsburgh, Learning Research and Development Center. Retrieved from https://files.eric.ed.gov/fulltext/ED155621.pdf

Goodman, Y, M, & Marek, A. M. (Eds.). (1996). *Retrospective miscue analysis: Revaluing readers and reading.* Richard C. Owens.

Gotlieb, R., Yang, X., & Immordino-Yang, M. H. (2022). Default and executive networks' roles in diverse adolescents' emotionally engaged construals of complex social issues. *Social Cognitive and Affective Neuroscience, 17*(4), 421-429. https://doi.org/10.1093/scan/nsab108

---(2021). Measuring learning in the blink of an eye: Adolescents' neurophysiological reactions predict long-term memory for stories. *Frontiers in Education, 5.* https://doi.org/10.3389/feduc.2020.594668

Gotlieb, R. J. M., Immordino-Yang, M. H., Gonzalez, E., Rhinehart, L., Mahjouri, S., Pueschel, E., & Nadaya, G. (2022). Becoming literate: Educational implications of coordinated neuropsychological development of reading and social-emotional functioning among diverse youth. *Literacy Research, 71*(1), 80-132. https://doi.org/10.1177/23813377221120107

Gore, J. (2023, Jul 6). Teaching degrees are set for a major overhaul, but this is not what the profession needs. *The Conversation.* Retrieved from https://theconversation.com/teaching-degrees-are-set-for-a-major-overhaul-but-this-is-not-what-the-profession-needs-209223

Gough, P. B. (1972). One second of reading. *Visible Language, 6*(4), 291-320.

Gough, P. B., & Hillinger, M.L. (1980). Learning to read: an unnatural act. *Bulletin of the Orton Society 30*, 179–196. https://doi.org/10.1007/BF02653717

Gough, P. B., Hoover, W. A., & Peterson, C. L. (1996). Some observations on a simple view of reading. In C. Cornoldi & J. Oakhill (Eds.), *Reading comprehension difficulties: Processes and intervention* (pp. 1–13). Erlbaum.

Gough, P. B., Juel, C., & Roper-Schneider, D. (1983). Code and cipher: A two-stage conception of initial reading acquisition. In J.A. Niles & L.A. Harris (Eds.), *Searches for meaning in reading/language processing and instruction* (pp. 207– 211). National Reading Conference.

Gough, P. B., & Tunmer, W. E. (1986). Decoding, reading, and reading disability. *Remedial and Special Education, 7*(1), 6–10. https://doi.org/10.1177/074193258600700104

Graham, S. (2020). The sciences of reading and writing must become more fully integrated. *Reading Research Quarterly, 55*(S1), S35-S44. https://doi.org/10.1002/rrq.332

Green, J. L., Dai, Y., Joo, J., Williams, E., Liu, A., & Lu, S. C.-Y. (2015). Interdisciplinarydialogues as a site for reflexive exploration of conceptual understandings of teaching-learning relationships. *Pedagogies, 10*(1), 86-103. https://doi.org/10.1080/1554480X.2014.999774

Green, J.,Skukauskaite, A., & Castanheira, M. L. (2012) Studying the discursive construction of learning lives for individuals and the collective. In O.Erstad & J. Sefton-Green (Eds.), *Identity, community, and learning lives in the digital age* (pp.126-145). Cambridge University Press. https://doi.org/10.1017/CBO9781139026239.010

Grigorov, S. K., & Fleuri, R. M. (2012). Ecopedagogy: Educating for a new eco-social intercultural perspective. *Visão Global, Joaçaba, 15*(1-2), 433-454.

Gutiérrez, K. D. (2008). Developing a sociocritical literacy in the third space. *Reading Research Quarterly, 43*(2), 148-164. https://doi.org/10.1598/RRQ.43.2.3

Gutiérrez, K. D., Cortes, K., Cortez, A., DiGiacomo, D., Higgs, J., Johnson, P., Lizárraga, J. R., Mendoza, E., Tien, J., & Vakil, S. (2017). Replacing representation with imagination: Finding ingenuity in everyday practices. *Review of Research in Education, 41*(1), 30-60. https://doi.org/10.3102/0091732X16687523

Gutiérrez, K. D., & Penuel, W. R. (2014). Relevance to practice as a criterion for rigor. *Educational Researcher, 43*(1), 19-23. https://doi.org/10.3102/0013189X13520289

Hall, C., Dahl-Leonard, K., Cho, E., Solari, E. J., Capin, P., Conner, C. L., Henry, A. R., Cook, L., Hayes, L., Vargas, I., Richmond, C. L., & Kehoe, K. F. (2023). Forty years of reading intervention research for elementary students with or at risk for dyslexia: A systematic review and MetaAnalysis. *Reading Research Quarterly, 58*(2), 285-312. https://doi.org/10.1002/rrq.477

Halliday, M.A.K. (2010). Introduction: On the "Architecture" of human language. In J. Webster (Ed.), *On language and linguistics* (pp. 1-30). Continuum International Publishing Group. https://doi.org/10.5040/9781474211932.0005

--- (1975). *Learning how to mean: Explorations in the development of language.* Edward Arnold.

Hammill, D., & Swanson, H. (2006). The national reading Panel's Meta-Analysis of phonics instruction: Another point of view. *The Elementary School Journal, 107*(1), 17-26. https://doi.org/10.1086/509524

Han, I. (2009). *Evidence-based reading instruction for English language learners in preschool through sixth grades: A meta-analysis of group design studies* (Order No. 3371852) [Doctoral dissertation, University of Minnesota]. ProQuest Dissertations Publishing. Retrieved from https://www.proquest.com/dissertations-theses/evidence-based-reading-instruction-english/docview/304958206/se-2?accountid=14656

Han, S., Northoff, G., Vogeley, K., Wexler, B. E., Kitayama, S., & Varnum, M. E. W. (2013). A cultural neuroscience approach to the biosocial nature of the human brain. *Annual Review of Psychology, 64*(1), 335-359. https://doi.org/10.1146/annurev-psych-071112-054629

Hanford, E. (2022, Oct–Nov). Sold a story [Podcast]. *APM Reports.* American Public Media. https://features.apmreports.org/sold-a-story/

--- (2020, Aug 6). What the words say. *APM Reports*. American Public Media. https://www.apmreports.org/episode/2020/08/06/what-the-words-say

--- (2019a, Dec 6). Perpetual laggards leap ahead in reading. *The New York Times*. https://www.nytimes.com/2019/12/05/opinion/mississippi-schools-naep.html?smid=url-share

--- (2019b, Aug 22). At a loss for words: How a flawed idea is teaching millions of kids to be poor readers. *APM Reports*. https://www.apmreports.org/story/2019/08/22/whats-wrong-how-schools-teach-reading

--- (2018, September 10). Hard words: Why aren't kids being taught to read? *APM Reports*. American Public Media. Retrieved from https://www.apmreports.org/episode/2018/09/10/hard-words-why-american-kids-arent-being-taught-to-read

Harris, C., & Grace, R. (2023, July 6). Universities who fail would-be teachers to be stripped of accreditation. *Sydney Morning Herald*. https://www.smh.com.au/national/universities-who-fail-would-be-teachers-to-be-stripped-of-accreditation-20230706-p5dm3t.html

Harrison, C. (2006). Sustaining myths, necessary illusions, and national literacy policies: Some U.S. and U.K. comparisons. *The Elementary School Journal, 107*(1), 121-131. https://doi.org/10.1086/509529

Harste, J. C. (2021). Researching literate lives: *The selected works of Jerome C. Harste* (World Library of Educationist Series). Routledge. https://doi.org/10.4324/9781003083054

Harste, J. C., Woodward, V. A., & Burke, C. L. (1984). *Language stories & literacy lessons.* Heinemann Educational Books.

Helfand, M., Aguilar-Gaxiola, S. A., & Selker, H. P. (2009). Comparative effectiveness research: An approach to avoiding "overgeneralized medicine." *Clinical and Translational Science, 2*(6), 444-445. https://doi.org/10.1111/j.1752-8062.2009.00158.x

Hiebert, E. H., & Tortorelli, L. S. (2022). The role of word-, sentence-, and text-level variables in predicting guided reading levels of kindergarten and first-grade texts. The Elementary School Journal, 122(4), 557-590. https://doi.org/10.1086/719658

Hiltzik, M. (2023, Jul 3). How Mississippi gamed its national reading test scores to produce 'miracle' gains. *Los Angeles Times*. https://www.latimes.com/business/story/2023-07-03/how-mississippi-gamed-national-reading-test-to-produce-miracle-gains

Hoffman, J. (2023). Research and practice in literacy teacher education: Imagining, designing, and engaging in "what could be." In R. J. Tierney, F. Rizvi, & K. Ercikan (Eds.), *International Encyclopedia of Education* (4th ed.) (Vol. 10, pp. 474– 479). Elsevier. https://doi.org/10.1016/B978-0-12-818630-5.07099-8

Hoffman, J. V., Hikida, M., & Sailors, M. (2020). Contesting science that silences: Amplifying equity, agency, and design research in literacy teacher preparation. *Reading Research Quarterly, 55*(S1), S255-S266. https://doi.org/10.1002/rrq.353

Holdaway, D. (1979). *The foundations of literacy.* Ashton Scholastic.

Hoover, W. A., & Gough, P. B. (1990). The simple view of reading. *Reading & Writing, 2*(2), 127-160. https://doi.org/10.1007/BF00401799

Hoover, W. A., & Tunmer, W. E. (2022). The primacy of science in communicating advances in the science of reading. *Reading Research Quarterly, 57*(2), 399-408. https://doi.org/10.1002/rrq.446

--- (2020). *The cognitive foundations of reading and its acquisition: A framework with applications connecting teaching and learning.* Springer International Publishing. https://doi.org/10.1007/978-3-030-44195-1

--- (2018). The simple view of reading: Three assessments of its adequacy. *Remedial and Special Education, 39*(5), 304-312. https://doi.org/10.1177/0741932518773154

Howe, K., & Eisenhart, M. (1990). Standards for qualitative (and quantitative) research: A prolegomenon. *Educational Researcher, 19*(4), 2-9. https://doi.org/10.3102/0013189X019004002

Hunter, J., Stobart, A., & Haywood, A. (2024, Feb). *The reading guarantee: How to give every child the best chance of success.* Grattan Institute. Retrieved from https://grattan.edu.au/wp-content/uploads/2024/02/The-Reading-Guarantee-Grattan-Institute-Report.pdf

Immordino-Yang, M. H., Christodoulou, J. A., & Singh, V. (2012). Rest is not idleness: Implications of the brain's default mode for human development and education. *Perspectives on Psychological Science,* 7(4), 352-364. https://doi.org/10.1177/1745691612447308

Immordino-Yang, M. H., & Gotlieb, R. (2017). Embodied brains, social minds, cultural meaning: Integrating neuroscientific and educational research on social-affective development. *American Educational Research Journal, 54*(S1), 344S-367S. https://doi.org/10.3102/0002831216669780

Immordino-Yang, M. H., & Knecht, D. R. (2020). Building meaning builds teens' brains. *Educational Leadership,* 77(8), 36.

Immordino-Yang, M. H., McColl, A., Damasio, H., & Damasio, A. (2009). Neural correlates of admiration and compassion. *Proceedings of the National Academy of Sciences (PNAS), 106*(19), 8021-8026. https://doi.org/10.1073/pnas.0810363106

Immordino-Yang, M. H., & Yang, X. (2017). Cultural differences in the neural correlates of social–emotional feelings: An interdisciplinary, developmental perspective. *Current Opinion in Psychology,* 17, 34-40. https://doi.org/10.1016/j.copsyc.2017.06.008

International Dyslexia Association (IDA). (2020). Dyslexia and the brain [Fact sheet]. The International Dyslexia Association. https://dyslexiaida.org/dyslexia-and-the-brain/

Jackson, R., McCoy, A., Pistorino, C., Wilkinson, A., Burghardt, J., Clark, M., Ross, C., Schochet, P., & Swank, P. (2007). *National evaluation of early reading first: Final report.* U.S. Department of Education, Institute of Education Sciences. U.S. Government Printing Office. Retrieved from https://files.eric.ed.gov/fulltext/ED498085.pdf

Jago, C. (Ed.). (2022, Nov). When students' right to read is at risk [November Issue]. *California English, 48*(2). California Association of Teachers of English. Retrieved from https://www.cateweb.org/journals/november-2022/

Javal, L. È. (1905). *Physiologie de la lecture et de l'écriture.* Alcan.

Jenkins, H. (with Purushotma, R., Weigel, M., Clinton, K., & Robison, A. J.). (2009). *Confronting the challenges of participatory culture: Media education for the 21st century.* MIT Press.

Johns, A. (2023). *The science of reading: Information, media, and mind in modern America.* University of Chicago Press.

Johnston, M. (1997). *Contradictions in collaboration: New thinking on school/university partnerships.* Teachers College Press.

Johnston, P. (2004). *Choice words: How our language affects children's learning.* Stenhouse Publishers. https://doi.org/10.4324/9781032680828

Johnston, P., & Scanlon, D. (2021). An examination of dyslexia research and instruction with policy implications. *Literacy Research, 70*(1), 107-128. https://doi.org/10.1177/23813377211024625

Kim, J. S. (2008). Research and the reading wars. In F. M. Hess (Ed.), *When research matters: How scholarship influences education policy* (pp. 89-111). Harvard Education Press. Available from https://scholar.harvard.edu/sites/scholar.harvard.edu/files/jameskim/files/bookch2.pdf

Kim, Y. G. (2017). Why the simple view of reading is not simplistic: Unpacking component skills of reading using a direct and indirect effect model of reading (DIER). *Scientific Studies of Reading, 21*(4), 310-333. https://doi.org/10.1080/10888438.2017.1291643

Kincheloe, J. L. (1991). *Teachers as researchers: Qualitative inquiry as a path to empowerment.* Routledge. https://doi.org/10.4324/9780203801550

Kraft, M. A., Blazar, D., & Hogan, D. (2018). The effect of teacher coaching on instruction and achievement: A meta-analysis of the causal evidence. *Review of Educational Research, 88*(4), 547-588. https://doi.org/10.3102/0034654318759268

Kristoff, N. (2023, Feb 11). Two-thirds of kids struggle to read, and we know how to fix it. *The New York Times.* https://www.nytimes.com/2023/02/11/opinion/reading-kids-phonics.html

Ladson-Billings, G. (1994). *The dreamkeepers: Successful teachers of African American children.* Jossey-Bass Publishers.

--- (1995). Toward a theory of culturally relevant pedagogy. *American Educational Research Journal, 32*(3), 465-491. https://doi.org/10.3102/00028312032003465

Landi, N., Perfetti, C. A., Bolger, D. J., Dunlap, S., & Foorman, B. R. (2006). The role of discourse context in developing word form representations: A paradoxical relation between reading and learning. *Journal of Experimental Child Psychology, 94*(2), 114-133. https://doi.org/10.1016/j.jecp.2005.12.004

Language and Reading Research Consortium (LRRC) & Chiu, Y. D. (2018). The simple view of reading across development: Prediction of grade 3 reading comprehension from prekindergarten skills. *Remedial and Special Education, 39*(5), 289-303. https://doi.org/10.1177/0741932518762055

Lather, P. (2004). This is your Father's paradigm: Government intrusion and the case of qualitative research in education. *Qualitative Inquiry, 10*(1), 15-34. https://doi.org/10.1177/1077800403256154

Lave, J., & Wenger, E. (1991). *Situated learning: Legitimate peripheral participation.* Cambridge University Press.

Lee, C. D. (2020). Social and cultural diversity as lens for understanding student learning and the development of reading comprehension. In E. B. Moje, P. P. Afflerbach, P. Enciso, & N. K. Lesaux (Eds.), *Handbook of reading research, Volume V* (pp. 37-56). Routledge. https://doi.org/10.4324/9781315676302

Lee, C. D., Meltzoff, A. N., & Kuhl, P. K. (2020). The braid of human learning and development: Neuro-physiological processes and participation in cultural practices. In N. S. Nasir, C. D. Lee, R. Pea, & M. M. de Royston (Eds.), *Handbook of the Cultural Foundations of Learning* (pp. 24-43). Routledge. https://doi.org/10.4324/9780203774977

Lenneberg, E. H. (1967). *Biological foundations of language.* Wiley.

Loewenberg Ball, D., Thames, M. H., & Phelps, G. (2008). Content knowledge for teaching: What makes it special? *Journal of Teacher Education, 59*(5), 389-407. https://doi.org/10.1177/0022487108324554

Lonigan, C. J., Burgess, S. R., & Schatschneider, C. (2018). Examining the simple view of reading with elementary school children: Still simple after all these years. *Remedial and Special Education, 39*(5), 260-273. https://doi.org/10.1177/0741932518764833

Luke, A. (2011). Generalizing across borders: Policy and the limits of educational science. *Educational Researcher, 40*(8), 367-377. https://doi.org/10.3102/0013189X11424314

--- (2004). Teaching after the market: From commodity to cosmopolitan. *Teachers College Record, 106*(7), 1422-1443. https://doi.org/10.1111/j.1467-9620.2004.00384.x

Lukianoff G., & Schlott, R. (2023). *The canceling of the American mind: How cancel culture undermines trust, destroys institutions, and threatens us all.* Penguin.

MacPhee, D., Handsfield, L. J., & Paugh, P. (2021). Conflict or conversation? Media portrayals of the science of reading. *Reading Research Quarterly, 56*(S1), S145-S155. https://doi.org/10.1002/rrq.384

Maisog, J. M., Einbinder, E. R., Flowers, D. L., Turkeltaub, P. E., & Eden, G. F. (2008). A meta-analysis of functional neuroimaging studies of dyslexia. *Annals of the New York Academy of Sciences, 1145*(1), 237-259. https://doi.org/10.1196/annals.1416.024

Malatesha Joshi, R., Binks, E., Graham, L., Ocker-Dean, E., Smith, D. L., & Boulware-Gooden, R. (2009). Do textbooks used in university reading education courses conform to the instructional recommendations of the National Reading Panel? *Journal of Learning Disabilities, 42*(5), 458-463. https://doi.org/10.1177/0022219409338739

Malatesha Joshi, R., Binks, E., Hougen, M., Dahlgren, M. E., Ocker-Dean, E., & Smith, D. L. (2009). Why elementary teachers might be inadequately prepared to teach reading. *Journal of Learning Disabilities, 42*(5), 392-402. https://doi.org/10.1177/0022219409338736

Manzo, K. K. (1998a). Drilling in Texas. *Education Week, 17*(39), 32–37.
--- (1998b). NRC panel urges end to reading wars. *Education Week, 17*(28), 1.
--- (1998c). More states moving to make phonics the law. *Education Week, 17*(33), 24.
--- (1997). Study stresses role of early phonics instruction. *Education Week, 16*, 1.

Martin, B. (1983). *Brown bear, brown bear, what do you see?* (E. Carle, Illus.). Henry Holt and Co.

Mathews, M. M. (1966). *Teaching to read, historically considered.* University of Chicago Press.

McArthur, G., Eve, P. M., Jones, K., Banales, E., Kohnen, S., Anandakumar, T., Larsen, L., Marinus, E., Wang, H., & Castles, A. (2012). Phonics training for english-speaking poor readers. *Cochrane Database of Systematic Reviews, 12,* CD009115-CD009115. https://doi.org/10.1002/14651858.CD009115.pub2

McEneaney, J. E. (2006). Agent-based literacy theory. *Reading Research Quarterly, 41*(3), 352-371. https://doi.org/10.1598/rrq.41.3.3

McGee, L. M., & Richgels, D. J. (1990). *Literacy's beginnings: Supporting young readers and writers.* Allyn and Bacon.

Meek, M. (1982). *Learning to read.* Bodley Head.

Meeks, L. J., & Kemp, C. R. (2017). How well prepared are Australian preservice teachers to teach early reading skills? *The Australian Journal of Teacher Education, 42*(11), 1-17. https://doi.org/10.14221/ajte.2017v42n11.1

Metzler, J., & Woessmann, L. (2010). *The impact of teacher subject knowledge on student achievement: Evidence from within-teacher within-student variation* [Discussion Paper No. 4999]. Institute for the Study of Labor.

Milner, H. R. (2020). Disrupting racism and Whiteness in researching a science of reading. *Reading Research Quarterly, 55*(S1), S249-S253. https://doi.org/10.1002/rrq.347

Misiaszek, G. W. (2020). *Ecopedagogy: Critical environmental teaching for planetary justice and global sustainable development.* Bloomsbury Academic. https://doi.org/10.5040/9781350083820

Moats, L. C. (2023). Creating confident readers: How LETRS supports teachers—and their students. *American Educator, 47*(1), 4.

--- (2020). Teaching reading is rocket science: What expert teachers of reading should know and be able to do. *American Educator, 44*(2), 4. Retrieved from https://www.aft.org/sites/default/files/moats.pdf

--- (2014). What teachers don't know and why they aren't learning it: Addressing the need for content and pedagogy in teacher education. *Australian Journal of Learning Difficulties, 19*(2), 75-91. https://doi.org/10.1080/19404158.2014.941093

--- (2000). *Whole language lives on: The illusion of "balanced" reading instruction.* Thomas B. Fordham Foundation.

--- (1999). *Teaching reading is rocket science: What expert teachers of reading should know and be able to do.* American Federation of Teachers, AFL-CIO, & the National Institute of Child Health and Human Development (NICHD). https://files.eric.ed.gov/fulltext/ED445323.pdf

Morris, J. M. (1966). *Standards and progress in reading: Studies of children's reading standards and progress in relation to their individual attributes, home circumstances and primary school conditions.* National Foundation for Educational Research in England and Wales.

Mukherjee, S. (2010). *The emperor of all maladies: A biography of cancer.* Scribner.

Murphy, P. K., Wilkinson, I. A. G., Soter, A. O., Hennessey, M. N., & Alexander, J. F. (2009). Examining the effects of classroom discussion on students' comprehension of text: A meta-analysis. *Journal of Educational Psychology, 101*(3), 740-764. https://doi.org/10.1037/a0015576

National Academies of Sciences, Engineering, and Medicine (NASEM). (2018). *How people learn II: Learners, contexts, and cultures.* The National Academies Press. https://doi.org/10.17226/24783

National Assessment Governing Board (NAGB). (2021). Reading framework for the 2026 National Assessment of Educational Progress. National Center for Education Statistics (NCES), U.S. Department of Education, Institute of Education Sciences. U.S. Government Printing Office. Retrieved from https://www.nagb.gov/content/dam/nagb/en/documents/publications/frameworks/reading/2026-reading-framework/naep-2026-reading-framework.pdf

National Council for Accreditation of Teacher Education. (2010). *Transforming teacher education through clinical practice: A national strategy to prepare effective teachers.* Report of the Blue Ribbon Panel on clinical preparation and partnerships for improved student learning. National Council for Accreditation of Teacher Education. Retrieved from https://files.eric.ed.gov/fulltext/ED512807.pdf

National Early Literacy Panel (NELP) & Eunice Kennedy Shriver National Institute of Child Health and Human Development (NICHD) (2010). *Developing early literacy: Report of the National Early Literacy Panel.* The National Institute for Literacy (NIFL), National Center for Family Literacy, National Institutes of Health (NIH), & U.S. Department of Health and Human Services (DHHS). U.S. Government Printing Office. https://www.nichd.nih.gov/sites/default/files/publications/pubs/documents/NELPReport09.pdf

National Education Policy Center. (2022, September 22). Nine ways to hold teacher prep programs accountable for equity [Online Newsletter]. National Education Policy Center. https://nepc.colorado.edu/publication/newsletter-teacher-prep-equity-092222

National Reading Panel (NRP) & Eunice Kennedy Shriver National Institute of Child Health and Human Development (NICHD) (2000). *Report of the National Reading Panel: Teaching children to read: An evidence-based assessment of the scientific research literature on reading and its implications for reading instruction* (NIH Pub. No. 00-4769). National Institutes of Health (NIH). U.S. Government Printing Office. https://www.nichd.nih.gov/sites/default/files/publications/pubs/nrp/Documents/report.pdf

National Research Council. (2002). *Scientific research in education.* Committee on Scientific Principles for Education Research, R. J. Shavelson & L. Towne (Eds.). Center for Education, Division of Behavioral and Social Sciences and Education. National Academy Press. https://nap.nationalacademies.org/read/10236/chapter/1#ix

--- (1999). How people learn: Brain, mind, experience, and school. National Academy Press. https://nap.nationalacademies.org/read/9457/chapter/1

Neuman S. B., Wright T. S. (2010). Promoting language and literacy development for early childhood educators: A mixed-methods study of coursework and coaching. *The Elementary School Journal, 111*(1), 63–86. https://doi.org/10.1086/653470

Nicholson, T. (2011). Beyond Reading Recovery®—what works best? *Perspectives on Language and Literacy, 37*(4), 7.

Olson, D. R. (1977). From utterance to text: The bias of language in speech and writing. *Harvard Educational Review, 47*(3), 257-281. https://doi.org/10.17763/haer.47.3.8840364413869005

Olson, L. (2023). *The reading revolution: How states are scaling literacy reform.* Future-Ed. Available from https://www.future-ed.org/wp-content/uploads/2023/06/The-Reading-Revolution.pdf

Ontario Human Rights Commission (OHRC) (2022). *Right to read inquiry report: Public inquiry into human rights issues affecting students with reading disabilities.* Government of Ontario. https://www.ohrc.on.ca/en/right-to-read-inquiry-report/introduction

Orton, S. (1966). The Orton-Gillingham approach. In J. Money (Ed.), *The disabled reader: Education of the dyslexic child.* John Hopkins University Press.
--- (1937). Reading, writing, and speech problems in children. Norton.

Palincsar, A. S., & Brown, A. L. (1984). Reciprocal teaching of comprehension-fostering and comprehension-monitoring activities. *Cognition and Instruction, 1*(2), 117-175. https://doi.org/10.1207/s1532690xci0102_1

Palincsar, A. S., Fitzgerald, M. S., DellaVecchia, G. P., & Easley, K. M. (2020). *The integration of literacy, science, and engineering in prekindergarten through fifth grade.* Committee on Enhancing Science in Prekindergarten through Fifth Grade National Academies of Sciences, Engineering, and Medicine. https://nap.nationalacademies.org/resource/26215/Integration-of-Literacy-Science-and-Engineering-PreK-5.pdf

Paris, D. (2012). Culturally sustaining pedagogy: A needed change in stance, terminology, and practice. *Educational Researcher, 41*(3), 93-97. https://doi.org/10.3102/0013189X12441244

Pattinson, S. D. (2015). The human rights act and the doctrine of precedent. *Legal Studies (Society of Legal Scholars), 35*(1), 142-164. https://doi.org/10.1111/lest.12049

Pearson, P. D. (2021). Toward a complete SoR. In J. V. Hoffman, S. Q. Cabell, S. Barrueco, E. R. Hollins, & P. D. Pearson, *Critical issues in the science of reading: Striving for a wide-angle view in research* (pp. 98-100). *Literacy Research, 70*(1), 87-105. https://doi.org/10.1177/23813377211032195
--- (2004). The reading wars. *Educational Policy, 18*(1), 216-252. https://doi.org/10.1177/0895904803260041
--- (2000). Reading in the 20th century. In T. Good (Ed.), *American Education: Yesterday, today, and tomorrow* (pp. 152-208). Yearbook of the National Society for the Study of Education. National Society for the Study of Education. Distributed by the University of Chicago Press.
--- (1989). Reading the Whole-Language movement. *The Elementary School Journal, 90*(2), 231-241. https://doi.org/10.1086/461615

Pearson, P. D., & Cervetti, G. N. (2017). The roots of reading comprehension instruction. In S. E. Israeli (Ed.), *Handbook of research on reading comprehension* (pp. 12–56). Guilford Press.

Pearson, P. D., Madda, C. L., & Raphael, T. E. (2023). Current issues and best practices in literacy instruction. In L. M. Morrow & L. B. Gambrell (Eds.), *Best practices in literacy instruction* (7th ed.) (pp. 3-40). The Guilford Press.

Pearson, P. D., McVee, M. B., & Shanahan, L. E. (2019). In the beginning: The historical and conceptual genesis of the gradual release of responsibility. In M. B. McVee, E. Ortlieb, J. Reichenberg, & P. D. Pearson (Eds.), *The gradual release of responsibility in literacy research and practice* (pp. 1-21). Emerald Group Publishing.

Pearson, P. D., Palincsar, A. S., Afflerbach, P., Cervetti, G. N., Kendeou, P., Biancarosa, G., Higgs, J., Fitzgerald, M., & Berman, A. I. (2020). Taking stock of the Reading for Understanding initiative. In P. D. Pearson, A. S. Palincsar, G. Biancarosa, & A. Berman (Eds.), *Reaping the rewards of the Reading for Understanding Initiative* (pp. 251-292). National Academy of Education. Retrieved from https://naeducation.org/wp-content/uploads/2020/06/Reaping-the-Rewards-of-the-Reading-for-Understanding-Initiative.pdf

Pearson, P. D., Palincsar, A.S., Biancarosa, G., & Berman, A.I. (Eds.). (2020). *Reaping the rewards of the Reading for Understanding initiative.* National Academy of Education. https://naeducation.org/wp-content/uploads/2020/07/NAEd-Reaping-the-Rewards-of-the-Reading-for-Understanding-Initiative.pdf

Peirce, C. S. (Author), & Burks, A. W. (Ed.). (1958). *Collected papers of Charles Sanders Peirce, Volumes VII and VIII: Science and philosophy and reviews, correspondence and bibliography.* Harvard University Press. https://www.hup.harvard.edu/books/9780674138032

Peirce, C. S. (Author), & Hartshorne, C., & Weiss, P. (Eds.). (1935). *Collected papers of Charles Sanders Peirce, Volumes V and VI: Pragmatism and scientific metaphysics.* Harvard University Press. https://www.hup.harvard.edu/books/9780674138025

--- (1933). *Collected papers of Charles Sanders Peirce, Volumes III and IV: Exact logic (published papers) and the simplest mathematics.* Harvard University Press. https://www.hup.harvard.edu/books/9780674138018

--- (1932). *Collected papers of Charles Sanders Peirce, Volumes I and II: Principles of philosophy and elements of logic.* Harvard University Press. https://www.hup.harvard.edu/books/9780674138001

Perfetti, C. A. (1980). Verbal coding efficiency, conceptually guided reading, and reading failure. *Bulletin of the Orton Society, 30*(1), 197-208. https://doi.org/10.1007/BF02653718

Perfetti, C. A., & Hart, L. (2002). The lexical quality hypothesis. In L. Verhoeven, C. Elbro, & P. Reitsma (Eds.), *Precursors of functional literacy* (pp. 189–213). John Benjamins. https://doi.org/10.1075/swll.11

Perry, M. (2023, Apr 15). Response to "The socio-cultural chasm in the Science of Reading" by R Tierney & P. David Pearson [Discussant]. *American Educational Research Association Annual Meeting, Chicago*, Illinois, April 13-16.

Pinnell, G. S., DeFord, D. E., & Lyons, C. A. (1988). *Reading Recovery: Early intervention for at risk first graders.* Educational Research Service. https://files.eric.ed.gov/fulltext/ED303790.pdf

Primary National Strategy (2006). *Phonics and early reading: An overview for headteachers, literacy leaders and teachers in schools, and managers and practitioners in Early Years settings.* U. K. Department for Education and Skills. Retrieved from https://dera.ioe.ac.uk/id/eprint/5551/3/5d970d28fc535dc54eb4dee9995bef36.pdf

Pugh, A., Kearns, D., & Hiebert, E. (2023). Text types and their relation to efficacy in beginning reading interventions. Reading Research Quarterly, 58(4), 710-732. https://doi.org/10.1002/rrq.513

Purcell-Gates, V. (2007). *Cultural practices of literacy: Case studies of language, literacy, social practice, and power.* Lawrence Erlbaum Associates.
--- (1995). *Other people's words: The cycle of low literacy.* Harvard University Press.

Purcell-Gates, V., Jacobson, E., Degener, S. (2004). *Print literacy development: Uniting cognitive and social practice theories.* Harvard University Press. https://doi.org/10.4159/9780674042377

Purcell-Gates, V., & Tierney, R. J. (2008). Public policy brief: Increasing literacy levels of Canadian students [Unpublished working paper]. University of British Columbia. Available from https://www.uky.edu/cpls/sites/www.uky.edu.cpls/files/ctools/33LiteracyPolicyBrief.pdf

Radio New Zealand (RNZ). (2023, May 16). Reading level of 10-year-olds tested against international counterparts. *New Zealand Herald.* https://www.nzherald.co.nz/nz/reading-level-of-10-year-olds-tested-against-international-counterparts/EUVVEZEKG5CPLCNRO67ZBRKFJ4/

RAND Reading Study Group (RRSG). (2002). *Reading for understanding: Toward an R&D program in reading comprehension.* RAND Education. Retrieved from https://www.rand.org/pubs/monograph_reports/MR1465.html

Raphael, T. E., & Au, K. H. (Eds.). (1998). *Literature-based instruction: Reshaping the curriculum.* Christopher-Gordon Publishers, Inc.

Rayner, K., Foorman, B. R., Perfetti, C. A., Pesetsky, D., & Seidenberg, M. S. (2001). How psychological science informs the teaching of reading. *Psychological Science in the Public Interest, 2*(2), 31-74. https://doi.org/10.1111/1529-1006.00004

Reinking, D., Hruby, G. G., & Risko, V. J. (2023). Legislating phonics: Settled science or political polemics? *Teachers College Record, 125*(1), 104-131. https://doi.org/10.1177/01614681231155688

Reynolds, M., & Wheldall, K. (2007). Reading Recovery 20 years down the track: Looking forward, looking back. *International Journal of Disability, Development, and Education, 54*(2), 199-223. https://doi.org/10.1080/10349120701330503

Richardson, V. (1998). Professional development in the teaching of reading. In J. Osborn & F. Lehr (Eds.), *Literacy for all: Issues in teaching and learning* (pp. 303-318). Guilford Press.

Rigney, L-I. (2021). Aboriginal child as knowledge producer: Bringing into dialogue Indigenist epistemologies and culturally responsive pedagogies for schooling. In B. Hokowhitu, A. Moreton-Robinson, L. T. Smith, C. Andersen, & S. Larkin, Routledge Handbook of Critical Indigenous Studies (pp. 578-590). https://doi.org/10.4324/9780429440229

Rivkin, S. G., Hanushek, E. A., & Kain, J. F. (2005). Teachers, schools, and academic achievement. *Econometrica, 73*(2), 417-458. https://doi.org/10.1111/j.1468-0262.2005.00584.x

Rockoff, J. E. (2004). The impact of individual teachers on student achievement: Evidence from panel data. T*he American Economic Review, 94*(2), 247-252. https://doi.org/10.1257/0002828041302244

Romano, A. (2020, Oct 9). A history of "wokeness." *Vox*. https://www.vox.com/culture/21437879/stay-woke-wokeness-history-origin-evolution-controversy.

Rose, J. (2006). *Independent review of the teaching of early reading: Final report.* UK Department for Education and Skills. https://dera.ioe.ac.uk/5551/2/report.pdf

Rose, M. (1995). *Possible lives: The promise of public education in America.* Houghton Mifflin. Retrieved from https://www.proquest.com/books/possible-lives-promise-public-education-america/docview/59713738/se-2

Rowe, K., & National Inquiry into the Teaching of Literacy (Australia). (2005). *Teaching reading: Report and recommendations.* Department of Education, Science and Training, Australian Council for Educational Research. https://research.acer.edu.au/tll_misc/5

Rumelhart, D. E. (1977). Toward an interactive model of reading. In S. Dornic˘ (Ed.), *Attention and performance VI: Proceedings of the sixth international symposium on attention and performance,* Stockholm, Sweden, July 28–August 1, 1975 (pp. 573–603). Lawrence Erlbaum. https://doi.org/10.4324/9781003309734

Rumelhart D. E., & McClelland J. L. (Eds.). (1986). *Parallel distributed processing, Vol. 1: Foundations.* The MIT Press.

Sailors, M., & Hoffman, J. V. (2019). T*he power of practice-based literacy research: A tool for teachers.* Routledge. https://doi.org/10.4324/9780429057571

Sailors, M., & Price, L. (2015). Support for the improvement of practices through intensive coaching (SIPIC): A model of coaching for improving reading instruction and reading achievement. *Teaching and Teacher Education, 45*, 115-127. https://doi.org/10.1016/j.tate.2014.09.008

Salinger, T., & Weinberg, E. (2021). Evaluation of the Teachers College Reading and Writing Project (TCRWP) Approach. American Institutes for Research. https://www.air.org/sites/default/files/Teachers-College-Reading-and-Writing-Project-Jan-2021.pdf

Sanden, S., MacPhee, D. A., Hartle, L., Poggendorf, S., & Zuiderveen, C. (2022). The status of phonics instruction: Learning from the teachers. *Reading Horizons, 61*(1), 69-92.

Saville-Troike, M. (2003). *The ethnography of communication: An introduction* (3rd ed.). Blackwell. https://doi.org/10.1002/9780470758373

Scanlon, D. M., & Anderson, K. L. (2020). Using context as an assist in word solving: The contributions of 25 years of research on the interactive strategies approach. *Reading Research Quarterly, 55*(S1), S19-S34. https://doi.org/10.1002/rrq.335

Scanlon, D. M., Anderson, K. L., Barnes, E. M., & Sweeney, J. M. (2024). *Early literacy instruction and intervention: The interactive strategies approach* (3rd ed.). Guilford Press.

Scarborough, H. S. (2023). *The Reading Rope: Key ideas behind the metaphor.* The Reading League. Retrieved from https://www.thereadingleague.org/wp-content/uploads/2023/11/TRLC-Educators-and-Specialists-The-Reading-Rope-Key-Ideas-Behind-the-Metaphor.pdf

--- (2001). Connecting early language and literacy to later reading (dis)abilities: Evidence, theory, and practice. In S. B. Neuman & D. K. Dickinson (Eds.), *Handbook for research in early literacy* (pp. 97-110). Guilford Press.

Schnellert, L. M., Butler, D. L., & Higginson, S. K. (2008). Co-constructors of data, co-constructors of meaning: Teacher professional development in an age of accountability. *Teaching and Teacher Education, 24*(3), 725-750. https://doi.org/10.1016/j.tate.2007.04.001

Schön, D. A. (1983). *The reflective practitioner: How professionals think in action.* Basic Books.

School Library Journal (SLJ). (2023). *Controversial books survey: 2022 to 2023 data comparisons.* Retrieved from https://s3.amazonaws.com/ImageCloud/Research/SLJ+2023+Controversial+Book+Survey+Report+with+comparisons.pdf

Schwartz, R. M. (2015). Ideology and early literacy evidence: A response to Chapman & Tunmer. Reading Recovery Community: Responding to Critics. *Reading Recovery.* https://readingrecovery.org/wp-content/uploads/2016/12/chapman_tunmer_2015_response.pdf

--- (2005). Literacy learning of at-risk first-grade students in the Reading Recovery Early Intervention. *Journal of Educational Psychology, 97*(2), 257-267. https://doi.org/10.1037/0022-0663.97.2.257

Schwartz, R. M., Hobsbaum, A., Briggs, C., & Scull, J. (2009). Reading Recovery and evidence-based practice: A response to Reynolds and Wheldall (2007). *International Journal of Disability, Development, and Education, 56*(1), 5-15. https://doi.org/10.1080/10349120802681564

Schwartz, R. M., & Stanovich, K. E. (1981). Flexibility in the use of graphic and contextual information by good and poor readers. *Journal of Reading Behavior, 13*(3), 263-269. https://doi.org/10.1080/10862968109547413

Schwartz, S. (2022a, July 20). What is LETRS? Why one training is dominating 'science of reading' efforts. *Education Week.* https://www.edweek.org/teaching-learning/letrs-program-teacher-training

--- (2022b, July 20). Which states have passed "science of reading" laws? What's in them? *Education Week.* https://www.edweek.org/teaching-learning/which-states-have-passed-science-of-reading-laws-whats-in-them/2022/07

Scribner, S., & Cole, M. (1981). *The psychology of literacy.* Harvard University Press.

Seidenberg, M. S. (2023a, Dec 4). Where does the "Science of Reading" go from here? [Video]. Presentation at the Yale Child Study Center. Video available from https://videos.files.wordpress.com/CJUEjfc9/video3767746143-1.mp4. Slides available from https://seidenbergreading.net/wp-content/uploads/2023/12/Yale-talk.pdf

--- (2023b, June 6). Decoding "The Simple View of Reading" III. *Reading Matters: Connecting science and education.* Mark Seidenberg. https://seidenbergreading.net/2023/06/06/decoding-the-simple-view-of-reading-iii/

--- (2023c, Mar 31). About the science in "The Science of Reading." *Reading Matters: Connecting science and education.* Mark Seidenberg. https://seidenbergreading.net/2023/03/31/about-the-science-in-the-science-of-reading/

--- (2017). *Language at the speed of sight: How we read, why so many can't, and what can be done about it.* Basic.

--- (2013). The science of reading and its educational implications. *Language Learning and Development, 9*(4), 331-360. https://doi.org/10.1080/15475441.2013.812017

Seidenberg, M. S., Borkenhagen, M. C., & Kearns, D. M. (2020). Lost in translation? Challenges in connecting reading science and educational practice. *Reading Research Quarterly, 55*(1), S119-S130. https://doi.org/10.1002/rrq.341

Selfe, C. L., & Hawisher, G. E. (2004). *Literate lives in the information age: Narratives of literacy from the United States.* Lawrence Erlbaum Associates. https://doi.org/10.4324/9781410610768

Siegel, M. (2006). Rereading the signs: Multimodal transformations in the field of literacy education. *Language Arts, 84*(1), 65-77.

Shanahan, T. (2023, Apr 29). *Which reading model would best guide our school improvement efforts?* [Blog post]. Shanahan on Literacy. https://www.shanahanonliteracy.com/blog/which-reading-model-would-best-guide-our-school-improvement-efforts

--- (2020). What constitutes a Science of Reading instruction? Reading Research Quarterly, 55(S1), S235-S247. https://doi.org/10.1002/rrq.349

Shanahan, T., Kamil, M., & Tobin, A. (1982). Cloze as a measure of intersentential comprehension. *Reading Research Quarterly, 17*(2), 229-255. https://doi.org/10.2307/747485

Share, D. L. (1995). Phonological recoding and self-teaching: Sine qua non of reading acquisition. *Cognition, 55*(2), 151-218. https://doi.org/10.1016/0010-0277(94)00645-2

Shaywitz, B. A., & Shaywitz, S. E. (2020). The American experience: Towards a 21st century definition of dyslexia. *Oxford Review of Education, 46*(4), 454-471. https://doi.org/10.1080/03054985.2020.1793545

Shaywitz, S. E. (2003). *Overcoming dyslexia: A new and complete science-based program for reading problems at any level.* A.A. Knopf.

Shaywitz, S. E., & Shaywitz, B. A. (2008). Paying attention to reading: The neurobiology of reading and dyslexia. *Development and Psychopathology, 20*(4), 1329-1349. https://doi.org/10.1017/S0954579408000631

--- (2005). Dyslexia (specific reading disability). *Biological Psychiatry, 57*(11), 1301-1309. https://doi.org/10.1016/j.biopsych.2005.01.043

Shaywitz, S. E. & Shaywitz, J., (2020) *Overcoming dyslexia.* (Second edition). New York: Alfred A. Knopf; ISBN: 9780385350327

Shaywitz, S., Shaywitz, B., Pugh, K., Skudlarski, P., Fulbright, R. K., Constable, R. T., Bronen, R. A., Fletcher, J. M., Liberman, A. M., Shankweiler, D. P., Katz, L., Lacadie, C., Marchione, K. E., & Gore, J. C. (1996). The neurobiology of developmental dyslexia as viewed through the lens of functional magnetic resonance imaging technology. In G. R. Lyon & J. M. Rumsey (Eds.), *Neuroimaging: A window to the neurological foundations of learning and behavior in children.* Paul H. Brookes.

Sherman, K. H. (2007). *A meta-analysis of interventions for phonemic awareness and phonics instruction for delayed older readers* (No. 3285626) [Doctoral Dissertation, University of Oregon]. ProQuest Dissertations Publishing. Retrieved from https://www.proquest.com/dissertations-theses/meta-analysis-interventions-phonemic-awareness/docview/304825094/se-2?accountid=14656

Shulman, L. S. (1987). Knowledge and teaching: Foundations of the new reform. *Harvard Educational Review, 57*(1), 1-22. https://doi.org/10.17763/haer.57.1.j463w79r56455411

Simon, H. A. (1996). *The sciences of the artificial* (3rd ed.). The MIT Press. (Original work published 1969) https://doi.org/10.7551/mitpress/12107.001.0001

--- (1973). The structure of ill structured problems. *Artificial Intelligence, 4*(3), 181-201. https://doi.org/10.1016/0004-3702(73)90011-8

Simos, P. G., Fletcher, J. M., Bergman, E., Breier, J. I., Foorman, B. R., Castillo, E. M., Davis, R. N., Fitzgerald, M., & Papanicolaou, A. C. (2002). Dyslexia-specific brain activation profile becomes normal following successful remedial training. *Neurology, 58*(8), 1203-1213. https://doi.org/10.1212/wnl.58.8.1203

Sleeman, M., Everatt, J., Arrow, A., & Denston, A. (2022). The identification and classification of struggling readers based on the simple view of reading. *Dyslexia, 28*(3), 256-275. https://doi.org/10.1002/dys.1719

Smith, F. (2015). Twelve easy ways to making learning to read difficult, and one difficult way to make it easy. In F. Smith, *Landmarks in literacy: The selected works of Frank Smith* (pp. 13–26). Routledge. https://doi.org/10.4324/9781315744490

--- (2012). *Understanding reading: A psycholinguistic analysis of reading and learning to read* (6th ed). New York: Routledge. (Original work published 1971) https://doi.org/10.4324/9780203142165

--- (1973). *Psycholinguistics and reading.* Holt, Rinehart and Winston, Inc.

Smith, G. H. (2000). Protecting and respecting indigenous knowledge. In M. Battiste (Ed.), *Reclaiming indigenous voice and vision* (pp. 209-224). University of British Columbia Press. https://doi.org/10.59962/9780774853170-020

Smith, L. T. (2005). On tricky ground: Researching the native in the age of uncertainty. In N. K. Denzin & Y. S. Lincoln (Eds.), *The Sage handbook of qualitative research* (pp. 85–108). Sage.
--- (1999). *Decolonizing methodologies: Research and indigenous peoples.* Zed Books.

Snow, C.E., Burns, M.S., & Griffin, P. (Eds.). (1998). *Preventing reading difficulties in young children: A report of the National Research Council.* National Academy Press. Retrieved from https://files.eric.ed.gov/fulltext/ED416465.pdf.

Somerby, B. (2023, Jul 4). Mississippi's Miracle: Do we really have a "Mississippi mirage?" The Daily Howler [Blog]. https://dailyhowler.blogspot.com/2023/07/mississippis-miracle-could-we-have.html

Spiro, R. J., Coulson, R. L., Feltovich, P. J., & Anderson, D. K. (1988). *Cognitive flexibility theory: Advanced knowledge acquisition in ill-structured domains* [Technical Report No. 441]. U of Illinois Center for the Study of Reading & Bolt, Beranek and Newman, Inc. Retrieved from https://files.eric.ed.gov/fulltext/ED302821.pdf

Stanovich, K. E. (1984). The interactive-compensatory model of reading: A confluence of developmental, experimental, and educational psychology. *Remedial and Special Education, 5*(3), 11-19. https://doi.org/10.1177/074193258400500306
--- (1980). Toward an interactive-compensatory model of individual differences in the development of reading fluency. *Reading Research Quarterly, 16*(1), 32-71. https://doi.org/10.2307/747348

Stanovich, K. E., & West, R. F. (1979). The effect of orthographic structure on the word search performance of good and poor readers. *Journal of Experimental Child Psychology, 28*(2), 258-267. https://doi.org/10.1016/0022-0965(79)90088-2

Stephens, D. (2023, May 17). Open letter: To curriculum coordinators in South Carolina school districts. Available from https://radicalscholarship.com/2023/05/17/open-letter-to-curriculum-coordinators-in-south-carolina-school-districts-diane-stephens/

Stockard, J., Wood, T. W., Coughlin, C., & Khoury, C. R. (2018). The effectiveness of direct instruction curricula: A meta-analysis of a half century of research. *Review of Educational Research, 88*(4), 479-507. https://doi.org/10.3102/0034654317751919

Strauss, S. L. (2014). The political economy of dyslexia. *Monthly Review, 66*(4), 35-35. https://doi.org/10.14452/MR-066-04-2014-08_4

Strauss, S. L., Goodman, K. S., & Paulson, E. J. (2009). Brain research and reading: How emerging concepts in neuroscience support a meaning construction view of the reading process. *Educational Research and Review, 4*(2), 021–033.

Suggate, S. P. (2016). A meta-analysis of the long-term effects of phonemic awareness, phonics, fluency, and reading comprehension interventions. *Journal of Learning Disabilities, 49*(1), 77-96. https://doi.org/10.1177/0022219414528540

--- (2010). Why what we teach depends on when: Grade and reading intervention modality moderate effect size. *Developmental Psychology, 46*(6), 1556-1579. https://doi.org/10.1037/a0020612

Suskind, D. C. (2020, Oct 24). The critical story of the "Science of Reading" and why its narrow plotline is putting our children and schools at risk [Blog post]. NCTE Blog: *Literacy & NCTE*. https://ncte.org/blog/2020/10/critical-story-science-reading-narrow-plotline-putting-children-schools-risk/

Taylor, B. M., Pearson, P. D., Clark, K., & Walpole, S. (2000). Effective schools and accomplished teachers: Lessons about primary-grade reading instruction in low-income schools. *The Elementary School Journal, 101*(2), 121-165. https://doi.org/10.1086/499662

Taylor, B. M., Pressley, M. P., & Pearson, P. D. (2002). Research-supported characteristics of teachers and schools that promote reading achievement. In B. Taylor & P. D. Pearson (Eds.), *Teaching reading: Effective schools, accomplished teachers* (361–373). New York: Routledge. https://doi.org/10.4324/9781410612489

Teacher Education Expert Panel. (2023, July 6). *Strong beginnings: Report of the Teacher Education Expert Panel 2023.* Australian Government Department of Education. https://www.education.gov.au/quality-initial-teacher-education-review/resources/strong-beginnings-report-teacher-education-expert-panel

Teale, W. H. (1982). Toward a theory of how children learn to read and write naturally. *Language Arts, 59*(6), 555-570.

Teale, W. H., & Sulzby, E. (Eds.). (1986). *Emergent literacy: Writing and reading.* Ablex Publishing.

The Reading League. (2023). The Reading League (Website). https://www.thereadingleague.org/

Tierney, R. J. (2018). Toward a model of global meaning making. *Journal of Literacy Research, 50*(4), 397-422. https://doi.org/10.1177/1086296X18803134

--- (2009). Literacy education 2.0: Looking through the rear vision mirror as we move ahead. In J. Hoffman & Y. Goodman (Eds.), *Changing literacies for changing times: An historical perspective on the future of reading research, public policy, and classroom practices* (pp. 282-303). Routledge. https://doi.org/10.4324/9780203875186

--- (2001). An ethical chasm: Jurisdiction, jurisprudence, and the literacy profession. *Journal of Adolescent & Adult Literacy, 45*(4), 260-276.

--- (1992). On matters of subjectivity, knowledge claims, the art of method and ethics in literacy research. In C. K. Kinzer & D. J. Leu (Eds.), *Literacy research, theory, and practice: views from many perspectives.* Forty-first Yearbook of the National Reading Conference. National Reading Conference.

Tierney, R. J., & Pearson, P. D. (2023). Epilogue: Literacy practicing: Repositioning teachers as cultural workers and ecopedagogues toward creating learning cultures. In L. M. Morrow, E. Morrell, & H. K. Casey (Eds.), *Best practices in literacy instruction* (7th ed.) (pp. 453-465). Guilford Press.

--- (2021). *A history of literacy education: Waves of research and practice.* Teachers College Press.

Tierney, R. J., & Shanahan, T. (1991). Research on the reading-writing relationship: Interactions, transactions, and outcomes. In R. Barr, M. L. Kamil, P. B. Mosenthal, & P. D. Pearson (Eds.), *Handbook of reading research, Vol II* (pp. 246-280). Routledge. https://doi.org/10.4324/9781315206349

Tierney, R. J., & Sheehy, M. (2005). What longitudinal studies say about literacy development/what literacy development says about longitudinal studies. In J. Flood, J. Jensen, D. Lapp, J. R. Squire, & J. M. Jensen (Eds.), *Methods of research on teaching the English language arts: The methodology chapters from The handbook of research on teaching the English language arts, 2nd ed.* (pp. 79-124). Lawrence Erlbaum Associates.

Tommy G. Thompson Center on Public Leadership. (2023, Mar 6). Thompson Center Summit on Early Literacy (YouTube Video). University of Wisconsin-Madison. https://www.youtube.com/watch?v=w_SNMp4brTw

Torgerson, C., Brooks, G., Gascoine, L., & Higgins, S. (2019). Phonics: Reading policy and the evidence of effectiveness from a systematic 'tertiary' review. *Research Papers in Education, 34*(2), 208-238. https://doi.org/10.1080/02671522.2017.1420816

Tortorelli, L. S., Lupo, S. M., & Wheatley, B. C. (2021). Examining teacher preparation for Code-Related reading instruction: An Integrated literature review. *Reading Research Quarterly, 56*(S1), S317-S337. https://doi.org/10.1002/rrq.396

Van den Akker, J., Gravemeijer, K., McKenney, S., & Nieveen, N. (Eds.). (2006). *Educational design research.* Routledge. https://doi.org/10.4324/9780203088364

Vellutino, F. R., & Scanlon, D. M. (2002). The interactive strategies approach to reading intervention. *Contemporary Educational Psychology, 27*(4), 573-635. https://doi.org/10.1016/S0361-476X(02)00002-4

Walsh, K., Glaser, D., & Wilcox, D. D. (2006). *What education schools aren't teaching about reading and what elementary teachers aren't learning.* National Council on Teacher Quality. https://www.nctq.org/nctq/images/nctq_reading_study_app.pdf

Washington Post (WP) Editorial Board. (2023, Mar 11). Cut the politics. Phonics is the best way to teach reading [Editorial]. The Washington Post. https://www.washingtonpost.com/opinions/2023/03/11/phonics-schools-students-read-learn/

Weale, S. & Adams, (2023). Reading ability of children in England scores well in global survey. *The Guardian*, May 16, 2023. https://www.theguardian.com/education/2023/may/16/reading-ability-of-children-in-england-scores-well-in-global-survey

Wenger, E. (1998). *Communities of practice: Learning, meaning, and identity.* Cambridge University Press.

Westall, J., & Cummings, A. (2023). *The effects of early literacy policies on student achievement* [Policy brief]. Educational Policy Innovation Collaborative, Michigan State University. https://www.edworkingpapers.com/sites/default/files/ai23-788.pdf

Wexler, N. (2023, Oct 10). The science of reading isn't just 'phonics,' but what else is it? *Forbes.* https://www.forbes.com/sites/nataliewexler/2023/10/10/the-science-of-reading-isnt-just-phonics-but-what-else-is-it/?sh=63bf41c5763a

Willingham, D. T. (2017). *The reading mind: A cognitive approach to understanding how the mind reads.* Jossey-Bass.

Wilson, A. (2021, Jan 25). Reading between the lines of the phonics debate. *New Zealand Herald.* https://www.nzherald.co.nz/nz/alice-wilson-reading-between-the-lines-of-the-phonics-debate/IVH3ULRPUWDYTQMMNKHDOXQPYY/

Wittgenstein, L. (1953). *Philosophical investigations* (G. E. M. Anscombe, Trans.). Macmillan.

Wolf, M. (2018). *Reader, come home: The reading brain in a digital world* (C. J. Stoodley, Illus.). Harper, an imprint of HarperCollins.
--- (2008). *Proust and the squid: The story and science of the reading brain* (C. J. Stoodley, Illus.). Harper Perennial.

World Health Organization (WHO) Regional Office for the Western Pacific. (2007). *People-centred health care: A policy framework.* WHO Regional Office for the Western Pacific. https://iris.who.int/handle/10665/206971

Woulfin, S., & Gabriel, R. E. (2020). Interconnected infrastructure for improving reading instruction. *Reading Research Quarterly, 55*(S1), S109-S117. https://doi.org/10.1002/rrq.339

Wyse, D., & Bradbury, A. (2023, Feb 17). The politics of 'scientifically-based' teaching: Phonics for reading and grammar for writing [Blog post]. *BERA Blog Special Issue: Spotlight on Language and Literacy.* British Educational Research Association. https://www.bera.ac.uk/blog/the-politics-of-scientifically-based-teaching-phonics-for-reading-and-grammar-for-writing
--- (2022). Reading wars or reading reconciliation? A critical examination of robust research evidence, curriculum policy and teachers' practices for teaching phonics and reading. *Review of Education, 10*(1). https://doi.org/10.1002/rev3.3314

Wyse, D., & Goswami, U. (2008). Synthetic phonics and the teaching of reading. *British Educational Research Journal, 34*(6), 691-710. https://doi.org/10.1080/01411920802268912

Yaden, D. B., Jr., Reinking, D., & Smagorinsky, P. (2021). The trouble with binaries: A perspective on the Science of Reading. *Reading Research Quarterly, 56*(S1), S119-S129. https://doi.org/10.1002/rrq.402

Yaden, D. B., Jr., Rowe, D. W., & MacGillivray, L. (2000). Emergent literacy: A matter (polyphony) of perspectives. In M. L. Kamil, P. B. Mosenthal, P. D. Pearson, & R. Barr (Eds.), *Handbook of Reading Research, Volume III* (pp. 425-454). Lawrence Erlbaum. https://doi.org/10.4324/9781315200613

Yaden, D. B., Jr., & Templeton, S. (Eds.). (1986). *Metalinguistic awareness and beginning literacy: Conceptualizing what it means to read and write.* Heinemann.

Yang, X., Pavarini, G., Schnall, S., & Immordino-Yang, M. H. (2018). Looking up to virtue: Averting gaze facilitates moral construals via posteromedial activations. *Social Cognitive and Affective Neuroscience, 13*(11), 1131-1139. https://doi.org/10.1093/scan/nsy081

Zeichner, K. (2020). Preparing teachers as democratic professionals. *Action in Teacher Education, 42*(1), 38-48. https://doi.org/10.1080/01626620.2019.1700847

Zhou, J., & Fischer, K. W. (2013). Culturally appropriate education: Insights from educational neuroscience. *Mind, Brain and Education, 7*(4), 225-231. https://doi.org/10.1111/mbe.12030

Made in United States
North Haven, CT
28 May 2024

53053892R00109